In Those Days

A book in the ADST-DACOR

Diplomats and Diplomacy Series.

James W. Spain

IN THOSE DAYS

A Diplomat Remembers

THE KENT STATE
UNIVERSITY PRESS
KENT, OHIO, & LONDON

Library of Congress Catalog Card Number 98-5729

ISBN 0-87338-606-X

Manufactured in the United States of America

Published in cooperation with
the ADST-DACOR Diplomats and Diplomacy Series.

04 03 02 01 00 99 98 5 4 3 2 1

Library of Congress Cataloging-in-Publication Data

Spain, James W. (James William)

In those days : a diplomat remembers / James W. Spain

p. cm.

Includes index.

ISBN 0-87338-606-X (alk. paper) ∞

1. Spain, James W. (James William) 2. Diplomats—United States—Biography. 3. United States—Foreign relations—20th century. 4. United Nations—Biography. I. Title. II. Series

E748.S734A3 1998

327.73'0092—dc21

[B] 98-5729

British Library Cataloging-in-Publication data are available.

The ADST-DACOR
Diplomats and Diplomacy Series

For more than 220 years, extraordinary men and women have represented the United States abroad under all kinds of circumstances. What they did and how and why they did it are not well known by their compatriots. In 1995 the Association for Diplomatic Studies and Training (ADST) and Diplomatic and Consular Officers, Retired (DACOR) created a book series to increase public knowledge and appreciation of the involvement of American diplomats in the events of world history. The series seeks to demystify diplomacy by telling the story of those who have conducted our foreign relations, as they saw it and lived it.

If the twentieth century was the American Century, James Spain was its classic product. From Chicago in 1926 to Sri Lanka in 1997, he has blazed a trail of high adventure and highly intelligent public service. His is a tale of the son of Irish immigrants who spent his childhood in "Al Capone country" and moved on, through military, academic, CIA, and Foreign Service encounters, to deal with mountain tribesmen and U.S. senators, African and Asian heads of state, and U.S. secretaries of state. It is diplomatic life on the edge, told with a bluntness leavened with feeling and humor. His delightful, incisive, often touching account of those years spent bouncing around the world with his family while ably serving his country is a very human one, with its full share of accomplishment and tragedy. In the process we also learn a lot about the practice of U.S. foreign relations.

Edward M. Rowell, President, ADST
Joan M. Clark, President, DACOR

CONTENTS

LIST OF ILLUSTRATIONS

Preface

THIS IS NOT A RAGS TO RICHES tale. Somehow during my three score years and ten I have managed to avoid both poverty and wealth. And, since I was never a part of the corporate, athletic, or entertainment fraternity, there is no advantage in laying claim to a Horatio Alger background.

If there is any psychological unity in this account, I suppose it is that, like so many others, I sought during my life what I did not have at its beginning and, as its end approaches, have gone away from what I did best.

When I was a boy, my family was not hungry or ill-clothed, but it did lack power, a respected place in the establishment, and knowledge of much beyond its own narrow world.

My effort to remedy these deficiencies was as close as I ever came to a cause. It has occurred to me occasionally that I might have had a better one. However, success, even if modest, is satisfying, and it hardly ever occurred to me in my youth that to achieve it, it helped enormously to be Christian (even Catholic) and the right color and sex.

I saw a good bit of a remarkable society. I brushed against a lot of people who are or will be in the history books. I saw horse-drawn wagons delivering ice in an alley and men and machines reaching for the stars in space, statesmen defending truth and right and politicians lying for profit and self-protection, brave soldiers dying in war, and clever spies conspiring in peace.

It is possible that readers, from animal trainers to astronauts, might pick up a fact or an idea here or there in this book. But it is not facts and ideas nor personal accomplishments that I wish to emphasize. I have deliberately not laid the narrative chronologically. Rather, my aim is to suggest in the matrix of family, school, work, and retirement the extraordinary diversity and opportunity of "those days" in twentieth century America that brought us to where we are now.

Edith, my wife, used to say that everything was history. It was the only thing you could count on. She got the whole family in the habit of dating the family's affairs by its great events: "during the Cuban missile crisis when Bill [our youngest] was born . . . ," or "the summer Daddy had to stay in Ankara for the Cyprus invasion and we went on leave to California alone. . . ."

It is small wonder then that this account of my life is more historical than biographical, that there is in it more of the times than the man.

There will be other and greater End of the Century books, some more interesting than others. For me, though, twentieth century America, where melting pot and ethnic pride combined and the world became a global village, is something for which I am grateful.

Acknowledgments

MY PROFOUND THANKS GO TO the Association for Diplomatic Studies and Training for including this volume in its ADST-DACOR Diplomats and Diplomacy Series; to longtime friend and former ADST president Stephen Low for invaluable advice and assistance; and to Margery Boichel Thompson, ADST's superb book publishing coordinator, who exceeded all normal human effort in editing and polishing the manuscript and finding the right publisher for it.

I am indebted to John T. Hubbell, director of the Kent State University Press, and his associates for accepting a work different from the usual diplomatic memoir or scholarly study and for their patience and skill during its preparation for publication.

To all those mentioned in the book who gave me the opportunity to make bits of their lives a part of my own, I offer truly humble thanks. Often their role in the world was greater than my own. I hope only that they remember those bits in something like the way I do.

Above all, I am grateful to the family who shared the adventure with me—to my parents, Patrick and Mary Ellen, who sent me off on it; to my late wife, Edith, whose love and wisdom kept me steady on the way; to my late daughter, Sikandra, who packed an extraordinary amount of activity into the scant thirty years she had on earth; and to my sons, Patrick, Stephen, and William, who remain the most vital part of my life.

Finally, in accord with a theme of the book, admiration and thanks must go to my grandchildren, present and to come, their children, and children's children, and to all of the Spains, Forristals, Jameses, and Burkes who preceded me on the way to and through the last seventy years of the twentieth century.

In Those Days

1

Enduring Icons

GANGSTERS WERE THE TRUE establishment figures in the Chicago into which I was born. Infants of all social degrees absorbed a feel for them with mother's milk, often supplemented by nipple bottles of bootleg beer or illicit home brew. This was considered less risky and more nutritious than the new pasteurized milk being flogged in the dairy wars in which Borden's, Bowman's, and the other young national chains fought for supremacy in the still-horse-drawn home delivery market.

There was a host of colorful names for a small boy to fasten on: "Spike" O'Donnell, "Golf Bag" Hunt, "Machine Gun" Kelly, "Mad Dog" Dillinger (or was it Hersh?), and others. But as with most things in the Chicago of the day, the top of the line was ethnic: Dion O'Bannion, the Irish Gangster; Al Capone, the Italian Gangster; and Moses Annenberg, the Jewish Gangster.

I and my preschool chums in the Ogden Park playground on the South Side favored O'Bannion, Irish, Catholic, and dealing exclusively in bootleg liquor, as opposed to Annenberg, who had supplementary activities in illegal horse-betting, and Capone, who was also busy in prostitution and narcotics. ("Dope" we called it in those days and, following Dick Tracy, its users, "dope fiends.")

No one in our family had ever met O'Bannion, but while on excursions on the North Side we often went by his flower shop opposite Holy Name Cathedral on State Street. My mother and I would stop in the cathedral for a prayer, from which I was released early to join my devout but anticlerical father in a stroll up and down the other side of the street to pay homage to the saintly florist who so bravely and effectively defied the hated Eighteenth Amendment.

A particularly poignant association with O'Bannion came through the family priest, Father Patrick Molloy, who may or may not have been a distant relative of my father's, but in any event was the only clergyman of whom he approved. "Father Pat" had been a boy with O'Bannion in an Irish slum in Chicago in the late years of the nineteenth century and had never ceased to be his friend and adviser, thereby earning from Col. Robert R. McCormick's righteous *Chicago Tribune* the dubious title the "Gangster Priest."

The grandest of our family legends centered on Father Pat's occasional visits to our house on his way to or from a funeral at one of the South Side cemeteries. He blessed the premises and handed out quarters to all small boys in sight. He talked of the great outside world, not only of the gangsters, but of Heavyweight Boxing Champion Jack Dempsey, whose uncanonical marriage Father Pat was always on the verge of straightening out. "Sure, half the things they say at the chancellery office about that boy aren't true," he explained charitably.

Indeed, the only subject on which Father Pat would not speak was Archbishop (later Cardinal) George Mundelein, his boss, Chicago's chief prelate, friend of President Franklin D. Roosevelt, and German-descended pillar of propriety, who ruled over the rowdy Irish, Italians, and Poles of the largest and richest diocese in Christendom. (There were Black, Greek, French, German, and other Catholics in Chicago, but they didn't really count.) Molloy drank silently, but not dissentingly, when my father at the end of the conversation raised the single glass of whiskey they each allowed themselves and offered "Desolation to the Dutchman!"

Then came the awful morning when the *Tribune* headlined O'Bannion's death as the climax of an accelerating gang war for control of Chicago's booze business. The Irish Gangster had been shot down by henchmen of the Italian Gangster in the door of his florist shop. Even as my mother called for a prayer for "the poor dead man," my father exploded in rage. The *Tribune* also noted that O'Bannion had been designated a "public sinner" and denied Christian burial by Archbishop Mundelein.

"Damnation to the Dutchman!" was my father's verdict on this.

My mother had a little trouble with the intricacies of the faith that could send a consecrated archbishop to Hell, but was satisfied with my father's assurance that George Mundelein would not find himself alone among his kind there. We were all on O'Bannion's side anyway. There was a denouement a few days later. This time the *Tribune* announced in banner headlines "Gangster Priest Buries O'Bannion." Two pages of pictures showed Father Pat saying prayers at the fallen warrior's grave. Eventually, "The Dutchman" had his revenge. Molloy was dispatched to the mission fields in Argentina. The blessings of the house ended. Father Pat was not seen in Chicago for years.

In due course, O'Bannion's boys loaded themselves into eight touring cars and drove slowly past Capone's Cicero headquarters in broad daylight, emptying their machine guns into it. Somehow, they missed "Scarface Al," and he finished off the O'Bannion mob not long after in the historic St. Valentine's Day Massacre in a dreary garage on North Clark Street. After that there was no doubt in anyone's mind as to who controlled the booze business in Chicago.

A note on methodology is in order here. History, for most of us, is not what we see or read but what we know. From my boyhood I knew what I have just recounted. It was not until after World War II that I discovered the "scientific method" in Social Sciences 101 at the University of Chicago and checked the documentary record. It was disturbing to discover that Dion O'Bannion had been killed before I even came into this world and that the retaliatory raid in Cicero had taken place the very year that I was born. I began to doubt even my vivid memory of standing on the front porch in my pajamas to brush the snow off the morning *Tribune* to get at the story of St. Valentine's Day 1929. After all, I would have been not quite three years old and barely into my ABCs, never mind the peculiar phonetic spelling that the *Tribune* periodically imposed on its readers in those days.

Fortunately, my mother lived on. She certified my memories to fine detail: "Yes, of course, you brought in the paper that morning. It's a wonder you didn't get your death of cold out on the porch. Looking for a late Valentine from the little girl next door, I think you were. . . . Well, you may not have actually been there when your dad and Father Pat used to drink 'Desolation to the Dutchman' but we would have told you about it often when you were a little boy, so, of course, you'd know. . . ."

She seemed relieved that my interests were so innocent. "If that's what you're studying over at the university, why don't you go and talk to Father Pat himself. After the Dutchman died, they brought in Archbishop Stritch. His mother was Irish and he has a niece who's an actress. He's much better. He brought Father Pat back and made him a monsignor."

I found an aged but still hearty Father Pat (apparently no one but his housekeeper ever called him "Monsignor") presiding over a large parish on the West Side. He confirmed all: "I never enjoyed a drink more than with your father! How we used to talk! 'Desolation and damnation,' eh? The very words! Sad it was to go to South America and leave the city to Capone . . . and His Eminence!"

From the St. Valentine's Day Massacre on, my memories take on greater plausibility, gradually upgraded to reliability when I checked them in the library stacks. One day—it would have been in the winter of 1932–33, after FDR was elected but before Prohibition was repealed in December 1933—my father took me out of first grade and in a rare excursion *à deux* brought me downtown to the Loop. We went to a movie in one of the pleasure palaces newly built as an antidote to the Depression.

Although the figures on the screen must have been some of the Hollywood "greats" of the era, Greta Garbo, John Barrymore, W. C. Fields, Boris Karloff, Jean Harlow, Clark Gable, or their like, I have no memory of whom or what we saw. I do recall vividly the speakeasy we visited afterward, where I was allowed to partake of the "free lunch" at the end of the bar and sip from my father's beer. At a little before three o'clock, we took up our stand in the center of the City Hall/County Building, whose intersecting east-west and north-south corridors provided sheltered transit for Chicagoans between La Salle and Clark, Washington and Randolph Streets.

"What are we waiting for, Daddy?" I asked, hopping from foot to foot in the way of children who neglect to take advantage of toilet facilities when

James W. Spain, first grade, Chicago, 1932.

they are available. My father responded that he wanted me to see something. It would happen in a few minutes. Before five had passed, it did.

Four "hoods" strode down the corridor, and in their midst, walking from his office on La Salle Street to be picked up by his limousine on Clark Street, was "Scarface Al," out on bail pending appeal of a conviction on income tax evasion. A scattering of citizens and municipal employees looked on indifferently. I knew the face from newspaper pictures and was impressed, but I had a question.

"Daddy, if his office is on La Salle Street, why doesn't he have his car pick him up there, instead of walking over to Clark?"

"Because he likes to walk through City Hall to show that he still owns it. That's what I wanted you to see," was the reply.

My personal contact with the Jewish Gangster was later and limited. My mother was a great walker. Occasionally on our treks about the city, she would point out a cracked place in the sidewalk where some banker or broker had ended his struggle against the Depression from twenty stories up. Once in a while she'd note a particularly well-known bookie joint, where Annenberg added to his prosperity, suggesting that I meditate on the implications of their proximity. Despite her fondness for going to the track to see the ponies run, she would, of course, never enter such illicit premises herself.

Not so the mother of my best friend in the fourth and fifth grades. She was a confirmed bettor, and when she couldn't get away from household chores to put down her daily fifty cents, her son and I would stop in on the way to school in the morning to place the bet, and again on the way home in the afternoon to pick up her rare winnings.

The bookie's was an exciting place with blackboards recording the races of the day and an announcer who did "live" commentaries based on data received (à la the movie *The Sting*) via Annenberg's wire service from observers stationed on hills or the roofs of private houses overlooking the tracks. The two eleven-year-olds were given the same courtesy and respect as other bettors. The addict's son hated his task and was never tempted on his own, but I occasionally saved up fifty cents to play a hunch. I never had a winner, or even a place or show.

It was soon over. O'Bannion was dead. Father Pat was in Argentina. Capone was firmly ensconced in federal prison. Annenberg moved east to establish himself as a respectable publisher and to put his son into an elite prep school. Booze was legitimate. More people were able to afford the dollar train tickets to the tracks where betting with a two-dollar minimum had always been legal. The city bookie joints became "mom and pop" operations. Prostitution was said to have been taken over by the Democratic party, but everyone knew that was just Republican propaganda. The real world war was coming.

A nostalgic schoolboy could find only an occasional reminder of Chicago's good old days. At my eighth birthday party, July 22, 1934, My chums and I were listening to *Jack Armstrong, the All-American Boy* when the broadcast was interrupted by a news bulletin that John Dillinger had been shot down by the FBI outside the Biograph Theater on the North Side. As a freshman in high school, I rode the same "El" train occasionally with an aged Spike O'Donnell, a minor but well-known Irish gangster. Once he invited me to share a pineapple soda with him when we got off, and we talked a little about what it was like when he was young, but he was forgetful and confused.

As the years took their toll and I became eighteen—"draft bait"—I pretty much forgot about my glamorous youth. At any rate, I had other things to think about when, as a private in the U.S. Army, I arrived for basic training at Camp Polk, Louisiana, the first time I had been any further away from Chicago than a few nights at Boy Scout camp in Michigan and Wisconsin. Camp Polk is now called Fort Polk, which, I believe, in army terminology designates greater permanence. If so, I shudder for generations of recruits yet uninducted. In my day the place was referred to by permanent cadre and transient trainees alike as "the asshole of creation." Coral snakes, scorpions, buried unexploded shells, and twenty-year-old drill sergeants from South Carolina conspired to make the epithet accurate.

I was the only midwesterner in my training company. Otherwise, by some precomputer precision, it was composed of one-third redneck farm boys from Georgia, one-third street-smart denizens of New York City and environs, and one-third equally urban-urbane punks from Southern California. The three groups had their own folkways and tended to socialize only amongst themselves. None of them thought much of me after they had to take turns explaining to me what Bernard John Grimes of Newark meant when he shouted from his bunk after lights-out "Come on, boys! Once you've had B.J., you'll never go back to women. Only a buck a throw!"

One evening the loudspeaker news at the end of the day reported that Al Capone's twenty-fifth (or maybe it was his thirty-seventh) appeal from the sentence he was serving in Alcatraz had been turned down. Desperate to contribute something after miserable weeks of being odd man out, I mentioned that I had seen the man. My bunk mate shouted out the fact for all to hear. The Georgians gave up their reminiscing of cross-burnings. The New Yorkers cut short their talk of mailbox-robbing. The Californians interrupted their reliving of gang-bangs. They all gathered round to hear of the greatest gangster of them all from one who had actually shared the air with him. My lonely days in uniform were over.

Subsequently, at the University of Chicago, Robert Maynard Hutchins, Mortimer Adler, Daniel Boorstin, and their fellow intellectuals were more impressed with the fragments of Aristotle and Thomas Aquinas that I had picked up in my Catholic secondary education than they were with my connections with the city's gangster past. But that was of little account. I was trying to get the coed (we used the term in those days) I loved to marry me. She was from Montana and working on a master's degree. I populated (often fictitiously) every bar to which I managed to get her to accompany me with shades of the great men of my boyhood. She was impressed. Soon she had her own real-life experience.

One night, while strolling along the Midway opposite Billings Hospital, a car pulled up near her. Two men emerged and dumped a moaning, semi-conscious third on the grass. They tipped their hats—"Fedoras, for God's sake!" she reported—and suggested politely that she might want to let the hospital know. Then they fingered their hats again and drove off.

She ran over to the hospital, and emergency room attendants came to get their patient. "He'll be all right," they told her. "Two bullet wounds; neither in the head. They always dump them here when they don't mind if they live." The police who sought her out in her dormitory the next morning to complete their report of the incident were equally relaxed. She tried to reconstruct the license plate number. They discouraged her. "These people don't mean any harm to decent citizens, Miss," they assured her. "But don't go walking alone at night. Some of the students at this place are dope fiends and worse. There's no telling what they might do!"

Not much later, after my Girl of the Golden West moved to a university-approved student rooming house near 63rd Street, she came home one night to find her landlady in tears. A faded, late middle-aged widow, the proprietress was given to staying up until her half-dozen coed charges returned, whereupon she plied them with tea and brownies and the late evening news. This night she was weeping copiously. "The radio just had it," she proclaimed. "Al is dead. He was such a sweet fellow! I don't know what I'd have done if he hadn't helped me after my husband passed away. He bought this house for me and you young ladies, you know! Then they sent him up and I never got a chance to thank him!"

I appeared the following night to take my date out to a modest student dinner at the University Commons and was treated to a full litany of the recently departed's virtues. When I remarked (without context) on my father's having taken me to see the great man when I was a boy, we were rewarded first by a further storm of tears and then with an opulent sirloin roast the grieving widow had prepared for herself but was unable to eat.

Catching the spirit—and showing off a bit—I offered to take both ladies out to the hotel bar at 67th and Stony Island Avenue where Al's living brother, Ralph, still hung out. The landlady couldn't go. Her only black dress wasn't good enough. She'd gotten it for the funeral of her late husband (one of Al's faithful hoods deceased decades earlier in the line of duty, she revealed). She'd have to get a better one tomorrow. But the young peoples' knowledge and respect were touching. The night would be on her. She pressed a twenty-dollar bill into my hand and shooed us out to be alone with her sorrow.

We had a couple of beers at Ralph's hangout. He wasn't there. "On the lam!" the bartender explained. "From the cops?" I asked. "Nah, from the lawyers and the reporters!" Not sure I could find Cicero on the far West Side where Al had his headquarters in the old days, we went on down the lake to an even seedier bar in Calumet City, which I mendaciously assured my Montana innocent was true Capone country. I needn't have made it up. There too the talk was all of death and grief (if not much of resurrection). We had free drinks on the basis of my boyhood recollections. Anyway, good came of it. Although it was another four years before we exchanged formal vows, I'm pretty sure that my beloved privately pledged her troth that night.

Later at Columbia University in New York, our fellow graduate students, normally incapable of accepting Chicago as anything other than a "second city," were always willing to provide a spaghetti dinner in return for our reminiscences about gangsters. More important, my professorial mentors in Comparative Government, old New Yorkers Schuyler Wallace and Lindsay Rogers, could often be distracted from my limited knowledge of the British parliamentary and French presidential systems by responses drawing tenuous parallels with O'Bannion's, Capone's, and Annenberg's differing approaches to ruling Chicago. Indeed, I managed to chew up forty-five minutes of a vital two-hour oral examination pontificating on the subject.

Eventually, we went off into the Foreign Service. In those days, young diplomats were trained to keep in mind a subject of general interest that they could introduce when necessary to sustain a dying cocktail or dinner party conversation with peoples of different educations and cultures, thereby establishing rapport. My choice while on a first assignment in Pakistan in the early 1950s was "ghosts." Everyone had them, I reasoned, and there were possibilities for inoffensive controversy between those who did and did not believe in them. I soon learned that the Islamic World strictly limits interaction between Heaven and Earth to the Holy Prophet Mohammed. While respectable Moslems might admit to having heard of ghostly experiences, they didn't much enjoy talking about them.

Ah, but gangsters were something else!

As soon as I admitted to coming from Chicago, I was treated to a swinging arm gesture and a cry of "Rat-a-tat-tat, hey? Tell us all about it!" At a Fulbright Scholars' dinner in Peshawar, a local professor introduced me as "probably the only man in all of Pakistan who has actually seen Al Capone." With scholarship and civic pride, he pointed out that since records began to be kept in the nineteenth century, his own notoriously violent Pathan city had the highest murder rate in the world—except for a brief period in the 1920s and 1930s when Chicago bested it.

The distinction accorded me was less than overwhelming, but I had a sure-fire subject to keep small talk from dying. I used it next in New Delhi, where a kindly Ambassador Chester Bowles took the still neophyte diplomat along to a Congress Party rally and the opportunity came to meet Prime Minister Jawaharlal Nehru. When I responded to the Pandit's question as to where I was from, he didn't go "Rat-a-tat-tat!" but he did remark "Oh, yes, Mr. Capone's town!"

"Yes, sir," I said. "Saw him when I was a boy!" and we held up the receiving line for five minutes while he asked me more. Poor Ambassador Bowles didn't have a word to say. He'd been to Chicago but had never seen Al Capone.

Turkish experts later disputed the Pakistani professor's claim. Their turbulent city of Malatya, they insisted, had for one year at least held the world's murder record, albeit no one could remember just which year. They had no doubts about the preeminence of Chicago in the gangster field, however, and the greatest respect for my connection with it. Indeed, when a diplomatic incident threatened to develop between our ambassador (born and brought up on the East Coast) and a group of senior Turkish officials whom he had jovially greeted with "Hi, gang!" I was called in privately to confirm, as the ambassador had desperately tried to explain, that he wasn't calling them criminals. After all, who could be trusted to know better than the man who had seen Al Capone?

In Tanzania a cabinet minister going on an official visit to the United States pressed me for the name and phone number of someone who could help him see Chicago. I proposed a son at the university. That wasn't quite what he had in mind. What about one of "them," the people we talked about all the time? I had to confess that there might well be none of "them" left and that I had been away too long to know any live ones.

When Walter (son of Moses) Annenberg was at the top of the U.S. diplomatic ladder as ambassador at the Court of St. James's during the Nixon administration, our paths crossed a few times. I was careful not to talk of Chicago, although my wife teased me that I was missing a last chance to get back my half-dollars spent in the neighborhood bookie joint so long ago. That was not to be the end of the story, however. A few years later our daughter, on her own, sought and won a generous two-year fellowship at the Annenberg School of Communications at the University of Pennsylvania. Those fifty cent bets turned out to be the best investment I had ever made. Like the university landlady, I regret that I have never had a chance to say thanks.

One day on Capitol Hill I found myself with people reminiscing about where each of us had been when John F. Kennedy was killed. Senator Charles Percy of Illinois, then chairman of the Senate Foreign Relations Committee, was present. Having exchanged stories about November 22, 1963, we discovered that both of us also remembered what we were doing on July 22, 1934, when John Dillinger was shot down by the FBI outside the Biograph theater on Chicago's North Side.

Recently, during the retirement in which this memoir was written, I rummaged my books to check on the St. Valentine's Day Massacre. I found still in print in a recent *World Almanac* the event of February 14, 1929—after a note on Amelia Earhart's flying the Atlantic and before those on the Stock Market Crash and Al Capone's first conviction for tax evasion.

What is there to say about American gangsters now that they are long gone? Citing brutal killer Gary Gilmore or financial manipulator Ivan Boesky as evidence that they live on misses the nature of O'Bannion, Capone, Annenberg, and their times.

They were greedy, vicious, and, like frontier cowboys and Hollywood stars, at once overblown and fly-specked. But they were brave rather than cowardly. Their victims were their competitors rather than society. They gave something back for what they stole. They provided an alternative to corrupt local governments. They offered a distraction from the dreary demands of everyday life, something that, other than the Brinks robbers and the early skyjacker who collected his loot and parachuted into the Rockies, no post–World War II wrongdoer has really been able to do. And what little boy, however perverse, would choose Gary or Ivan as role models?

All in all I have derived a great deal of satisfaction from my criminal connections of more than six decades.

2

Getting an Education

I HAD FINISHED MY EDUCATION and was out making a living before I realized that the schools people go to often have a lifelong influence on them. A Ford Foundation executive whom I once escorted on a tour of the Peshawar Museum proudly gave as his "profession," when he signed the visitors' book, "Princetonian."

A high foreign affairs official who was otherwise fond of me as a young bureaucrat lamented the fact that I hadn't gone to Harvard, the only subject of conversation on which he was truly enthusiastic. And what is there to say about graduates of the Yale Law School? Well, most of us know at least one.

Then I ran across the Berea and Oberlin fanatics, whose college years had been the best of their lives. I found that my mother-in-law, wife, and daughter, all Beloit alumni, misted up when they reminisced about their common alma mater in Wisconsin. Even my two youngest sons showed emotion when they talked about the New England prep schools in which they spent much time on disciplinary restriction and academic probation.

Thinking about my own academic experiences, I conclude that they were pretty good, at once impersonal, ethnic, and pluralistic in a way not equaled today, and as adequate as an education is ever likely to be. The Dominican nuns at St. Brendan's Parochial School, Marquette Road and Racine Avenue on Chicago's South Side, got first whack at me. In those Depression years, the tuition was ten dollars a year. It was sent in a dollar at a time with the monthly report card. From the first grade on, this covered reading (phonetic), writing (Palmer Method), spelling, arithmetic, history, geography, religion, effort, and deportment. Grading on such things as social adjustment and peer consciousness was unknown. Each child was what he or she was.

I was mixed material. Taught to read and write at home by my mother and given an interest in civic affairs by my father, I was an only child, known in the neighborhood as "spoiled." I did not like people, including nuns, telling me what to do, especially when it involved doing it in coordination with other children. I was not sent to St. Brendan's because it was considered better academically than the equally nearby Altgeld public school. In Chicago, as in most other places in those days, the superiority of the public schools in resources was generally acknowledged and their higher qualifications for teachers conceded.

My mother made the decision "to make sure that I got a good Catholic education right from the beginning." There might have been other reasons also. She, of course, would not have thought of, or been respected, working outside the home and hence had plenty of time to devote to me. Indeed, she confessed in later years that she was acutely aware that St. Brendan's didn't have a kindergarten, while Altgeld did, and she therefore got to keep me under her wing for an extra year. My father supported her. He was suspicious only of priests; he had a high regard for nuns.

Eight years at St. Brendan's brought me to literacy and competency in mathematics, history, and geography above that imparted by most secondary schools today. Why this should be bothers me—especially every time I visit Chicago and drive quickly and cautiously through what is now a ghetto, past a closed and abandoned church and school with cast-off young blacks lounging in the street. They are only a little poorer than I was. Yet, their preparation for the outside world is immensely inferior.

The eloquently described traumas that assailed the Catholic childhood of Mary McCarthy, and indeed of my own children, passed lightly over my head. My first few years included fear of having my hands whipped by Sister's rosary. That ended when the practice was outlawed by a new pastor. The rumor was that he objected to the desecration of the sacramental object rather than the abuse of the child. From then on we got our knuckles rapped with a ruler—as they did in the public school.

Naturally, I was told that to talk back to priests, nuns, and parents was a venial sin, which would keep me in purgatory, that to have "bad thoughts," take the Lord's name in vain, or eat after midnight before taking Communion were mortal sins, which, unless compensated for by vigorous pursuit of indulgences, would result in prolonged and severe punishment. To marry a Protestant or divorce a Catholic meant roasting in Hell forever. I didn't doubt that Sister believed all of this. It seemed fitting that she should. But it didn't occur to me to take these things literally. A child lives in a child's world. Hell and damnation can be frightening, but for most they are no more lasting and meaningful than the Yellow Brick Road to Oz or the ritual spitting we did every time we passed the local Methodist Episcopal Church on the way to and from St. Brendan's.

In the eighth grade, I discovered the Inquisition in an encyclopedia and challenged Sister Mary Amelia about it. She did as good a job of explaining as my Columbia and Chicago professors in later years, mostly atheist liberals who never in their lives hit anyone's hand with either a rosary or a ruler. As my eight years under the Dominican sisters drew to a close, I was ungratefully concerned about one thing in high school: I did not want any more women teachers! This excluded the local public high school, which was also dominated by females, although "smart" Cousin Aidan, my mother's aunt's boy, was an assistant principal there. (Sadly, he had "lost his faith" at the University of Chicago on the way to academic eminence.)

My mother, like most Irish mothers, cherished the notion that she might have a son who was a priest. My father, perhaps sensing his own not-distant death, did not pursue his anticlerical sentiments. So I visited Quigley, the archdiocesan preparatory seminary on Rush Street on the near North Side to consider and be considered for admission. I had a question: "If I sign up, will I have to be a priest no matter what?"

"Certainly not, young man!" the rector replied testily. "We take in three hundred here every year and we have to kick out five out of six of them before they graduate." Of the sixty that went on to St. Mary of the Lake (the seven-year major seminary), only half were ordained. "You'll probably not make it even halfway through prep!" he added with Jesuitical cleverness.

Quigley's course of studies involved a suit-shirt-tie-clad five years with three hours of homework each night. Its five years of Latin and four of Greek outshone that of the Chicago Latin School, a posh secular preparatory institution. The object was deliberate, if unspoken: to give the sons of blue-collar and lower-middle-class Catholics, whether they became priests or not, a better education than the scions of the Chicago establishment.

Quigley did that. Later, at the University of Chicago and at Columbia, I was to find that these august institutions delighted in my familiarity with Achilles, Aeneas, and Xenophon and that I had already read eighty out of a hundred of Mortimer Adler's "Great Books." Twenty were missing because of their presence on the *Index Librorum Prohibitorum,* which was still taken seriously in those days. I soon made up the deficiency.

Except for the Italians clustered several blocks to the west beyond Ashland Avenue, no one in my neighborhood spoke anything but English. My experience of Latin had been limited to a dozen or so phrases, such as "*Dominus vobiscum*" and "*Et cum spiritu tuo,*" memorized as an altar boy. I simply did not understand the concept of language; and if someone had told me the subject was a branch of mathematics, I would have accepted the notion calmly.

My studies did not begin well. The sample word for learning the "easy" first declension was *agricola.* Singularly unsuited for this lot of urban youth, the word means "farmer." It is accented on the antepenult—"a-*gríc*-ola." Thirty of us chanted the cases in unison: *agrícola, agrícolae, agrícola, agrícolam, agrícola.* Then we were called on individually to demonstrate our knowledge.

I recognized the parts and thought I had it. Agriculture meant farming; cola was a popular drink. But what I had somehow missed at St. Brendan's was any concept of accent. So I intoned "ágri-cóla, ágri-cólae . . ."—an eraser thrown by the notoriously short-tempered Father Kenny clipped the side of my ear—"ágri-cóla, ágri-cólam . . ." I went bravely on. That brought a book which just missed my head. When I crescendoed "ágri-cóla," he kicked the metal wastebasket across the front of the room.

"No! Damn it!" he screamed. "*Agrícola!*"

"Ágri-cóla" I repeated.

There was nothing left to throw or kick, so he pounded his head on his desk and ordered, "Sit down, you ass!"

If the incident had taken place at St. Brendan's, the girls would have giggled loudly and the boys chanted softly, "Sister says James is an ass!" It was different at Quigley. After class, one of my fourteen-year-old peers took me aside. He was Italian, repeating his first year because he could barely count to ten, but he was skilled in the use of accents.

"Don't let old Kenny get to you," he advised. "He's a bad one, but we'll fix him next time." He then took me through the declension until I was mouthing *agrícola* as well as he. Next day, he showed up with a "one-incher," a small but powerful firecracker obtained at his church's fiesta. Before class we rigged it with a long string fuse inside the metal wastebasket.

It went off in the middle of class just as Father Kenny was about to launch one of his frequent kicks. He clutched his chest and collapsed over his desk. The room prefect, designated as such each month for exemplary behavior, shot out of his first-row seat and returned with the school prefect of discipline, a priestly martinet. Father Daniel Culhane eyed the class coldly and ordered, "Some of you had better come to see me about this!" as he helped the shaking Latinist from the room.

Convinced that we had provoked a fatal heart attack, my friend and I went to confess, promising to pray for Father Kenny.

"Save your prayers for yourselves. Father Kenny will survive," the prefect of discipline informed us. "Before he went home, he told me that he thought you two would be in here. It's a good thing you are!" He gave us ten demerits each (two hours "in the jug" after class). Then, unbelievably, he chuckled and sent us on our way. "Don't ever get caught doing a thing like this again!"

At priestly poker parties, the story spread of how Kenny had scared the bejesus out of a pair of smart alecks by faking a heart attack. I finally figured out what the charade was all about. Our scatterbrained act had no moral malice in it. Our sin was indeed "getting caught," so the punishment was light. At the same time, demerits added up. If you got more than twenty-five in a year, you were kicked out. That needed to be taken seriously.

Later on I was exposed to other equally subtle instructions in practical theology. One day a chum in third year, a German boy, viewed with suspicion for his artistic inclinations, brought a book of Eric Gill's etchings to school. A mob of classmates seized the volume—naked women with hair, for God's sake!—and dragged it and its owner down to the building's boiler room. The offending edition was consigned to the flames and its owner threatened with them. Motivated by I had no idea what, I plunged an arm into the boiler and managed to get the book out only slightly scorched. Turning to fight off the righteous, I saw the same prefect of discipline standing on the stairs.

"You boys had better stop whatever it is you are doing and tell me about it!" he instructed.

The book fell open to a particularly explicit drawing as he took it from my hand, and I figured that I had truly "had it." The more articulate members of the lynch mob told their stories. "Merschel brought these dirty pictures to school, Father, and showed them around. So we decided to teach him a lesson, and Spain tried to stop us. . . ."

Danny Culhane gave them ten demerits each and sent them off. He addressed Merschel. "Eric Gill may have been a Catholic, and he could draw well, but he was a disgusting homosexual. It's something you will have to watch out for, young man. If you want to look at his pictures, do so at home. Five demerits!"

He turned to me. "Well done, boy. Gentlemen do not burn books. Now get out of here, or I'll give you two demerits for being in the boiler room without authorization!"

Not long afterward the lesson was repeated on another plane. All students were required to eat in the school cafeteria. Perversely, I took to exploring the neighborhood's restaurants, where in those days a "businessman's lunch" could be had for ninety-nine cents. I found that a beer was available (regardless of age—this was Chicago) for another fifteen cents. One day, to my horror, I looked up from my table at Rickett's to see Father Donald Temple, another professor, observing me. A few days later the boom seemed about to fall. He stopped me in the corridor and said, "I see you eat at Rickett's. I see you drink beer."

I envisaged twenty-five demerits and the end of my time at Quigley. "Well, yes, Father, but not very often."

"Tell your mother that next Tuesday you are going to stay late and have dinner with me. Bring a clean shirt."

I was relieved but still unsure what next Tuesday portended. I found out when "Doc" Temple (he was one of the few faculty members to have a doctorate of sacred theology) took me off to Jacques's, an elegant French restaurant on Michigan Avenue, and invited me to have whatever I wanted to eat and drink. An elderly, white-tied waiter asked about Doctor Temple's health and that of his young friend and unfolded our napkins on our laps. He inquired what I would like. I said that I would have a beer. And the purpose of the dinner invitation became evident.

"You may eat anything you want," said Doc, "but gentlemen do not drink beer. You may have Scotch whisky. Soda or water?"

Looking back even from our current libertarian times, it seems to me that life at Quigley was reasonably free and flexible. There were things you absolutely could not do, such as "going out with a girl" or cheating on examinations. However, other straying from the norm was ignored or actually admired (often, I suspect, in proportion to excellence of grades). My evasion of the requirement that all students attend Mass daily was known and overlooked. I was allowed to wear a grey homburg hat, a personal talisman. My working nights for the Associated Press during my senior year was accepted, if not officially sanctioned.

I turned eighteen and finished Quigley as World War II drew to a close. I took a look at the major seminary for a few months and promptly went off into the army. Even after all these years, I remain convinced that being in uniform was a major part of my education; but more about that later. Let us skip over the next two years and come to the University of Chicago in 1947.

When I got out of the army, I was a pretty cocky young man with five stripes on my arm and the GI Bill in my pocket to pay for any education I wanted. I wonder now how my widowed mother stood me when I moved back into her small, rent-free-for-me apartment on the South Side. Still impressed with Jesuit education, I headed first for Loyola University on Chicago's North Side. I didn't see a Jesuit anywhere, but a grumpy layman in the Admissions Office glanced over my collection of Quigley credits, disallowed one year of Latin and two of Greek, and indicated a willingness to give me provisional admission as a college freshman—if I was prepared to make up high school chemistry and biology.

Smoldering at this humiliation, on my way back home on the "El" I transferred at 59th Street from the Englewood train, which terminated near our apartment, to the Hyde Park line, which served the University of Chicago. Now firmly in the control of Chancellor Robert Maynard Hutchins, who had abolished both football team and fraternities, the "Midway's" academic reputation was fearsome and its admission standards reportedly the same.

I hadn't yet read James Farrell's *Studs Lonigan*, and if I had, I doubt I would have recognized Studs in myself as I prowled among the grey Gothic buildings to find the Admissions Office. I was a mixture of fear and fascination, doubting my ability to measure up. (Oddly, the University of Chicago was the only institution that ever inspired this reaction. The Foreign Service certainly did not.)

The rumpled young man I finally ran to earth, an instructor in Classics moonlighting in Admissions, studied my transcript carefully. "Five years of Latin and four of Greek!" he exclaimed. "How splendid! Good on history and English. Weak in physical science. What do you want to get your degree in?"

"Political science" was the best I could come up with.

"What a waste of all that Latin and Greek! But if you do well in the placement exams, it should work out all right!" This time my provisional admission was directly into a three-year program for a master's degree (another Hutchins invention). I was told to file my GI Bill claims with the Registrar.

My horizons had widened when I went to Quigley and again when I spent time in the army. Now they swung open to encompass the universe. In those days the University of Chicago was described as an institution where "atheists" (most of the faculty) taught Catholic philosophy (Thomism) to Jews (most of the student body) with Baptist (John D. Rockefeller) money. In fact, everyone taught and talked to everyone else about everything. Mortimer Adler extolled the virtues of the Great Books. Hans Morgenthau debated the visiting East German Communist leader, Gerhardt Eisler, on what was the only American campus to open its rostrum to him. Quincy Wright preached that the United Nations, like seventeenth- to nineteenth-century antidueling laws, would succeed if only given time enough.

Herman Finer, fresh from the London School of Economics, taught that all public acts should be covered by "unwritten" (like the British Constitution) government regulations. Jerome Kerwin (the only Catholic on the faculty), inhibited by traditional doctrine, struggled to keep up as Hutchins and Adler expanded scholastic philosophy far beyond conventional horizons. Daniel Boorstin, presiding over the Committee on Social Thought, perhaps the first interdisciplinary arrangement on an American campus, brought me to realize that the Puritan Ethic was something much deeper than I had always thought, namely, producing Thanksgiving as a counterweight to Papist Christmas.

Charles Merriam, the only university professor ever to hold elective office (Chicago alderman) until Economics Professor Paul Douglas went to the U.S. Senate in 1948, preached that government was most important at the municipal level. Leonard White insisted that good public administration solved everything.

Robert Maynard Hutchins took on Col. Robert Rutherford McCormick's *Chicago Tribune,* saying that he did not understand why the colonel cared about what he taught at the University of Chicago; no one at the university cared about what he printed in his newspaper. Hutchins defied a member of the Illinois Legislature, a onetime halfback of the moribund Mighty Maroons football team, by replying when asked whether it ever occurred to him to exercise, "Once in awhile it does. I lie down for a nap until it goes away."

Like a cerebral pope with a sense of humor (out of three hundred there must have been one), Hutchins lectured *urbi et orbi* on all subjects. Sometimes he went too far. One day extolling books as essential for survival of the mind, he remarked that an intellectual had as much right to them as a starving man to food. The next day students stripped the University Book Store and the chancellor was in trouble with the trustees again. So we brought back our loot.

The Illinois National Guard had a recruiting van on the Midway. A deep-cover U.S. intelligence officer brought his artificial, ostensibly liberal, world government organization to the campus. Henry Wallace, the third party presidential candidate in 1948, joined his vice presidential running mate, Rexford Guy Tugwell, a University of Chicago professor, in campaigning for votes. Americans for Democratic Action made their pitch. The even-then suspect Students for a Democratic Society made theirs. (I warned my Montana girlfriend about SDS. She joined anyway.) Three Trotskyite groups competed at one end of the political spectrum and two fascist organizations fought it out at the other.

We booed and picketed, cheered and marched. The important thing was not to miss anything. On those rare nights when nobody was on the rostrum, we went down to the university tavern to study the graffiti. "Kilroy" still proclaimed his presence in those post–World War II years, but the universal favorite was "Mulligan is a neo-Platonist dog!" None of us had ever met Kilroy but we knew Tom Mulligan, a classicist turned law student who spent all his time at the bar explaining his conversion. His girlfriend, the ultimate JAP (Jewish American Princess) in beauty and wealth, had written the denunciation.

Neither I myself nor student and faculty associates ever challenged my religion. They just didn't care, although all were interested in whether I was an Aristo-Thomist or a Plato-Augustinist and whether I stood with Hans Morgenthau on geopolitics or Quincy Wright on international law as the answer to the world's woes.

One thing that Hutchins and Adler and the rest of us humanists faced uncertainly in those far-off days was the challenge to the established curriculum, not as at present from Black Studies, Native American Studies, Women's Studies, or Alternate Lifestyles, but from science. We knew what Enrico Fermi and his colleagues had started when they produced the world's first sustained nuclear reaction under Stagg Stadium. We weren't all that fond of scientists and tended to keep them in the basement. (My Montana girl worked part-time filing papers for one of them, and she had a cold all the time from working in his damp office.) But we did recognize reality. Divisions of biological and physical science were promptly established in both college and graduate schools.

Eventually something like integration took place, and we all benefited. Maybe it will happen again when the now embattled politically correct, non-Western-centered advocates find themselves joining forces with the traditionalists to oppose demands for such courses as "DNA Psychosociology" and "Extraterrestrial Individuality," with the debate being conducted in electronic megabytes. And, after that . . . ?

In August 1949 I got my master's degree with a thesis on "Gilson, Thomism, and Politics," as my beloved got hers with "Vigilantism in the Montana Gold Camps." She still wouldn't marry me, so we went our separate ways, she to teach at a posh girls' school in Los Angeles, I to a cushy but temporary civilian job "reorienting" education in Japan, found for me by a friend in an influential place in the Pentagon.

I came back to the United States in 1950 to continue my unsuccessful courting while using up what was left of my GI Bill benefits at the University of Southern California. I had managed at Chicago to pass the State Department's Foreign Service examination, and at the end of the year I was called to Washington. More about that later.

To continue with my education, in 1953 I ended up at Columbia on a university fellowship and a Ford Foundation grant to do a book on the Pathans, the wild tribes along the North West Frontier of Pakistan with whom I had become fascinated during a two-year Foreign Service tour in that country.

Columbia was different from Chicago, associated longer and more closely with the metropolis in which it stood and more old-fashioned in its academic structure. After minimal consultation I found myself a Ph.D. candidate in the Department of Public Law and Government of the Faculty of Political Science. (At Chicago it had been the Department of Political Science of the Social Science Faculty.)

Here too were towering figures: Lindsay Rogers in comparative government, Schuyler Wallace in international affairs, Phillip Jessup in international law, L. D. Goodrich in international organization, W. T. R. Fox in international politics, Nathaniel Peffer in diplomatic history, and J. C. Hurewitz in all things Middle Eastern. I really wanted only to write my book on the Pathans and go back to government, or maybe journalism, but they devoted a flattering amount of time and energy to encouraging me to complete the Ph.D. and become a fellow academic.

An apparently insurmountable obstacle to my doctorate was that, apart from English, I could read only French. Columbia required two "recognized languages of scholarship" for the Ph.D. I was reluctant to start from scratch with German, Spanish, Italian, or Russian. What good were they anyway to someone who was interested only in the Pathans (none of whom, like me, spoke any of the above)?

Browsing through the university's graduate degree guide (only slightly smaller and less complex than the FAM, the U.S. government's Foreign Affairs Manual of regulations), I discovered that Latin was still listed as an acceptable language and promptly signed up for the examination given every three months by the Classics Department. One look at the dozen pages of Livy, Ovid, and Juvenal made clear that this was not Quigley's kind of Latin, and I handed it back, claiming there was a mistake. What I needed was Medieval Latin. I was sent to the History Department where a young instructor ran me through a couple of paragraphs of the *Gesta*

Romanorum, twelfth century folk tales in the simplest Church Latin, and certified me as "essentially qualified."

A friendly (God bless her!) secretary to the Department of Public Law and Government did a course credit calculation with me, throwing in a few credits left over from the University of Chicago, and I was ready for the oral comprehensives. This formidable two-hour affair involved two majors and four minors. I did reasonably well in comparative government and political theory, waxed loquacious on Middle Eastern affairs to chew up a solid hour, and scraped past in international politics and international law. With only two minutes left, I met my nemesis in diplomatic history.

Professor Nate Peffer was famous around Columbia for two things: being the only full professor with no more than a bachelor's degree and harboring a hostile attitude toward graduate students who desired to acquire the title of "doctor" (which was used at Columbia, as it was not at Chicago). With an eye on the alarm clock that would end the session, he handed me scribbled on the back of an envelope a list of twenty classic high points of diplomatic history, beginning with the Roosevelt Corollary to the Monroe Doctrine. "Identify these in one sentence or less!" he ordered.

I got the first, followed by nineteen "Don't knows" and "Not sures." The alarm went off, and I left the room while the faculty discussed my performance. After a half hour, I was called back. The chairman, Lindsay Rogers, announced that I had passed. Leaving, he shook my hand and offered congratulations.

I responded "Thank you, sir. I'm grateful."

He turned back and looked at me. "God damn it, boy, you should be!"

None of the others, including Professor Peffer, had anything to add.

Thus the way was opened for me to go off to England, India, Pakistan, and Afghanistan on a Ford Foundation grant and write my book. Eventually I came back again to offer it as my dissertation and defend it in another two-hour oral session. This time things were more relaxed. The cast of characters was pretty much the same: Rogers, Wallace, Fox, Goodrich, and Hurewitz. (Nate Peffer had declined an invitation to attend.) I knew more about my obscure tribes than anyone else, including the young anthropology assistant professor who had been assigned to participate under a university regulation requiring the presence of "a representative of a relevant discipline within the faculty but outside the candidate's home department."

My mentors had concluded by now that I was going to leave the groves of academe. (Indeed, I was already back on the government payroll.) Old-school gentlemen that they were, they decided to send me off benevolently. I responded happily and at length to such questions as "Why is it that there are Pathans in both Pakistan and Afghanistan?" and "Are they really descended from the lost tribes of Israel?"

The young anthropologist, having his own way to make in the university, bored in. He pointed out that there was no trace of anthropological methodology in my work and suggested correctly my utter ignorance of that subject. "Now, Mr. Spain, if you are to do a proper job of scholarship on these 'Pay-thans,'" he began, "you must go back and . . ."

Recalling the agony inflicted on me over "agri-cóla," I interrupted in a voice in which my brief spell in diplomacy had taught me how to mix apology and contempt. "Please, Professor! Pa*thans.* Accent on the last syllable!"

The seniors, instinctively siding with an amiable graduate student they were about to get rid of over an aggressive colleague with whom they must live, guffawed. The flustered young academic lapsed into incoherence. The remaining twenty minutes of the session were waived. I was a Doctor of Philosophy. So ended my formal education.

Looking back, I'm pretty well satisfied with it. I missed the emotional and spiritual attachment that places like Harvard and Oberlin produce, but I don't think I lost out on any of the ideas that circulate there. Perhaps I even acquired a few techniques that are unknown or discounted in such institutions. Peter McDonough, in the book *Men Astutely Trained: A History of the Jesuits in the American Century,* stresses how intellectual strain, divided personal loyalties, and the "fatal success" of Jesuit education have succeeded in propelling Catholics out of their subculture and into the mainstream.

Maybe so. But I never found anything deadly in my bits and pieces of education. On the contrary, they seemed to me to fit well into both the subculture and the mainstream. Anyway, I got a lot out of them—and I may even have given a little back to both God and Caesar.

3

Wearing a Uniform

WHAT HAVE I LEARNED OVER the years about the role of the military in America and the role of the American in the military?

The citizen volunteer was paramount in the Revolution. The U.S. Military Academy at West Point, New York, was established in 1802 to provide leadership, and indeed it did in the 1812, Mexican, and Spanish-American wars. The draftee–citizen soldier appeared in the Civil War, played a substantial role in World War I, and came to full glory in World War II, bearing by far the larger share of a million casualties. The idea that it was proper for civilians involuntarily in uniform to die for their country carried on through Korea and Viet Nam.

Then the Selective Service System, which had begun with violence in the New York Draft Riots of 1863, ended with violence in the "Hell no! We won't go!" demonstrations of a century later. After that, volunteer professional soldiers using "smart" weapons won virtually casualty-free victories in Central America and the Persian Gulf. (Some of their less lucky companions were blown up in Beirut and shot in the back under the UN flag in Somalia.)

Public debate on military conscription, after waxing and waning for more than a hundred years, seems over—for the twentieth century at least. Focus is now on some kind of national service bill that provides for voluntary service in a modest organization resembling the Civilian Conservation Corps, devoted to social and environmental welfare. Its alumni would receive educational benefits to enable them to hold their own in an affluent society. Most Americans seem to like it that way.

I turned eighteen as the war in Europe raced to a close. By the time I was actually in uniform, the war in the Pacific had ended also—and with it the threat of dying on the beaches of Kyushu or Honshu. My military education began during unspeakable weeks of basic training in Camp Polk, Louisiana.

The army makes sure that, whatever else its men suffer, they get more than enough to eat. My training company was experimenting with "family messing," in which each small unit had its own dining hall with food put in platters on tables of ten. We had our own cooks, but the troops still had to provide a dozen or so men every day for hated KP (kitchen police) duties. Much of the rest of the huge camp used a consolidated mess, and by some exercise in military logic we had to provide it with another dozen KPs regularly, too.

On my KP morning, I had trouble finding the place and arrived ten minutes after the prescribed 5:00 A.M. deadline. The marshaling of pot scrubbers, dishwashers, food servers, and the like was still going on. A snarling sergeant checked his list and gestured me to a small cluster over at the side—the punishment group, I assumed. Then, having dispersed the rest to their assigned tasks, he came over to us.

"Get out of here, you fuck-offs!" he ordered. "You got the rest of the day off. Go to the PX or the movie or wherever you want. Report back to your companies before 2100 hours."

I addressed one of my unknown companions. "What's this all about?"

He shrugged. "It's Yom Kippur, that's all. The bastard can't make us work in noncombat situations." He stuck out a hand. "I'm Sidney Greenberg. That's Mel Goldstein over there. The first movie's at 9:00 A.M. We'll fool around at the PX until then."

"But I'm not Jewish! Why am I off?"

"What's your name? Oh, 'Spain.' Well, old know-it-all told us it was Yom Kippur before you came along and warned us not to try to cheat. He said he knew Jewish names; they all ended in 'stein' or 'berg' or places, like a fellow he'd read about called Isaac of York. Welcome to the tribe! Enjoy it while you can."

We went to the movies four times, the library twice, and in between stuffed ourselves with PX food, beer, and jukebox music. I became aware of a hidden asset. My dog tags might say "R.C.," but my surname had limitless possibilities. I went through the rest of my time in the army claiming both Jewish and Christian holidays. On something like this the khaki machine has no institutional memory, and none of my various commanders later had individual ones—even when Passover and Easter came within days of each other.

I learned quickly that standing silent when volunteers were asked for to do sanitary details (latrine digging) or demonstrate crawling through barbed wire under machine gun fire had no demonstrable effect. You had to do these things anyway. I abandoned the traditional army wisdom of "Never volunteer!" Instead, I volunteered for everything and anything that might get me out of Camp Polk: Officer Candidate School, parachute training, even poison gas experiments.

The world's greatest military machine was breaking up and Camp Polk felt the effects. Veterans poured home from Europe and the Pacific on long-service "points." Replacements were urgently needed. Our seventeen-week basic training course was cut to eight and suddenly we were full-fledged soldiers. There wasn't time for a passing-out parade, but our company commander, a much-decorated captain who had already proclaimed his intention to be a thirty-year army "lifer," talked informally with me.

"War's over now, so I guess we don't need so much training about how not to get killed," I offered.

He shook his head sadly. "You got it bassackwards, boy. The war's over, so you don't need so much training in how to kill people!"

He told me that one of my offers to volunteer had been picked up. I was off to Combat Photographer School at the Signal Corps Photo Center (SCPC) in Long Island City, New York. The rest of the training company were going to occupation duty in remote and dismal Korea, least desirable of overseas assignments in those days.

SCPC revealed a different side of the military machine. It was run by captains and majors from Hollywood and the big newspapers, who had come in to make professional-quality recruiting films and produce a high-standard pictorial record of U.S. victories in World War II. Some of them still didn't have enough points for discharge. While waiting, they lived in luxury Manhattan hotels and made deals for their postwar careers. They came over to SCPC for a couple of hours each day to teach teenage draftees the rudiments of photography and assign them to training exercises taking pictures of everything from the Metropolitan Opera to the New York Police Department maintaining order in Chinatown.

We trainees worked a five-day week and had the rest of our time free to take advantage of free dinners, play tickets, and more provided by the USO (United Services Organization) in a city in love with uniforms. We were given handfuls of subway tokens for our assignments, with no accounting for private travel required. My personnel records went to Korea with those of the rest of my training company, but the SCPC sergeant major allowed me to draw my private's seventy-two dollars a month by signing a paper certifying that I was in the army and assigned to SCPC.

"'Course, there's another side to it," he told me. "Without an assignment order I can't draw for you on the food and quarters roster, and you'd be sleeping and eating off the rest of us. We'll get by, though. There's only sixty now, but I've still got three hundred on the roll like there used to be. So, if you ever have a hot date and want to take a couple of steaks to her apartment, let me know. Those fucking Hollywood officers do it all the time!"

The normal seventeen-week course at SCPC was not shortened. There was no longer any combat, so combat photographers overseas could be brought home without replacements. We trainees learned by doing. We took pictures of everything. In the process I mastered driving, tooling a jeep across the Queensborough Bridge and through Times Square. I got myself into the press box for Yankees, Giants, and Dodgers games and backstage at theater, ballet, and opera presentations. I rode with the NYPD on night patrols, ate free at the Stork Club, played tennis with Jinx Falkenberg, joined the mayor for dinner at Gracie Mansion, and dated a model whose picture was on the cover of *Cosmopolitan* magazine. I discovered that with luck and skill the army, for all its ferocious practices, could be made to work for me.

However, the army never entirely loses sight of its purposes. The day came when I was handed orders for a brief furlough in Chicago en route to Camp Stoneman in California, whence I was to proceed to join the 16th Signal Services Company, which was thought to be in Japan. I was given cash to cover civilian transportation to San Francisco. In hope of adding to my leave funds, I went to Mitchell Field in another part of Long Island and hitched a free ride on a decrepit C-47 allegedly heading for Chicago. I was flattered when, the only passenger, I was called to the cockpit by the two lieutenants who piloted the craft. One pointed at a chart showing an obscure airfield in the middle of Michigan.

"Here's where we're going in," he explained. "Have you ever done it before?"

Confused over the difference between Michigan and Chicago and between "landing" and "going in," I was not about to admit that this was my first airplane ride. "Well, not in this kind of a plane," I hedged.

"Nothing to it," he assured me. "Just stay buckled up. There'll be a lot of bumping and sparks, but we probably won't even catch fire!"

From subsequent chatter between the lunatics to whom I had entrusted my life, I figured things out. The C-47 was a derelict. The landing gear wouldn't stay down. They were flying it to a facility specializing in cannibalization for spare parts. They were going to crash land it there. We all walked away, but a taxi to Detroit and bus fare to Chicago wiped out anticipated savings.

In 1946 most people still crossed the country by train. I got a reserved seat on the Santa Fe El Capitan, planning a night in Los Angeles and another in San Francisco before reporting to Camp Stoneman. On the train I found another SCPC trainee, a lab technician from Minneapolis. We savored our trip across America, hanging out the window to spit in the Mississippi and grabbing fistfuls of snow as we climbed slowly up the Rockies. Elderly couples (even in those days, anyone over thirty) offered us sandwiches, and girls flirted with us in the bar car. One of them, just turned twenty-one, had to buy the drinks for the rest.

On our night out in Los Angeles, we shared a cab with a meanly drunk captain, who sneered at our lowly enlisted status. My friend, under the influence of two Tom Collinses, punched him in the nose. Contrary to what had been drilled into me at Camp Polk, no thunderbolts flashed from the sky. The driver merely pulled to the curb and said, "You kids had better get out." He nodded at the befuddled officer. "He'll pay."

Twenty-four hours later in San Francisco, we found that we had missed the last bus that would get us to Camp Stoneman in time to report as ordered. We sought help from Army Headquarters at the dignified Presidio. A bored OD (officer of the day) laughed and put us on a supply truck to the camp, up the bay near Vallejo. No one at Stoneman was sure where the 16th Signal Service Company was, but there was a transport for Yokohama leaving in forty-eight hours, so we were listed for that. The two of us—and several thousand others—had just marched aboard when we were marched back to the dock. Someone had discovered that the ship would pass through Aleutian waters. Trucks full of heavy army overcoats pulled up, and we were each issued one.

During the first two days of what we were told would be a voyage of thirty, we tried to adjust to the narrow, six-tier bunks in the steamy bowels of the converted ten-thousand-ton Liberty ship. The twice-a-day meals, eaten in a mess hall ankle-deep in vomit from cases of seasickness, were even harder to take. Then we volunteered again: for mine-watch duty in an abandoned gun turret on the starboard bow. We moved our overcoats and blankets up and "lived in," having swiped fifty-pound sacks of onions and bread from the galley. Sandwiches from these kept us alive and healthy, and I still have a partiality for them. We spotted no mines but got a brief sight of the Aleutians through banks of fog and mist. We thanked our stars that we weren't going there!

As we sailed into the waters of Tokyo Bay, a delegation of troops called on their nominal commander, a Medical Corps colonel who occupied a cabin next to the ship's captain all by himself. The delegation protested the overcoats issued at the last minute. They were heavy, looked awful, and wouldn't fit into already overstuffed duffle bags. Would they really be needed in Japan? Couldn't we get rid of them? The benign doctor looked up a temperature chart for the coastal regions of Honshu and Kyushu and then checked Army Clothing Regulations. The overcoats, he conceded, didn't appear to be necessary. We could dispose of them. Someone ran for the public address system and announced the new policy.

Within minutes, thousands of overcoats bobbed in the waters where General of the Armies Douglas MacArthur had accepted Japan's surrender aboard the battleship *Missouri* a few months earlier. From my post in the bow, I wondered which bold soul had been the first to fling his overboard. Surely, a field marshal's baton belonged in his duffle bag!

At the huge "Repple-Depple" (replacement depot) outside Yokohama, we found that there really was a 16th Signal Service Company. A proud and vigorous unit of three hundred, it had photographed most of the war in the Pacific. On arriving in Japan, its first concern was to send home its men with "big points." It now consisted of an alcoholic captain, a befuddled second lieutenant, an addled master sergeant (all of whom had committed themselves to becoming Regular Army "lifers"), and one photographer and two lab technicians from the SCPC class before ours. We brought its "order of battle" up to eight. We were supposed to stay in the Repple-Depple except while on official passes, but there was nothing to do there except lounge around the PX and movie hall. So we spent much of our time in Yokohama trading cigarettes and candy bars for pathetic souvenirs.

Fortunately, I was in my proper place one morning when a nervous Repple-Depple colonel led an impeccably dressed major with a cord on his shoulder to our four-tent-long company street and called for the 16th to assemble. Three of us turned out. The other two were lab technicians, so I was carried away by the major to become Official Photographer to Lieutenant General Robert L. Eichelberger, Commander of the Eighth United States Army, the American occupying force in Japan. On the way to headquarters I was further informed that I would occasionally go to Tokyo to do photographic jobs for SCAP (Supreme Commander Allied Powers) General of the Armies Douglas A. MacArthur. Under congressional pressure, SCAP had just dismantled the large personal public relations unit he had carried with him throughout the Pacific.

When we arrived, the Major tossed me the keys to the jeep. "This one's yours," he said. "Find a place to billet."

In the year that followed, I traveled all over Japan with the army commander on the special train he had acquired from the Imperial Palace. I photographed him giving medals to American officers and shaking hands with Japanese officials (discreetly disappearing when they insisted on handing him gifts of ancient weapons, lacquer, and china). I went to Tokyo to take pictures of General MacArthur. He never traveled beyond the Dai Ichi Building, where he had his headquarters, and the former American Embassy, where he lived. My Speed Graphic recorded him handing out medals and dominating the Allied Control Council (American, British, French,

James Spain, "official U.S. Army photographer," in Japan, 1946. *Courtesy U.S. Army*

Australian, Chinese, Dutch, and Russian field marshals and generals).

Things happened to me that should happen to every maturing young man. I discovered the beauty of Kyoto and Nikko, the mystery of the centuries-old tea ceremony, the visions of an ancient Frenchman in Karuizawa who made wood block prints with such materials as mother-of-pearl and amber ground into the ink. I enjoyed the charm of folk dances like the *Tanka Bushi* and the *Izu Bandi,* the bombast of the *kabuki,* and the quiet of the *noh* theaters. I savored strange food at tiny paper-and-bamboo-walled restaurants with mystic *kakemono* scrolls on the walls and gaudy paper banners flying outside—and the pleasures of being carried back drunk to my *ro-jo-han,* two-and-a-half *tatami* room, at country inns.

Through most of this I was still a private, wearing khaki adorned only by the red and white Eighth Army patch on my shoulder and the photographer's flash on my sleeve. My records were still lost, so I couldn't be promoted. I didn't mind. During my official duties, both MacArthur and Eichelberger called me "Sergeant" or "Son." (I don't suppose they could conceive of anyone more lowly serving them.) On my time off I had the same run of the newly founded Foreign Press Club as the rest of that motley crew. Occasionally, for fast food and drink I dropped into an Officers' Club near headquarters. I had trouble only once, and it was handled quickly. An officious captain at the bar, guessing my lowly lineage, remarked to a companion that he was going "to check out the kid." A major, a bright new medal on his chest, glanced at me. "Better be careful," he warned. "Whatever he is, he's the Old Man's kid."

Then my records finally caught up with me. I had been in the army more than six months without "major disciplinary infraction" and was therefore entitled to be a private first class at $76 a month (up from the $72 I was getting and the $28 a private drew for much of the war). I was ordered to report to the headquarters company orderly room with my one stripe sewn on my sleeve. I had barely signed the required paper when the phone rang. The officiating officer came to attention and shouted. "The general's giving medals. He wants Spain in his office right away. Quick!"

I grabbed my camera and performed as expected. As the ceremony ended and the honored officers filed out, I waited respectfully. General Eichelberger glanced at me and said, "Thank you, Sergeant." Then his eye caught the new stripe. He did a double take and asked, "You are a sergeant, aren't you, son?"

"No, sir," I replied sadly. "I'm only a private first class, but I do the best I can."

A kindly man, the general said, "You do work hard, and you're a good photographer. You really ought to be a sergeant."

I snapped "Thank you, sir!" and sped around to the little adjacent office of the senior aide, my original discoverer. "Major, sir," I reported, "the general says that I ought to be a sergeant!"

The aide pushed open his connecting door. "Sir, Spain is in here. He says that you said that he ought to be a sergeant."

"Well, yes. I did say something like that," the general admitted with a chuckle.

The major shut the door. "OK," he conceded. "What kind of a sergeant would you like to be?"

I was tempted to try for master sergeant (three stripes and three rockers) but feared to push my luck too far. "Well, sir, I'm a photographer. Photographers are technical people. I think tech sergeant (three stripes and two rockers) would be nice."

The major was close to enough points for discharge. "All right. You're a tech sergeant. For God's sake, get the stripes sewn on. I don't want to go through this again!" My monthly earnings soared to something like $152.

Before long, after less than two years in the army, my own points totaled up, and I was ready to go back to civilian life. A newly issued circular from ATS (Army Transport Command) announced that enlisted "first three graders" (master, technical, and staff sergeants) were eligible for air transportation for discharge in the Z.I. (Zone of the Interior), if so recommended by "Division or Higher Headquarters." That wasn't hard to arrange. I traveled back to Camp Stoneman, not in thirty days but in sixty hours, the DC-4 propeller-driven transport taking eight hours from Tokyo to Guam, eight to Kwajelein, eight to Johnson's Island, four to Honolulu, and fifteen to San Francisco. (Today's jets require less than a dozen hours for a nonstop trip.)

I turned in my uniform at Stoneman and refused an offer being made to all "first three graders" of a second lieutenant's commission in the Reserve. My military career was over and I knew what I wanted to do with the rest of my life: to represent America abroad as a civilian. There were, however, to be a few subsequent military blips on the screen. (The metaphor was just gaining currency in those days.)

In the 1948 election, the eminently liberal University of Chicago, almost to a person, got behind the Democratic candidates: Harry Truman for president, Adlai Stevenson for governor of Illinois, and Paul Douglas for U.S. senator. By training and instinct, I should have been with the others. But Douglas MacArthur, still ruling Japan, allowed his hat to be thrown into the ring for the Republican nomination for the presidency and I, dreaming of being the first twenty-two-year-old ambassador in history, wrote him an approving letter.

He replied, addressing me as "Dear Comrade-in-Arms" and accepting my support. I took the letter down to the local MacArthur headquarters, set foot in a Republican institution for the first time, and promptly found myself "Acting National Chairman, Veterans for MacArthur." Neither I nor the World War I general, chairman of Sears Roebuck, who replaced me got very far (for which I retroactively thank God!), but the die was cast, and I had to support Dewey, Green, and Busby. It did not do my popularity any good at the university, especially when the Democrats won both in Illinois and the nation.

In 1949, finished at the University of Chicago but not yet accepted by the Foreign Service, I prowled the State Department's Washington corridors for something to fill in. In a large but sparsely furnished office in the Pentagon, I found General Eichelberger serving out his last months before retirement, as advisor to the secretary of the army on the Far East.

The WAC (Women's Army Corps) major who had been his secretary in Japan rushed me in. She was obviously eager to find something, anything, to keep the Old Man busy. He greeted me warmly and, after reminiscing about the "old days," called in another aide, who took me off and fixed me up with a cushy six-month assignment "reorienting education" in Occupied Japan.

Years later, as a senior diplomat in Turkey, I tried to bolster rapport with the generals then running the country by recounting tales of my life as a private and sergeant. Turkey had universal conscription, but every high school graduate was commissioned. The pashas couldn't conceive of an ex-enlisted man who had risen in the world. Their politest reaction was that I must be joking. My service in uniform had finally been mined out.

Like everyone else who ever served in the U.S. military, my career in uniform was cumulatively unique. Those of the majority of involuntary civilian-soldiers of the time probably had more in common with Bill Mauldin's mud-and-blood-splattered cartoon characters, Willy and Joe. Even the most wretched of them, however, came away with the experience of having lived at risk for something other than themselves, and with an understanding of camaraderie of a kind beyond that to be found in Boy Scout troops, union baseball leagues, or the local country club. Most of them also had at least one story of how they had beaten the system and taught the military machine a lesson.

I wonder who is humanizing the machine now?

4

Family Values

IT IS EASY TO BE FLIPPANT about education, careers, even totems such as sports and automobiles. It is hard to deal lightly with our families. More than anywhere else in the uncharted waters through which we sail, "here be dragons!"

In childhood my "dragons" were few. My father was forty-six when I was born. He took me to see exciting things—the stockyards fire, Al Capone walking through City Hall, Franklin D. Roosevelt calling for a "quarantine of the Aggressor" at the dedication of the Outer Drive Bridge. But in a boy's mind, these did not entirely compensate for his failure to teach me batting, throwing, and catching, as my friends' more youthful and vigorous fathers did.

My younger mother, pretty and vivacious, skilled in domestic arts, font of all knowledge, for some reason mysterious to me but apparently known to all the neighborhood "could have no children" after me. In an era where an only child was a rare phenomenon, this made me a suspicious character at playground and school. I wondered if somehow I might myself be responsible for our misfortune. The fact that I had no grandparents—all four were dead—added to my oddity.

I had two bachelor uncles, one each paternal and maternal, whom the Depression pushed into alcoholism. Occasionally, they showed up at the door for a drink or the price of one and were dealt with singly and clandestinely by their particular sibling. I was early instructed, separately and secretly, how to handle an uncle if I should happen to be in the house alone: Be nice to the poor man. If there's fifty cents in the kitchen jar (this from my mother) or on my dresser (this from my father), give it to him. Don't tell your mother (from my father), or father (from my mother).

The most formidable dragon that everyone, including small boys, had to live with during those days was the Great American Depression (1929–39, for lack of a more precise definition). Our family was better prepared than most.

My father, born Patrick J. Spain in 1881 near Tullamore, Ireland, came to Chicago in 1897. In rare personal moments, he revealed that he had left "a jump ahead of the Queen's troopers" and that the Spains had been great people in their day. Their ancestor had been one Donal from a Kildare clan

The Spain family cottage (built circa 1798), the Grand Canal, Cappancur, County Offaly, Ireland, as it looked in the 1970s.

of the kingly Kavanaughs, who had remained loyal to the old church and who therefore in the seventeenth century had to be sent off to Spain for his education. Donal's impoverished descendants had at the turn of the nineteenth century moved to the King's County to tend a lock on the new Grand Canal.

There they had stayed until Pat took off for the New World. He had lived a quarter-century as a single man in Chicago, shoveling bones in the stockyards, carrying a hod on construction projects, and finally driving streetcars and promoting the cause of organized labor.

Handsome, over six feet tall, with black hair and white skin, he had only a few years of formal education, but spoke Shakespearean English without a trace of a brogue. He saved his money for the day when he would need a house of his own. He was as racially unenlightened as most American whites of his time but was proud of saving a black in the 1919 race riots by driving his streetcar into a mob and snatching away the lynch victim. Except for a single brief visit in 1921, he was finished with Ireland. His attendance at Mass was irregular, but after all the Kavanaughs and the Spains had gone through, no priest—or archbishop, either—was going to drive him out of the church.

My mother, born Mary Ellen Forristal in 1890 in New Ross, County Wexford, still cherished at her death more than ninety years later documents showing the name spelled "fforistal" in the old Norman way. She delighted in the legend (which may have been true) that her great-grandfather, one Captain Williams, had commanded the three-masted schooner that brought the Kennedys, also from New Ross, to Boston in 1848. She could never see the humor I did in the image of that top-hatted petit bourgeois, paid fifty pounds a year to captain a ship he did not own, looking down with scorn and pity on his wretched passengers in steerage.

She came to the United States in 1913, when she was fully grown, to visit an aunt in Chicago. Though she stayed on, she never gave up her Irishness—perhaps because it was in New Ross that the famous dialogue about the English-Irish "troubles" is supposed to have originated: "Q: When did they begin? A: When Strongbow crossed the Irish Sea [twelfth century]. Q: When will they end? A: When Cromwell gets out of Hell."

Energetic, pretty, vivacious, never deigning to disguise her brogue, the young colleen went to work in the garment factories fueled by World War I.

In a few years, she was a forewoman, with a small share in the profits and a foot in the boss class. She, too, saved her money and planned for the future.

In 1923, in lacy white gown, with a full trousseau in waiting cedar chests, she stood before the altar in St. Bernard's Church, where she was joined with Pat in the holy sacrament of matrimony. "The melting pot" was working well: Irish immigrants were supposed to marry only people from the same part of Ireland.

Mary Ellen quit her job at the "sweatshop" (Pat's word), and they settled down in a newly purchased house. It took three years for me to appear. Three years later came the Depression. The mortgage on the house was paid off. Pat had a steady job on the cars. A prized Atwater-Kent radio had been paid for in cash, so it was all ours. I heard Al Smith's gravelly voice as he fought for the Democratic nomination for president in 1932. Convinced that "they wouldn't let a Catholic have it because they know they're going to win," Pat and Mary Ellen nonetheless put Franklin D. Roosevelt's picture in the window. He ignored the threat from his streetcar bosses that he would be fired for it.

In November 1932, FDR triumphed over Herbert Hoover, the Republican candidate who said, if Roosevelt is elected "grass will grow in the streets." In early 1933, in the first grade, I absorbed my first historical fact. FDR would be sworn in in March because in the past it had required that much time for the victor to ride in from Tennessee or Illinois or wherever; but that was no longer necessary. Henceforth, inaugurations would be in January.

Almost simultaneously I came down with lobar pneumonia. The fluid that filled the young lungs turned septic and peritonitis set in, a recipe for death in those days before penicillin. Medical insurance was unknown, and all costs had to be borne by the family.

Sick leave was equally unheard of, not for the worker, and certainly not for him to sit at the bedside of a relative. Pat's vigil at the hospital threatened to cost him his job, but he was saved by his union connections. An uncle did lose his busboy job at the Union League Club for his absence without leave. Mary Ellen, standing anonymously in a hospital elevator, got the prognosis when she overheard two doctors chatting. "The kid in 309? Not a chance. He's finished!"

But the family pulled me through. An unconventional German woman doctor my mother found cut a hole in my back and put in a rubber tube to

The wedding of Patrick Joseph Spain and Mary Ellen Forristal (*at left*), Chicago, July 21, 1923. Best man John Sherlock and maid of honor Helen O'Keeffe (*at right*).

drain the worst lung (an operation the hospital surgeons had refused to perform). My father bullied the nurses and, at the first sign of returning appetite, brought in a tempting hot dog (which the hospital kitchen refused to supply).

Such were the uncertainties and simplicities of medicine in America in those days. The approach to convalescence was not much different from what it had been full centuries earlier. Returning from the hospital in an ambulance, I was cheered at the door of the house by friends and relatives—and not allowed out of it again until the safe warmth of summer.

The family savings were gone, and Pat's wages were cut to eighteen, then eleven, cents an hour. The day came when there were only two dollars in the house and payday was a week away. Mary Ellen took a recovered seven-year-old downtown. She carried a pair of gold cuff links she had given Pat on their wedding day and a gold ring of his mother's that he had given her. At a leading jewelry store on State Street, she presented the treasures. A supercilious clerk insisted on testing the metal before he would give an estimate. He offered ten dollars to a tearful woman and bewildered little boy. To the boy it was a lot of money, two weeks wages for his father. To Mary Ellen it was not enough, and the cuff links and the ring, with the sharp little notches the clerk filed in them, are still in the family.

Things gradually got better as FDR's economic recovery measures took hold. But there was a final blow still to come. Pat fell sick with a long terminal illness. Roosevelt's blessed Social Security had just come into effect, and the union provided a year's disability payments. But the psychology of a Depression-embittered generation was harsh. In a neighbor's house one day I was told, "Ah, you had it good all the time. Now you'll have no breadwinner, and you'll find out what it's like to be poor."

Compassion still reigned at home, however. To my chagrin, my father had always refused to take me to Comiskey Park to see a White Sox game. Devoted to the team in his younger years, he had turned on it during the "Black Sox" scandal of a crooked World Series in 1919 and swore never again to watch them play. When a union comrade came to visit the dying man, he pleaded to be allowed to do something, anything, to help. My father said, "Take the boy to see the Sox. I should have done it myself when I could."

World War II came. Pat died. Mary Ellen went back to running a garment factory. I finished school and went into the army. When I came back

Edith Burke James, U.S. Navy WAVE, North Island, California, 1945.

to the university, love and respect were still there between us. My mother and I stayed in close touch throughout the remainder of her life, but now we were two individual adults with different tastes and habits. The new postwar world was getting underway, and the old family intimacy and interdependence were going.

It took a few years, but I got it back again.

Edith was from Montana, almost four years older than I, fresh out of a WAVE navy uniform, tall, slim, and beautiful. She had been engaged twice and was at the University of Chicago to get a master's degree in history, writing her thesis on "Vigilantism in the Montana Gold Camps."

I fell instantly and totally in love and remain so fifty years later. She was alternately amused by my arcane knowledge of Chicago and frightened by the ardor with which I pursued her and by my constant proposals of marriage. She told me that she wanted someone strong when she married; and I, too ready to do anything that I thought might please or placate her, didn't seem a likely candidate. She even went to the extent of getting engaged a third time, possibly just to discourage me.

We did a lot of things together, but I never met her mother, a frequent visitor, and she never met mine. After three years at the university, we got our degrees and went our separate ways, she to Los Angeles to add a California teaching certificate to her portfolio and I to Washington to pursue a Foreign Service career.

On returning in 1950 from a brief civilian assignment in Japan, I stopped for a few months in Los Angeles to have another try at courtship. We found that we still liked to talk to each other and that we both considered Angelenos callow. This time under true political colors, I joined her in desultory campaigning for James Roosevelt and Helen Gahagan Douglas against a panoply of big-name Republicans, including a one-term congressman named Richard M. Nixon, whom we agreed was a sinister figure.

We were acutely aware that we were at the midpoint of the twentieth century. The Korean War began. We talked over 29¢ margaritas and $1.98 prime-rib dinners at Lowry's about the time that lay ahead and how important it was that the right things be done in it. She said that her right thing, for a while at least, was going to be teaching history to the girls of West Lake School. I said she should marry me and come away with me in the Foreign Service. She refused.

I went back to the spartan Beta Sigma Tau antifraternity house (only Negroes, Jews, Catholics, and foreigners), in which I had found cheap quarters, and stayed up all night painting a large wooden sign that proclaimed: "*Virtus! Veritas! Virginitas! Ineuntes, Spem Depone!*" which in bad Latin means, "Virtue! Truth! Virginity! Abandon Hope All Ye Who Enter Here!" I took it back and hung it over the door of the staid Soroptimist House, where she earned free rent by supervising female students. From there, I left for Washington, D.C.

So that was that—until January 1951. I got into the Foreign Service and, before I quite knew what was happening, was ordered to report as a vice consul in Pakistan by February 28. I wrote to tell her the news and to ask—for the last time, I emphasized—would she marry me? It took an airmail letter only two or three days to cross the country in those days, and an answer came back in exactly six. She would! But I'd have to come to Los Angeles for the ceremony, and she couldn't join me in Pakistan until July. She had a teaching contract and couldn't ruin her record by breaking it. She still might have to support herself—and maybe me—someday.

It all worked out. The airmail sacks between the United States and Pakistan that spring were laden with almost daily letters back and forth. (In those primitive days mail took a week each way.) Into one otherwise sweet and loving one, she tucked a sardonic account of how she had taken her history class to see General MacArthur's triumphal welcome home in Los Angeles after he had been fired for insubordination by President Truman. She had neglected to bring an ample supply of paper tissues, and all the girls had ruined their makeup.

She showed up in Karachi in July to open that wonderful world that belongs to newlyweds. We discovered each other. And we discovered that women were seldom seen on the streets, but that female foreigners weren't women; that the North West Frontier was everything Kipling had said it was; that Pakistan expected U.S. help to get Kashmir, and India expected U.S. help in keeping it; that unpaid Foreign Service wives had duties as demanding as their husbands'; and that $3,200 a year (my salary) didn't even have to be stretched to include six household servants.

Our cook composed his own menus. When he served a specially tasty appetizer, Edith asked what it was called. He replied "fuscus." When she asked for "fuscus" again, something entirely different appeared. Challenged, he had a simple explanation: "Yes, memsahib, always fus' course, then secon' course, main course, and, after sweet, savory."

At the funeral of assassinated Prime Minister Liaquat Ali Khan, she watched an opposition political worker being torn apart by a mob and came home in a horse-drawn carriage to wash the blood splatters away. We had hepatitis together. With the Rh factor still undiscovered (ours, it turned out later, were not favorable), we had our first baby, Patrick (1952). At the insistence of a transient Seventh Day Adventist doctor, I helped in the delivery. ("If you're going to stay in this business, you'd better know how! See, a piece of the placenta is missing. Let's go back in and get it.")

Today, almost all Foreign Service posts have American doctors and nurse practitioners and many, a psychiatrist. Even a normal birth entitles return to the States. Servants are fewer and more expensive, but commissaries, air-conditioning, and microwave ovens make up for them. I guess it's better now, but certainly the range of experience for young Americans overseas is less.

That older people, too, might have interesting experiences occurred to me when Edith's parents showed up in Pakistan. John ("Jesse," "Pop") and Edith ("Senior") James had been tied to a hospital while he was undergoing surgery at the time of our marriage, so I had not met them. They had never been out of the United States before, but couldn't resist when the

United Nations' Food and Agriculture Organization asked him to do a land and water survey in Baluchistan. "Figured this was the only way I'd ever get to know my new son-in-law," Pop announced on arrival in Karachi.

Younger son of an intellectual Baptist doctor, whose ancestors had come from Wales in the seventeenth century and who had moved west from Pennsylvania after the Civil War, "Pop" was born in Montana Territory in 1880. Taught Latin and Greek by his father, he could cap any line I offered and recite from memory whole works from Shakespeare. He was an engineer, known for the earth-fill dams that he built and the land and water legislation he wrote. He remembered, as a boy on the family ranch near Great Falls, the night of the "shivaree" for the wedding of Charlie Russell, the cowboy painter, and the day a rider came out from town to report the killing of Sitting Bull at Wounded Knee, because Old Yank, the hand, had been with Major Reno at the Little Big Horn. The folks in town thought he should know.

As casual racially as my own long-dead father, he told me to discount anything his "half-white" daughter (Edith "Senior" was an Irish Roman Catholic) might have told me about his attitude toward his other son-in-law. It was true that he had sworn to kill the other Jimmy, the worthless

The James ranch (built circa 1878) Chestnut Valley, near Cascade, Montana, as it looked in the 1960s.

Edith's father, John Sexton James, 1906 (*rear, second from left*), Montana State football team, Livingston, Montana.

cowboy who had eloped with his eldest daughter. But he had never done it. They were living happily in California and even came to visit Montana sometimes. Hell, he and his brothers had sworn to kill another cowboy who had married their only sister forty years earlier. The bastard was alive—and Annabel was still supporting him.

My mother-in-law was no less intriguing. Edith Beatrice Burke had been born in 1891 in a room above the railroad station in Calgary, Canada, when her father, a mysterious "boom and bust" railroad contractor, Patrick D'Orsey Burke, was down on his luck and drawing wages as roadmaster on the Canadian Pacific. The Indian Wars lasted longer in Canada than in the United States, and Calgary was tensed for an attack. "P. D." kept a locomotive with steam up on a siding, in case his wife and new baby had to be evacuated.

Dashing and arrogant, P. D. had told little about himself, except that he was a younger son of a Catholic landlord in County Westmeath, Ireland, had collected and absconded with the rents, immigrated to the United States sometime after the Civil War, and married Mary Nolan of Sparta, Wisconsin. Mary's father had come over during the 1848 famine and, in his forties, had left his farm and fought his way through that entire conflict.

Edith's mother, Edith Beatrice Burke, 1906 (*second from left*), with classmates at St. Vincent's Academy, Helena, Montana.

Edith Beatrice had childhood memories of mansions in St. Paul and Evanston and a six-dollar-a-month rented shanty behind the jail in Lamont, Illinois. From Lamont her father had taken her to see the 1893 Columbian Exhibition in Chicago and to hear William Jennings Bryan repeat his "Cross of Gold" speech on the hustings along the railroad tracks. In the Gold Rush of 1898, P. D. went off to the Klondike, where he died without ever hitting it rich again. Mary succumbed to a cancer caused by a breast injury inflicted when the trolley car on which she was riding in St. Paul turned over after hitting a cow.

After a few years in a convent in Sparta, young Edith Beatrice headed west to *au pair* for a British gold assayer in Helena, Montana. An elder brother who had become a high school principal in Omaha, Nebraska—and who was later to go to the U.S. Senate—helped Edith attend Beloit College in Wisconsin. She went back to Montana to teach in one-room schools in the mining camps, then returned east to graduate as a dietician from Fanny Farmer's School in Boston. Back west again, working at her profession at the U.S. Army Hospital in Hot Springs, South Dakota, she met and married the young John Sexton James.

Here, too, the melting pot was stirring away. And from my standpoint in the 1950s, it had stirred well. I had not only a beloved mate of soul and body but a whole new family as well—which later came to include brother-in-law Jack, an amiable but extremely competent Justice Department anti-trust attorney, who first brought to my attention that J. Edgar Hoover was not all that he was cracked up to be; and beautiful and kindly sister-in-law Catherine, who, with worthless cowboy-turned-successful-accountant Jimmy, produced three gorgeous daughters, who gave them a round dozen grandchildren and a score of great-grandchildren. In her widowhood, she took up golf.

What more could anyone want? Even the mothers-in-law kept in touch and got on well (except once when we naively invited both of them to come to our house in Washington and take care of our four kids while we stole away for a week together in Europe).

Edith age six, Helena, Montana, 1928.

My Edith was the center of it all. She bore three more children, a girl, Sikandra (1954), and two boys, Stephen (1958), and William (1962). Throughout the years she loved and nurtured them. Stationed in Washington, she worked as an editor but found time to assure a six-year old Patrick that his father was only joking when he called him a "BMV" (bad, mean, and vicious) little boy and chased him with a toasting fork. She bucked up a nine-year-old Sikandra who came home from school crying because she had been "snubbed" by not being invited to the birthday party of Ellen Fishburn, the most popular girl in the class. Her mother assured her that Ellen Fishburn might have been thoughtless or even rude, but Sikandra Spain was Sikandra Spain. How could anyone possibly snub or look down on her?

She convinced Stephen, grieving over his neglected position as "middle child," that everyone cared for him more than anyone else—and proved it by driving him to his remote soccer games twice a week. Drawing on her own experience, she persuaded "Wretched Willie" that to be a youngest child was the most fun. When the children were older, she saw them into—and once or twice out of—boarding schools and taught them to play bridge. Through endless dialogue, she worked them away from their absolute conviction that they were all going to die of nuclear explosions before their natural time.

Overseas, she graduated from giggling about "fuscus" in 1951 to hostessing superbly a visit by President and Mrs. Nixon, when we were on a second assignment in Pakistan as chargé d'affaires in 1969. In Istanbul, Turkey, in 1970, she paid regular visits to Billy Hayes (of *Midnight Express* fame) in Samalcilar prison and tried to distract his attention with yoga books and candy bars.

In the mid-1970s in Tanzania, she convinced a visiting Nancy Kissinger to persuade Secretary of State Henry to approve embassy acquisition of a recreational beach house and charmed Cyrus Vance, his successor, into a give-and-take with American residents. She argued the American, as opposed to the British, approach to mining law with President Julius K. Nyerere and inspired perennial houseguest Andrew Young to remark that the American Residence in Dar es Salaam was the best hotel he'd ever been in. On three hours' notice she organized a birthday party for Sam Nujoma, the exiled Namibian leader, the first occasion at which he ever socialized with Americans.

In 1980, back in troubled Turkey, we went to Adana so I could make a prison visit to some young American women there on long narcotics sentences. Soon-to-arrive reporters and congressmen were interested, and we needed a reliable, firsthand report. I mustn't go through with it, the U.S. consul on the spot insisted. The jail was full of leftist terrorists who had virtually taken over administration. As soon as the American ambassador went inside, they'd grab him as a hostage or kill him.

Then his eye fell on Edith. "Ah!" he said. "Perhaps, Mrs. Spain can go instead. No one will make anything of an American woman talking to the girls. And, if something should happen, well . . . you know . . . it wouldn't be like an international incident."

She went, got soaked in a torrential downpour, sidestepped a bottle thrown at a guard, and had an automatic rifle poked in her face on the way out. But she saw the prisoners and reported back. "Not too bad for them, despite the riots. They're in a separate section, and the guards are nice to them. Morale's good. All they need is more candy and magazines." She smiled sweetly at the consul. "And, oh yes, now I know the value the State Department puts on Foreign Service wives."

I fear that at times during these decades I cared more about—or at least devoted more attention to—the business of trying to promote the independence of Zimbabwe or keeping Turkey in NATO than to the sorrows and joys of my wife and our four children. I was an American male of my times. If things have changed a bit now, that's no doubt for the better—even in the Foreign Service.

Edith never suffered divided loyalties. Perhaps because of her devotion to history, children and current events were all of a parcel to her. She insisted that both must view and be viewed forward and backward, not just in general at the time. If Patrick, our eldest, was slim, strong, graceful, always ready for competition but contemptuous of team sports, his grandfather was as responsible as the fencing lessons we gave him. When later his interests turned from classics at the University of Chicago to the law and making money, his Uncle Jack and Great-grandfather P. D. could be assumed to have had a role. Appropriately, he found his place, in Texas in midlife, as president and chief operating officer of a leading business information company. He and his wife of a dozen years are further internationalizing the Spains by adopting a Chinese infant.

Sikandra's reserved manner and academic brilliance might be peculiarly hers, but her beauty, efficiency, independence, and utter fearlessness were not without debt to her grandmothers—and, I would add, the lesson she had so thoroughly learned from her mother: "I am Sikandra Spain. How can anyone look down on me?" A dozen years later her colleagues in the Peace Corps in Fiji and at the University of Pennsylvania's Annenberg School still remember the influence she had on them. She was our Golden Girl, but somehow neither she nor we thought that implied any superiority over the boys.

Stephen, gentle from the cradle, inheriting his Grandfather Spain's "Spanish" looks and his Grandfather James's athletic abilities, from his earliest years in grade school bested his Latin American contemporaries at soccer. His approach to the world was his own. He managed to keep from being thrown out of Phillips Exeter Academy (though he spent most of his time there on both "disciplinary restriction" and "academic probation"). He passed through the University of Florida, Emerson College, three years of driving a Boston taxi, and three more in the computer field while trying to write the Great American Novel.

Subsequently, he worked for a pittance for Save the Children in Quetta, Pakistan, and then served as a well-paid representative of the United Nations High Commissioner for Refugees in Afghanistan. Returning after four hazardous years in Quetta, Kandahar, Herat, Kabul, and Islamabad, he used his savings to earn a master's degree at Harvard's Kennedy School and undertook a peaceful career with not-for-profit foundations in Massachusetts. Along the way, he acquired a Boston wife and two children, another Sikandra and another James. He keeps up with his cosmopolitan brothers by referring to the children as "half-Boston." They are part of the continuum too.

William started big and clumsy (I got hereditary credit for that). The most thoroughly "Foreign Service" of this brood of "Foreign Service brats," he entered his ninth school in the ninth grade in Dar es Salaam. He went from the unconventional Vershire School in Vermont (where he lived alone in a cabin in the woods) to the University of Massachusetts at Amherst. Becoming skilled at editing and layout on the daily newspaper there, he went to work for *Advertising Age* magazine in Chicago. A freelance article in the *Chicago Tribune* Sunday magazine suggesting that there was value as well as danger in the old American custom of fireworks on the Fourth of July brought him a contract to promote that industry, of which his family, admittedly a minority in modern America, heartily approves. Later, he married a young woman from Kerala, India, and wrote for national magazines. He has a son, Aidan Sikander, and works happily as information director for the American Civil Liberties Union in Chicago.

Unusually, we were all in the States for Thanksgiving 1983 and found a five-day house rental at a resort in West Virginia. On Wednesday, Pat drove in from Chicago, Bill and Steve from Boston. Sikandra, now 29, with only her degree left to pick up in Philadelphia, took the Metroliner to Washington and rode out with Edith and me in the new family car. We had a lavish Thanksgiving dinner at the resort restaurant. We walked in the woods and basked before the fire in the house, eating, drinking, playing bridge, and talking.

We were not without concerns. Edith and I were bitter at being replaced prematurely in the Embassy in Ankara by a Reagan political appointee. Pat, general counsel for an electronic transnational, was furious at the company's new owners. Kanda had been promised a commitment on a hoped-for UN job before Thanksgiving but hadn't heard a word. Steve had a fight with his cab company in Boston over taking five days off. Bill was frustrated at being passed over for editor-in-chief of his paper.

The Spain family on its last Fourth of July, Washington, D.C., 1983. *From left:* Patrick, James, Sikandra, Edith, Stephen, and William.

But all these gripes were with other people. We were six adults now. Earlier family conflicts—about progress in school, attendance at Mass, the length of skirts and hair—were over. We were all together for the first time in years. We loved and were proud of each other. Present and future were promising. What more could any family want of God and country?

Then, the world, as it sometimes does, turned upside down.

On a sunny Sunday, Pat, Steve, and Bill took off on the holiday-dangerous turnpikes. Edith, Sikandra, and I wended our way through country roads back toward Washington. Near Leesburg, Virginia, our light fiberglass car was hit by a huge old station wagon going eighty-five miles an hour, driven by a local high school football player who was not wearing the glasses his license prescribed. He wasn't scratched, but we had to be evacuated to the Washington Hospital Trauma Center by helicopter.

The next morning when my brain came back to life, I was immobilized with a variety of fractures and bruises. Edith was clinging to life in an intensive-care unit. Sikandra was dead. The boys raced back to take care of us. I managed to get out of the hospital in time to help bury Sikandra after a funeral Mass I was not sure she would have wanted.

In a few months Edith, in a wheel chair, joined us at the grave in Rock Creek Cemetery, a stone's throw from the statue of "Grief" by Augustus St. Gaudens, which marked the resting place of Clover, wife of Henry Adams. Father Tom Duffy, a favorite priest from St. Thomas Apostle, said prayers. We all sang the Jesuit hymn, "Be Not Afraid," so fitting for the woman who had been our daughter and sister.

Weeks after that, Edith followed. Her last words to me from a Georgetown Hospital bed rigged with wires, tubes, and machines were, "Let me go. Please!" That very night, as stout-hearted as her mother and daughter, she too went off alone into the unknown. She had chosen the inscription on Kanda's grave: "Always Young, Always Beautiful." On hers we put, "Fresh and Brave Forever."

That was our family. The boys and I are still alive and thriving, in debt in no small way to the bravery and wisdom of our dead women. But every family is different. Each has its own set of joys and sorrows, of heredity and experiences. Might there be anything of use to others, now or in the future, to be derived from the Spains' particular passage through the world?

First, there is the very concept of family. It is good for individuals, even children, to be free to do anything they want. But they and society pay a price for it. One caring parent is better than two uncaring ones, but the chance of getting that one are only half as great. The Spains would not have been the same if they had been products of a single mother or father or of divorce. And they might not have existed at all if previous generations had embraced abortion.

Second, Edith went to her death heartened by the belief that she would be reunited with Sikandra. Despite all its accretions over the centuries, religion has its virtues. And, while we might have reasons to revolt against its organized ministers, we have none to despise those who hold to the fundamentals. How could God—or a rational natural order—provide for simple elimination from the cosmos of Edith and Sikandra and all those wonderful people who have gone before and will come after us?

Third, despite pollution, the Republican Party, Viet Nam, the Hiroshima bomb, the Depression, the Spanish-American War, Boston Brahmins, "Know-Nothings," the Draft Riots of 1863, racist chattel slavery, and Thomas Jefferson's mulatto bastards, it was easier for our family to achieve what it did in America than it would have been anywhere else.

Finally, whether or not there is an afterlife, we who inhabit this earth, and those who might live on other planets as well, are all part of a continuum. If we have responsibilities for preserving our environment, we have them also for ourselves. I hope that my descendants will set foot in space, but I suspect that they, as I, will find as much wisdom in our past on this planet as among the stars in the future.

We should spend more time looking for it.

5

A Working Apprenticeship

NOT LONG AGO I LISTENED IN at a dinner party in an affluent New Jersey suburb as two fathers talked about their teenage sons' employment for the summer of 1993. "McDonald's or Burger King?" the broker asked the professor.

"Burger King," the latter replied. "He's been there the last two years. It's closer to his girlfriend's house."

"Ted's back at McDonald's, his third summer, too. He likes it. They have reserved parking spaces for the employees."

They went on to praise the utility of summer employment, "Keeps them from just hanging around. Lets them earn their own gas money." They spoke of the desirability of having a choice of places to work. "Food's pretty much the same both places but atmosphere is different." They agreed on the virtue of stability even in temporary employment. "They get a chance to watch the same business grow every year and learn how it does it." They approved of the social broadening of the roadside restaurant. "They see all kinds of people, tourists, workers from the town, everybody, not like waiting table at the country club!"

Long an admirer of both McDonald's and Burger King, I welcomed this show of support for them. But it got me to thinking of the jobs, temporary and not so temporary, I had held over a cycle that started half a century earlier. I didn't think that these boys of the nineties were getting as much out of their first forays into the world of work as I did.

The first money I ever earned outside the house was about the time I turned twelve. A sixth-grade classmate and I reported to the local Democratic party precinct captain. He gave us sketch maps of sections of Mt. Olivet Cemetery on 111th Street, twelve cents trolley fare (three cents each way for children under twelve), notebooks and pencils, and instructions to copy down the names on the headstones of persons who had died during the previous two years. When we returned, we got to keep the pencils and the unused portion of the notebooks and were given a dollar each to boot.

My father explained it all that night. There was an "off-year" election coming up in November 1938. The Democrats needed to ensure continued control of the city and county. No one ever checked the electoral lists for deaths between presidential elections. The deceased would still be listed. The precinct captain would see to it that they voted Democratic one more time.

"Better put the dollar in the collection box at church tomorrow morning," he added.

Four years later, working in a tiny one-man hot dog stand on the lake front at 47th Street, I got my first lesson in entrepreneurial economics. The schoolteacher friend who leased it from the city during his summer vacation netted $25.00 a day during June, July, and August, about what my recently dead father had made in monthly wages "on the cars." Paid 10 percent of profits, I got $2.50 a day.

The following summer, as the war left fewer and fewer adult males in place, I found myself a sample man in Armour's Lard Refinery in the stockyards. My job was to dip ladles into arriving railroad tank cars and stationary storage tanks and bring the samples back to the laboratory chemists to test for content. My triumph was finding a 100,000-gallon storage tank from which some never-identified "war profiteer" (we had signs about them all over the plant) had pumped out and carried away the animal oil and replaced it with water. My disgrace was having to wear on the job a knee-length white coat, the traditional mark of "management" in the Yards. What would my father have said?

After that I spent a summer mixing tooth powder on the night shift at the Squibb plant, near Johnson and Johnson, in an industrial suburb where my mother was turning out uniforms. (We saw each other for an hour each day as shifts turned over.) My special task, for which I had to be bonded, was claiming a sack of the "secret ingredient" from a controlled storeroom and stirring it into the mix. The dust left me with periodic fits of sneezing for the next twenty years.

Then, two nights a week and one summer when I was in my last years at Quigley, came a job as "assistant night photo editor" at the Associated Press office at Randolph and La Salle Streets in the Loop. By now there were no able-bodied males at all out of uniform, and employers had to make do with what they could get. The lofty title was something of a fraud, given to me so I could get a press credential to do my real copyboy job of delivering wirephotos and lugging camera cases for aged professional photographers too old for the draft. But what experience it provided! I passed through police and fire lines with my magic credentials and invited myself to Mayor "Big Ed" Kelly's press conferences. He asked me where I was from and I replied, properly, "Eighteenth Ward, Eighteenth Precinct." He commented, "Jake Voglander, always carries for us! You're all right, son."

Both the Republican and Democratic conventions were held in Chicago in 1944. I saw keynote speaker Clare Booth Luce in her underwear, as she tried on dresses and hats in an afternoon rehearsal before delivering her "GI Joe and GI Jane" speech. I discovered the "voice from the sewers" in the basement of the Chicago Stadium, where Big Ed had set up loudspeakers that boomed out a recorded "We want Roosevelt! We want Roosevelt!" I neglected my Associated Press duties to get Democratic National Chairman Jim Farley a hot dog when he was hungry and was subsequently signaled by him from the podium to get him two more. When I delivered them, he introduced me to an obscure senator from Missouri, Harry S. Truman, about whom more was heard subsequently. (Roosevelt "ditched" Vice President Henry Wallace in Truman's favor.)

Then I, too, went off to the Army. When I came back to the University of Chicago on the GI Bill, I sought new ways of supplementing my income.

For a while I sold the Encyclopedia Britannica house to house—until I discovered that, however lofty the contents of the books, the sales techniques would make a busker blush. A stint as a baby photographer for a syndicate was pretty much the same. The pictures were all right. The prices and pressure on straitened young parents were pure exploitation. Next, I turned to honest labor, puddling steel on the night shift of the open hearth of the Carnegie Illinois Company in Gary, Indiana. Comments from mother, girlfriend, classmates, and faculty that I looked awful gave me an excuse to quit in less than a month.

Shortly afterward, my 1948 campus aberration in support of MacArthur as presidential candidate paid off. The Republicans somehow managed to win Cook County (in which Chicago is located), and I was offered a well-paying full-time night job in the County Building. Three other "college kids" and I actually came to work—for about three of the eight hours for which we were paid. Our updating of the records in the Tax Assessor's Office was sufficient to justify paying forty precinct captains on the payroll, who never came to work at all except once every two weeks to collect their paychecks.

In 1951 I entered the Foreign Service. It was not a bad place from which to watch a bureaucracy grow. In those days the State Department's employment roll numbered fewer than 10,000, of which the Foreign Service accounted for fewer than 3,000, compared to some 50,000 total in the Department of Agriculture. State now has about 25,000, of which perhaps 10,000 are Foreign Service, compared to Agriculture's total roll of 125,000. But then we citizens have gone from 150 million to 250 million. During forty years I moved, albeit in an erratic way, from FSO-6, third secretary and vice consul, $3,200 a year (1951) to career minister and ambassador, $89,000 a year (1989). Diplomatic services are very like military ones: lieutenant, captain, major, colonel, and, only if you are lucky, general.

Assigned first to Karachi, Pakistan (our embassy did not move from Pakistan's original capital to the new one of Islamabad until 1966), I paid a formal call on my ambassador in March 1951. Like most of his senior career colleagues, he had emerged from an Ivy League university around the time of World War I. Even more than most he seemed determined to confirm the stereotype of his time and class. He changed his white duck suit twice a day. He was a great sailor and hunter and would eat only game fish and meat. He had driven his wife into alcoholism and demanded that his subordinates' wives cover for her. He pushed noted journalist Marguerite Higgins down the Embassy steps when she dared to ask him why he couldn't get the Pakistanis to help us with troops in Korea.

This ambassador also called his senior subordinates in the embassy by title rather than name: "DCM [Deputy Chief of Mission], I want that done over. Now!" "Counselor! This is the worst draft I've ever seen. Do it again!" "Attaché! I called your office this morning and you weren't there. Why?" Juniors he called only "You."

"Do you crew?" were his first words to me.

The boy from Chicago wasn't sure what the word meant. "Not really, sir."

"Do you shoot?"

I thought he was asking if I were a marksman, unaware that the British use the word for hunting.

"No, sir, but I am going to try to learn Urdu!"

His Excellency turned beet red. Perhaps he had a momentary vision of what was going to happen to the Foreign Service during the lifetimes of officers such as I.

"Get out of here!" he roared.

Still, I learned a few things from him. One was that you couldn't be too careful about handling claimants to U.S. citizenship. "Bloody Mary," a mad Asian beggar woman who lived in the street outside the Embassy, clamored for a U.S. passport. She got her dirty hands all over the ambassador's white suit every time he passed. He in turn had her put in jail. When that failed to remove her permanently, he kicked and cuffed her. As it turned out, she was the widow of a high American official assassinated in Iran during World War II. She was, in fact, an American citizen, with an influential banker brother-in-law, who had spent years searching for her.

Another thing I learned was that, even in the Foreign Service, digging in on a matter of conscience could keep you out of, and get you into, trouble. Tapped as secretary-treasurer of the newly established Fulbright Foundation for the exchange of scholars ("Who can we best spare around here? Let that new fellow, what's-his-name, do it"), I soon came to have doubts about the large number of high-value checks made out to "Cash" being routed to me for signature by the Pakistani executive director. I refused to sign them. When the departure for the United States of the son of a cabinet-member friend of the ambassador was delayed by my adamancy, I got a tongue-lashing but still refused.

When an even newer vice consul, who, I was gleefully informed, had been a banker in Chicago, arrived, I was relieved of my Fulbright duties. Six months later a team of Foreign Service inspectors showed up and found a large sum of money missing. Faced with a choice of resignation or personally paying back what amounted to several years' salary, the too-agreeable young Foreign Service officer signed a resignation and went back to his bank—which wouldn't rehire him because of his financial peccadillos abroad.

Fulbright business took me to Pakistan's North West Frontier. Edith and I, both reared on Kipling, agreed that the fabled city of Peshawar and the Pathans who dwelt around it were worth a lifetime of study. The problem was that, except for Fulbright matters (which I soon lost anyway), the Frontier Province was the responsibility of the U.S. consul general in Lahore.

A less successful diplomat than his college and Foreign Service classmate, the ambassador in Karachi, the consul general was extremely jealous of his territory. The relationship between the two was one of mutual hatred. Each did everything he could to frustrate and humiliate the other, but the ambassador had the advantage. He was responsible for all U.S. government activities in the country. Putting the consul general's pride together with the interest of his lowliest "you" in the Frontier, he got a sum he liked. The developing Cold War gave the Frontier high priority in embassy reporting, and "an Asian scholar, what's-his-name," from the embassy was assigned responsibility for it.

In the beginning, the consul general tried to fight a rearguard action. In those days Orient Airlines (predecessor to PIA, Pakistan International Airlines) had a daily Convair flight from Karachi to Peshawar, with stops at Lahore and Rawalpindi. When it came down at Lahore the consul general was waiting for me on the tarmac. "Off!" he ordered. "Back to Karachi! You don't have permission to enter my consular district!"

I agreed and apologized. But what could I do? I was only a vice consul. The ambassador, nothing less than the personal representative of the president, had ordered me to Peshawar. The consul general fretted and fumed for the half-hour's stop but let me get back on the airplane. After all, what could he do? He was only a consul general. When I told the ambassador

New parents with infant son Patrick in Karachi, Pakistan, March 1952.

about the incident upon my return to Karachi, he guffawed. "Real burned up, was he? I would like to have seen that. Make sure he knows every time you go through Lahore!"

Vice Consul James Spain and Pathan chieftain Abdus Sattar Khan Mohmand (1953) at Takht-i-Bhai, North-West Frontier, Pakistan.

So began a half-century's devotion to the North West Frontier. I went up there often. Edith accompanied me when she could—at our expense, of course. It was a fascinating time for a young couple enamored of Kipling. We watched tent-pegging and polo with "the sahibs," the urbane and highly educated upper classes of officialdom, who had but recently taken over responsibility from the departing British. We talked to the pretender to the Afghan throne in exile in a remote village in Waziristan, surrounded by wild tribesmen. Their great event had been their participation a few years before in the "Kashmir Jihad." On their own they had stormed into the disputed state and started the first Indo-Pakistani war.

By the time our tour in Karachi ended in 1953, we were "hooked" on the Frontier. Notice of a next assignment as consular officer in Caracas left us restless and dissatisfied. Senator Joseph McCarthy with his lists of "Communists in the State Department," and the Eisenhower administration's less than forthright response, dampened our enthusiasm for the Foreign Service (although I was far too obscure for the senator from Wisconsin to even know my name). With the arrival of an offer of a teaching assistantship at Columbia and a Ford Foundation Fellowship to study the Frontier, I resigned and we moved to New York.

At Columbia in 1954, we followed McCarthy's antics on television. The tube was still a novelty, as yet available in few homes but increasingly common in bars. Our graduate student budget did not allow for many outings, but when the McCarthy hearings were broadcast, we managed to find enough money for a baby-sitter while we took our places with the faithful in a neighborhood bar. We jubilantly watched the hilarious exchange with

Edith during a stop on the Italian Riviera on the way back from Embassy Karachi, June 1953.

Army counsel Joseph Welch about "pixies" and "fairies," which helped turn opinion against McCarthy. Looking back now on the incident, in which Welch implied that McCarthy and/or his staff were homosexual, I wonder what today's reaction might be.

With everything but a dissertation in the bag at Columbia, I drew on the Ford grant for a nine-month trip to Britain and the Frontier. Edith took infants Patrick and Sikandra to camp with her parents in Montana and, after her father retired, California. Returning early in 1956, I had come to realize that I would rather "do" than teach. After a few weeks in the winter sunshine, we headed back to Washington to scout opportunities for getting back into the Foreign Service.

The eight-day trip in a 1948 Dodge club coupe had its trials: two restless infants in the cramped back seat, competing for space and attention with each other and with all the Spain worldly possessions (four suitcases). There were nervous hours with bald tires on ice-covered roads in Arizona and New Mexico and a constant focus on finding "economy" motels and restaurants.

However, the long days on the road and the fourteen-hour nights in motels, free of distraction (in those days, even of TV), had their charms. Edith and I took turns driving. In recognition of my origins on the midwestern flatlands, I handled the fast, level stretches of road. The trickier, twisting parts through the mountains went to her, to take advantage of her Montana skills and greater female patience. With half a year of separate experiences to catch up on, we talked our way across mountain and plain. We found out later that thirty-two-month-old Patrick listened to every word. For months afterward, he queried us on every detail of our dialogue on the trip.

In those days, Route 66 was the main transcontinental artery. Long stretches in the West were two-lane, undivided, and poorly graded. We followed it eastward as far as Oklahoma City and then stayed south as long as possible to avoid the January weather. In the ghost town of Williams, Arizona, Edith, holding Patrick by the hand while I carried Sikandra, expounded on the difference between placer and quartz-lode mining. As we crossed the Mississippi at Memphis, she told the story of King Cotton in the South and sang "Old Man River," adding a summary biography of Paul Robeson.

Coming up through the Virginia Piedmont, she gave us "The Wreck of Old Ninety-Seven" and told about meeting Mrs. Casey Jones when she was a schoolgirl. Patrick was rapt. Sikandra was at least subliminally interested. And I realized anew the treasure that was mine. That did not, however, prevent me from enjoining her, "For God's sake, don't be a nagging wife!" when she pointed out a missed turnoff or stop sign. Finally, on Route 50 approaching Washington we drove as far as Rosslyn at the Virginia end of the Key bridge before finding a motel for the night.

A very different capital city from the one we know today lay before us. From the center of the little town built around a half-dozen pawn shops, we looked across the Potomac at the spires of Georgetown University and decided against it in favor of the University of Chicago for Patrick. As far as Sikandra was concerned, the question did not arise. The Jesuit College was strictly male. And the thought that fifteen years later our little girl would be a boarder at the convent school on the campus there while we lived in Turkey was far from our minds. The view down the river ran straight to the massively graceful Lincoln Memorial. The Kennedy Center and Theodore Roosevelt Bridge were still in the future.

There were no motel chains to offer glossy brochures from which the traveler could select sites and rates. At our mom-and-pop establishment, a friendly Virginia-born proprietor provided milk for Pat and Sikandra from his own cow, tethered a few yards behind his office. Asked about an un completed wing, he replied that he was trying to find a loan to finish it. "Went into the Small Business Administration people in Washington the other day," he explained morosely. "Whole big room of 'em sitting at desks. Not a white man among 'em. Nothin' but Jews, Nigras, and Catholics. Wouldn't give me a thing!"

To me from Chicago, racial and religious stereotypes were commonplace, undesirable but often more humorous than vicious. I had to fight down a temptation to elaborate on the Virginian's theme, suggesting perhaps that a white man had to be particularly wary of Catholics. They were capable of sneaking out without paying their motel bills, saving the money to give to the Pope of Rome.

To my Montana girl, bigotry was a new thing. She didn't like it. "Do you remember just a couple of weeks ago when we were invited to that party in California," she asked, "and were warned that we might want to decline because a Nisei couple were going to be there? Now we have to look out for 'Jews, Nigras, and Catholics.' What a strange world! Let's never get so preoccupied with ourselves that we act like that!"

Thirty years later a similar young couple arriving in Washington might well have given job-hunting priority to Edith rather than to me. She had declared her education completed. She had an M.A. and a teaching certificate. I was still working on a Ph.D. Teachers were in demand. Asian scholars were not. But the mores of the time prescribed that first importance be given to my employment. Once I was reestablished, she might seek something that would pay for child care and housecleaning services.

My efforts began on a discouraging note. Again in contrast to thirty years later, the State Department's reaction to my coming back to the Foreign Service couldn't have been more negative if it had been the Society of Jesus and I a Jesuit who had jumped over the wall and run away with a nun. I had resigned, of my own free will, hadn't I, renouncing all the perks and privileges I had earned by being one of the select few who passed the entrance examination? One would have thought that I'd have had more pride than to come crawling back.

The fact that I now had a wife and two infant children to support only enhanced my sinfulness. (In those days, a male Foreign Service officer only had to get permission to marry. The few female ones had to resign.) Take the examination again? Well, yes, they couldn't stop me from doing that, since I was still below thirty-one (the maximum age for entry in those days, now below the average entry age).

But even if I passed the written exam, there was the oral to think about. How did I propose to handle the question of why had I resigned in the first place? Surely, there was no getting around that!

6

Falling in with the CIA

SALVATION CAME FROM ANother source. The Central Intelligence Agency, known simply as "the Agency," was expanding rapidly. Deputy Director Robert Amory, Jr., somehow heard that there was a South Asian specialist in town looking for a job. Arrangements were made for meetings on street corners. The Agency people couldn't tell me about the job I was being interviewed for—it was too secret—but they seemed satisfied with my background. ("You've actually been in Afghanistan!") I was told to report to the personnel office, the only part of the Agency that admitted to habitation at shabby old 2430 E Street, Northwest, in Foggy Bottom. (The marble palace at Langley was still a mere gleam in the eye of Director Allen Dulles.)

In those days CIA was the glamour agency in Washington. Its salaries were higher, its personnel rules more flexible, its reputation one of unblemished success, as in the ouster of Mossadegh and restoration of the Shah in Iran. Most glamorous of all was the clandestine services part of it, the "spooks" who served their country by brilliant, dangerous, and extralegal "dirty tricks." Many of the best people of the post–World War II generation were already serving in the CIA. What could be more challenging—and more patriotic?

Intrigued by such a destiny, I donned trench coat, Peshawar-made boots, and a thick tweed suit that dated back to my days in Japan. Puffing on my pipe, I reported to 2430 E Street. The personnel officer looked at my outfit and remarked that I wouldn't need that getup where I was going. Even a fledgling bureaucrat could tell, however, that, barring my having two heads, he had been ordered to hire me.

The terms were generous, GS-9, $3,900 a year, with a promise of GS-11, $4,800 a year, as soon as I got my Ph.D. There would be a lengthy security clearance before I could have access to classified material, but I could go on the payroll the following Monday. I would sign a statement of willingness to take a polygraph test and spend my time at the Library of Congress working on my dissertation until the security clearance was complete.

During the next months, I plugged away at my dissertation. Edith got us established in a small tract house in Fairfax County, Virginia: price $10,000, 3 percent GI loan, $500 down payment, and a Boxer pup. Soon word came in from friends and relatives everywhere either of us had ever lived of mysterious gentlemen "on government business" inquiring about our patriotism, morals, stability, and personal habits. Another young couple was off on the American Dream.

In the summer of 1955 I finally received word to "come aboard." That process began with another visit to the personnel office. I was dispatched to Building 13 to undergo two days of tests, which ranged from conventional IQ and ink blot to polygraph. The operator of the latter assured me there was nothing to worry about. "We know everybody is different. We've had gangsters, Harvard boys, actors, everything in here! Some of the fellows even say that the Pope is on the payroll. Boy, would I like to put him on the box!"

I fared less well in a long oral interview with the Agency psychiatrist. The only thing he wanted to talk about was my response to one item on a questionnaire. The instructions had been specific: "Answer quickly and instinctively." It had been easy to do so for most of the questions. "Which of your parents do you know and like best?" My mother—since my father had died when I was half-grown. "What is your favorite taste?" Chocolate marshmallow ice cream.

Two were difficult. "Which sock do you put on first, left or right?" I had no idea, so I said the right one during the week and the left on Sunday. "Name the thing that revolts you most." I thought about that for a while. Slugs under a rock? No. Physical deformity? No. In my rational world, the worst possible thing would be intellectual deformity. So, I put down mental illness. The shrink worked up to the kill slowly.

"Father dead. Cause?"

"Cancer of the stomach."

"Mother's health?"

"Fine."

"Brothers and sisters?"

"None."

"Insanity anywhere in the family?"

"God, no!"

"How long have you had this fear of going mad?"

"What fear?"

"It's obvious. Mental illness revolts you!"

"Oh, that. Now I see. Well, I just couldn't come up with anything, so I thought about it for awhile and put that down."

"Don't you see the significance?"

I explained the reasoning process I had gone through.

"You still don't see the real reason for your answer?"

"Not really. I've just explained why I answered that way."

"Hmm-m-m." He wrote on my file, sealed it in a large brown envelope and handed it back. "Finish your processing. It's not up to me to make a final decision, but I doubt the Agency will want someone like you. However, don't be distressed. There are undoubtedly many nonsensitive jobs in Washington you could fill."

In those days, the CIA was housed in a number of World Wars I and II temporary buildings scattered around Foggy Bottom. On my way to my next appointment, I rested on a bench beside the Potomac. I noticed that I could get a fingernail under the flap of the sealed envelope. Looking around I could see no evidence of surveillance by my new masters. Besides, what was this spying business all about? Shouldn't it be to my credit if they found me doing a little on my own? I pried the envelope open.

"Given to exotic and unseasonable clothing. Possibly a 'cowboy.' Wants a grade higher than justified by previous USG employment," the personnel officer noted.

"No subversive affiliation or sexual deviation but unduly concerned over trifles," the polygraph operator registered.

"No established pathological or psychotic conditions in family, but subject appears unstable, preoccupied by fear of insanity," the shrink recorded.

I sealed the envelope up again and trudged on the rest of my rounds. The last of them was "Cover." The man there told me simply, "On credit card applications and things like that, say you work for the Department of Defense. That's all."

"Couldn't I say 'State'?"

"Sure, if you want to."

Two days later I was back with the personnel officer. He shook his head sadly. "Amory says hire you."

"GS-9, and GS-11 when I get my degree?" I asked.

"Yeah. He says that too." I signed a variety of papers swearing to uphold the Constitution of the United States of America and not to reveal my employer to anyone. I was told to get a badge made down the hall and report to Building 8 Monday at 0800.

"Where's Building 8?"

He handed over a sketch map of CIA's real estate. I folded it and put it in my pocket. He insisted that I couldn't take it out of the building. I should memorize it and give it back. I did and went home, not sure anymore that I really wanted to work for CIA.

Things looked brighter Monday morning. I was welcomed to the Office of Current Intelligence (OCI) by the assistant director who ran it. He, I was told by the Middle East Division chief to whom he turned me over, was a former Price Waterhouse accountant who had done great things in the war. The division chief revealed that we were fellow graduates of the University of Chicago. He had been a Lutheran theology student but had "turned archaeologist." He hinted that he too had done great things during the war.

The division chief brought me to the South Asia Branch, where the chief, a Harvard Ph.D who had been a "missionary brat" in India, introduced me to the three other analysts. One was an aging young man who had spent the war in the Pentagon as a civilian analyst. He, I was told, "really knows how to write things up, anything!" Another was an elderly lady who had lived for years in South and Southeast Asia as the wife of an American bank manager. The third was another new employee, a gentleman whom I had met a few times during my assignment to the embassy in Karachi, where until his retirement he had been managing director of an American oil company. Both overcome by the CIA's mystique, it was weeks before we admitted knowing each other before.

OCI, I discovered to my mild disappointment, had nothing to do with "dirty tricks" or overseas activities. It produced the daily Top Secret Current Intelligence Bulletin, offering in condensed form reports and analysis on what was new, interesting, or dangerous in the world. Sources were press accounts and radio broadcasts, State and Defense department cables, and "TDCSs." The last was said to stand for "Telegraphic Dissemination: Clandestine Services," but no one knew for sure.

My responsibility would be Afghanistan and backup on Pakistan. OCI also did special briefings for Director of Central Intelligence Allen Dulles. He was fascinated with Afghanistan, so I could expect to get a lot of time with him.

Working in OCI was stimulating. Each analyst usually submitted at least one piece for the Bulletin every day; often, though, only one of a half-dozen sent to the editorial board during the course of a week got printed. My co-workers were pleasant and sophisticated people who went out of their way to make a neophyte feel at home, although I early came to suspect that they were—and knew they were—as far out of the mainstream of government affairs as I was. In those ancient, non–air-conditioned days, whenever the temperature rose above 90 degrees or dropped below 10 degrees, we got to shut down at noon and go home.

We all professed confidence that our product was being read by, and having an influence on, the great world of "policymakers," from the president on down to State Department desk officers. This view was undercut when I ran into a few State desk officers I had known in my previous incarnation and asked them about the Bulletin. One told me that, oh, yeah, he saw it sometimes, but it was always a week or more old and he didn't read it anyway. Another, perhaps not wanting to appear of lowly status, said the Bulletin was great. He never missed it—but went on to demonstrate that he didn't know what it looked like. It was what we of the Agency expected from the State Department "cookie-pushers."

What seemed to me good clandestine service reports on Europe and the Soviet Union came in occasionally, but most agent reports on South Asia were junk, self-serving gossip of a kind I wouldn't have bothered reporting a few years earlier when I was on the ground as an embassy officer. Some were copied verbatim from vernacular newspapers, which the American case officers in the field could seldom read, but the translation service supporting OCI could. Yet many were rated B-2: "Probably true from a usually reliable source in a position to know."

It was suggested that when possible we build our Bulletin pieces around the TDCSs, so others in the government could see the value of the Agency's recently increased clandestine collection in South Asia. To give Agency objectivity its due, when I reported my view to my bosses, their response was straightforward: "Don't use the stuff then! That's what OCI's paying you for, your knowledge and judgment." When I proposed that our brothers on the clandestine side of the house should be informed how bad their agents' output was, the answer was equally clear-cut: "Leave the spooks alone. TDCSs are what they're paid for, and they've got to make a living too. Besides, they wouldn't pay any attention to us."

During the remaining thirty-five years of my government service, reading what must have been ten thousand TDCSs, I saw a useful one now and then, particularly on Soviet weapons, but I always found it hard to take them seriously. I doubt that it is a fair judgment, but I wonder if U.S. interests would be any worse off if the peculiar art form had never developed.

OCI in the 1950s was a good place to learn the ways of Washington's rapidly developing bureaucratic culture. (In those days embassies overseas were still relatively free of it.) One Monday I ran a piece in the Bulletin suggesting the likelihood of a military coup in Country X after Wednesday's cabinet meeting. It didn't happen, and I submitted another piece on Friday explaining why. My wise old chief turned it down instantly. "No one will remember," he explained. "Why remind them of your mistake?"

OCI's principal bugbear was its security officer, a former Military Police captain of horrendous personality. His delight was to ring the alarm bell that gave us all five minutes to lock our safes and evacuate the building. Somehow he always managed to grab armloads of unsecured classified material during the exercise. This had to be retrieved later in a humiliating repentance ceremony at which the culprits acknowledged a security violation. Another of his joys was enforcing the regulation that required all employees to wear a photo identification badge on a chain around their necks. (OCI was virtually alone in the practice in those days.) The badge had to be visible within the building and covered outside it. Rumor had it that the security officer's proudest achievement was forcing an analyst driving home on Shirley Highway to the curb and grabbing the badge lying visible in his lap.

Our nemesis got his comeuppance. As he prowled the corridors, he habitually reached out to flip badges out of shirt pockets, where the wearer had tucked them while on some errand outside the building. He did it to a feisty young former WAC (Women's Army Corps) whose badge was concealed down the neck of her blouse, and a button popped off. It was long before the days of women's liberation, but she recognized an opportunity when she saw one. She screamed long enough to bring fellow employees out into the hall. Then, surrounded by eager witnesses, she marched off to the assistant director to report a "probable intended rape." The next morning we had a new security officer.

When the young Spain family came back from Pakistan in 1953, it was still very much "the thing" for a wife to stay home and take care of her husband and children. Attitudes were changing rapidly, however, as educated young women discovered how demanding and unsatisfying that role could be. Working couples became acceptable, even respectable. The traditional civil and foreign services still did not like the idea of both spouses being on the same department payroll, though. It smacked of nepotism and conflict of interest.

CIA was different. The required exhaustive security clearances were quicker and easier if one had already been done on a spouse. Although the marriage bond did not transcend the "need to know" restriction on sharing of information, spouses did talk to each other. If the Agency had them both on the payroll, it at least had some control over the situation.

So Edith, too, went to work at "the pickle factory." Elsie, an eminently respectable Fairfax County matron, came to take care of the children. The salary she needed to avoid digging into an inheritance from a great-grandfather, whose post–Civil War forty acres were now the site of a new shopping mall, coincided almost exactly with what was left after taxes from

Edith's Agency earnings. It was a satisfactory arrangement of a kind devised by many Civil Service families of the time.

Edith was assigned to the Analysis Branch of the Motion Picture Division in the Office of Collection and Records. She spent the next few years "looking at more motion pictures than I expected to see in a lifetime—and I'm a movie buff!" OCR was just as segregated from the clandestine services as OCI. Its *raison d'être* lay in World War II. Data on beaches, roads, airports, and cities all over the world had been readily available in the 1920s and 1930s. The U.S. government had never collected it, and between 1941 and 1945 landing ships floundered on uncharted reefs and paratroops lost their way on unknown roads. To ensure that this would never happen again, the postwar intelligence community set out to create a massive National Intelligence Survey based on all available information in existing books, maps, and motion pictures.

Edith pointed out that often there was no way of determining whether the settings she saw on film were the actual site or sets in a studio. In a rare contact with "the other side of the house," she found it didn't make much difference. An anonymous young agent about to go overseas showed up at the film library wanting to look at "alleys in Istanbul." Edith was able to produce several minutes from a recent French thriller but warned that she could not vouch for the authenticity of the alleys the actors flitted through. "Don't worry, honey," her client consoled her. "It's just that I have to check through here before they'll clear my assignment. Besides, alleys are pretty much the same all over the world."

I alternatively exulted and fretted over the processes of government. She was usually just amused. Only once did I see her really distressed. Somehow OCR had come into possession of some poorly made footage of what appeared to be medical experiments. The pictures showed the violent and erratic behavior of patients after having been injected with a drug. The name "LSD" was discernible on a bottle in the pictures. She could find no reference to the drug in a pharmacopoeia. "Some kind of lunatic asylum?" I suggested when told about the day's screening. "Maybe," she replied, "but they all had army uniforms on. I don't like it. Those fellows are going to get the country in trouble." Decades later press reports and court cases proved her right.

One December I had my own experience with "spookery." A call from an aide in Director Dulles's office asked me to go see "Frederick" in a specified room number in a building occupied by the clandestine services. "Mm-m-m," my old-timer branch chief observed, "could be old 'Shaky Freddie.' Be careful. He's a big-time operator down there."

Frederick had only two questions for me. Was I the young man who knew all about Afghans and Pathans? If so, would I be willing to take a quick trip out to Kabul, Peshawar, and environs and ask my friends if the tribes would be willing to take over Kabul and establish stability if anything were to happen to the "pro-Communist" regime of Afghan Prime Minister Mohammad Daud?

Edith and I consulted that night long after Elsie had gone home, when the children were asleep. Overriding troubled consciences with Kipling quotes about "a grey-coat guard on the Helmand ford" and "No man knoweth the mind of a king," we decided I should do it, even though it meant my being away from the family for Christmas.

I ended up spending the Holy Night in a broken-down lorry at twelve thousand feet, in the Lataband Pass between Kabul and Peshawar. The "well-informed" responses I collected on both sides of the border were casual and identical: "Sure—if the U.S. will provide the guns, pay us well, and allow us to loot Kabul." Frederick accepted the answers I brought back without comment and thanked me for my efforts.

My apparent intimacy with him brought attention from lesser "spooks," who would not ordinarily be caught dead talking to a "pointy-head" from OCI. From them I learned that "something big" was under consideration. The clandestine services were focusing on the fighting qualities of the warrior classes that lived along the underbelly of the Soviet Union: the Kurds, Pathans, and Gurkhas. What a confederacy they would make! It took the "pointy-head" from the other side of the house to point out that despite Kipling's glowing image of Kabul's "old Peshawar Gate, where Kurd and Kaffir meet," nowhere did these groups touch each other. In fact, thousands of miles separated their homelands. Nothing came of it all. The clandestine services boys were just "earning a living" thinking about it.

At home family life was pleasant. The little house in Falls Church, Virginia, was suburbia, but a rather different suburbia from that of today. We could drive into Washington in twenty minutes and park on the street near a theater or restaurant.

Edith and James with Sikandra and Patrick, Falls Church, Virginia, 1955.

One night we went to the Carter Barron Amphitheatre in Rock Creek Park to see Danny Kaye. Rain poured down as soon as he began. Performer and audience held out through a two-hour soaking. On the way home, due to some mysterious malfunction underneath, our ancient Dodge caught fire on Arlington Boulevard. The county fire department put it out and towed it away. The county police department took us home, the patrolmen joking about the risks they were taking by entering Fairfax County. Six-year-old Patrick was the star of his first grade the next day telling how the police brought Mummy and Daddy home last night.

One Labor Day we were sitting at home watching TV with the children. "Pick Temple," a pre–Sesame Street mentor who played games and sang songs for the young of the D.C. area, was their favorite character. After a few sugary remarks about the nobility of the working man, he broke into the old International Workers of the World ballad, "Joe Hill." Their mother, my Montana girl, clapped and sang with him, in honor of the "Wobbly" who had been executed by firing squad in Utah before World War I: "I dreamed I saw Joe Hill last night, alive as you and me. . . . 'But Joe, you're ten years dead,' says I. 'The copper bosses . . . shot you Joe.' 'I never died,' says he. . . . What they forgot to kill went on to organize, went on to organize. . . .'" What the children made of it, we never knew. What our prosperous civil-servant and small business neighbors thought, we never found out either.

We began to think of change. We acquired a big old house in Woodley Park in central Washington, just as the Agency moved out to Langley, Virginia. Edith quit to devote more attention to the children, the oldest two now in school. I was invited to join the Office of National Estimates (ONE), the Agency "think tank," an almost exclusively Ivy League establishment originally headed by Harvard historian William Langer and during my time by Yale professor Sherman Kent, with William Bundy (later to become one of "The Best and Brightest") as his deputy.

The years surrounding the turn of the decade from the 1950s to the 1960s were vibrant ones. The comfortably dull days of the Eisenhower administration gave way to the constantly exciting ones of the Kennedy presidency. In an agency that was in those days renowned for quick promotion, I went from GS-9 ($3,900 a year) to GS-15 ($24,000). Edith climbed from GS-7 ($3,600) to GS-11 ($4,800). By 1964 the house on Cathedral Avenue Northwest that we had purchased for $21,000 had a market value of more than $50,000. (When finally sold twenty years after that, it fetched $250,000, and in 1996 it was advertised for sale at $450,000.) The Spains acquired a summer house on the mouth of the Potomac River in Northumberland County, Virginia. A little red European sports car joined the sober family Buick station wagon.

Just after Kennedy's election, Edith's father died. I took care of the children while she went to California to pay a last farewell. The boy who had known Charlie Russell and danced with the Blackfeet was no more. Our personal link with the days of George Armstrong Custer and Sioux chief Sitting Bull was gone.

Less than two years later, our nuclear family was completed with the birth of a fourth child, William, on October 20, 1962, in the middle of the

Cuban missile crisis. Like his brothers, Patrick and Stephen, he was given the middle name of James, and the memory of those who had gone before was carried on.

In the years that followed, our four bright, energetic, handsome children were a source of pride—and often amusement. They did not interfere with their father's life in government nor with their mother's part-time job as an editor at American University. Edith wrote her widowed mother of their doings.

"Pat is the same Pat. Sunday afternoon it was raining and he and Kanda were playing on the porch. He looked out, walked over to the door and shouted: 'God! Stop this rain! Right now!' If I kept a baby book, I would enter that as his first prayer." Later, when he was an altar-boy master of ceremonies at an Easter Sunday Mass, she reported: "He did very well, clapping his hands with the right air of authority when they were all supposed to stand and kneel and keeping at everyone's elbow to oversee their activities. I suspect that's the way old P. D. Burke built his railroads."

Sikandra, slim, light-boned and tall, even as an infant, had the family appetite. "She eats like a young horse," her mother wrote. "All of it goes into the 'up' and none into the 'out.' She consumed her Easter basket entire. We never found anything except the handle and a piece of an artificial egg. Grass and all were gone. Still, she is the cutest thing to take out, good as gold, drifting around smiling silently, and being oh-so-ladylike. She doesn't have an ounce of self-preservative sense—fell off a bag of laundry yesterday!"

Some years later, when she was in her second year at Georgetown Visitation Convent School, Edith wrote: "Kanda's first dance was an unmitigated success. She danced every dance. One of them was with Bobby Kennedy, Jr., although she didn't know who he was, because she refuses to wear her glasses at parties. I remarked that her social life seemed to be doing well and she said, yes, she was doing all right 'for her age and condition,' but she was really going to get going when she (a) got contact lens, (b) got her teeth braces off, and (c) bleached her hair. And to think that I was afraid that she was going to be a shy and awkward teenager!"

Steve (born March 27, 1957) refused, in the first six months of his life, to eat any baby food other than cereal. His mother described him as "having four front teeth, trying to crawl, and yelling bloody murder," but "I hope to have a comrade in eating hot cereal on cold mornings. None of the rest of the family will touch it." When he was in grade school, she reported: "He's totally immersed in baseball, playing all morning and watching the unfortunate Senators on TV all afternoon and evening. That's what he does in the summer. In the winter it's the same with basketball and soccer. The biggest thing that has happened in his life was when his father took him to this year's opening Senators game."

William joined the family procession at the very end. Early on his mother convinced him that to be a youngest "way-behind" child, as she had been, was the most fun of all. He could be bad-tempered at times, she noted, but "there is a kind of incorruptible honesty and sincerity about him that makes up for much." One day when he was in kindergarten, a District of Columbia police officer showed up at home. An unidentified neighborhood five-year-old had broken a window in a garage down the alley, and the owner demanded legal action. Settling the officer at the kitchen table with a cup of coffee (Washington's way in those days), Edith asked, "Are you going over to Oyster School to pull him out of class?" "Not unless he turns up in our files as a hardened criminal. Would you just call the neighbor and calm him down?"

To return to affairs of state, OCI was like a newspaper office. Its attention span seldom exceeded twenty-four hours. There were dull days in the world, but the Bulletin had to be put out on even the least eventful of them. Thus, a minor tribal disturbance in Afghanistan might get attention one day and a major cabinet crisis in India be pushed aside the next in favor of a new Soviet missile test.

The Office of National Estimates was different. ONE was more like a university. Its two dozen people dealt in ideas. Its job was not to report current events or to try to influence them. We predicted what was going to happen. Our National Intelligence Estimates (NIEs) were "national," that is, not just CIA's but coordinated with all the foreign affairs agencies. There was ample evidence that the president and members of the National Security Council read them.

There were no editors, and every member of ONE had to know—or learn—how to write concisely and without ambiguity. In a way that would seem incredible today, it was an all-male organization. Women aspirants were deflected—for some years successfully—by the explanation that it was not a matter of sex discrimination, simply that Sherman Kent's language in heated discussion sessions was not suitable for gentle feminine ears.

ONE had its own absolutes. We drew on information from scholars, journalists, diplomats, and secret agents, but in reaching conclusions we made no concessions to the opinions of these "committed" people. "How can you expect some ambassador committed to a hundred million dollar aid program for his country to admit its economy is going down the drain?" Sherman Kent asked me one day. Bill Bundy's favorite remark was that he had never seen a memorandum of conversation "in which the drafting officer comes off second best."

We extended our analysis back into history. Quotes from Homer appeared in estimates on the Eastern Mediterranean. We projected our thoughts about the future by the most rigid social science methodology. The aim was to define alternatives and cast odds on them. Titles of the NIEs ran to such lyricism as "The Outlook for Greece over the Next Five Years" and "Prospects for Soviet Influence in the Third World." Inevitably, we were not always right. In the early 1960s, NIEs predicted that the regimes of the Saudi monarchy, the Shah of Iran, and King Hussein of Jordan (familiarly known in ONE corridors as the "BYK," for "Brave Young King") would not last out the decade.

An individual NIE might take months to complete. The staff member in charge was free to consult anyone he wanted, sometimes including a trip to the area concerned. His initial draft was gone over by the "board," eight senior members of ONE, mostly retired flag officers, ambassadors, and scholars. It might then be taken up to Princeton where, on a weekend retreat, it would be reworked by Allen Dulles and a selected group of public figures. Then it was distributed to the foreign affairs agencies. Further refined in week-long meetings with their representatives, it came to the United States Intelligence Board (USIB), chaired by Dulles. There State, Defense, the FBI, or the National Security Agency chiefs could take footnote dissents. In the spirit of ONE, our feeling was, "The more footnotes the better. It shows we made them think!"

All this intellectual stimulation did not destroy my long-standing hankering to return to the Foreign Service. I had only to ask myself, "Would you rather retire as an anonymous GS-18 in ONE or as ambassador to, well, almost anywhere?" Thus, when a chance came to participate in a new CIA/Office of National Estimates–State/Policy Planning Council annual exchange program, I grabbed it.

There was one last temptation to be resisted. In May 1963, just as I was shifting from National Estimates to State, a meeting on the Middle East was scheduled in Rome to be chaired by John McCone, Kennedy's new director of central intelligence, I decided to go on my own a few days early to try to get a personal feel for what was going on in the sweeping movement for change that was shaping the church under Pope John XXIII.

At the last minute, the venue of the official gathering was shifted to Frankfurt. I held to my plan and spent Saturday and Sunday in Rome before going on to Frankfurt. I had consulted the only "liberal" cleric I knew in Washington, Msgr. George Higgins, then with the National Catholic Welfare Conference. He had given me a few names and letters of introduction.

I sought out several of the young priests who surrounded the pope. By chance I also fell in with a school chum from Chicago, a network correspondent in Rome. He was full of information about the exciting new things happening in the church and had close contact with many of the men behind them. My time was taken up with eating, drinking, and talking with the pope's collaborators, although I also noticed that the Roman press was filled with coverage of another American visitor, Director of Central Intelligence John McCone, in town for an audience with the pope and allegedly to cast a suspicious eye on him as possibly "procommunist."

On Monday morning, still a little queasy from the last bottle of wine consumed a few hours before with voluble clerics and theologians, I flew to Frankfurt. I arrived at the meeting site late, just as everyone was sitting down to lunch. McCone was at the right hand of the host. As there were no place cards and bureaucratic diffidence had left the chair on the other side of the great man the only one still vacant, I had no choice but to fill it myself.

Over lunch McCone told of his visit to Rome and what he and the pope had said to each other. McCone's views were intelligent, albeit much on the conservative side. He admired the charismatic holiness of John XXIII but worried about the young men around him. "Some Italians say that a lot of them are communists," he remarked. When the general conversation died away, I told McCone that I, too, had been in Rome over the weekend, largely with the pope's young associates. Describing some of the things I had seen and heard, I suggested that the pope's men were "no more communist than President Kennedy's Boston Irish Mafia."

McCone listened and finally asked, "Who are you, anyway?" He was pleased when he learned that, technically, at least, I was on his payroll. The president, he said, was very interested in the subject. Would I do a memo on "all this" when I got back to Washington?

The meeting on the Middle East passed uneventfully. When I got home, I gave Sherman Kent, my ONE boss, a fifteen-page account of my two days in Rome. Not very interested in all this Catholic exotica, Kent sent it on to McCone, who, I discovered years later, gave it to Kennedy. Shortly afterward, I transferred back to the State Department to concentrate on another difficult charismatic, Gamal Abdel Nasser of Egypt.

I was back in Foggy Bottom only a few days when I got a telephone call from one James Jesus Angleton. A mysterious, powerful, and eccentric figure in the agency, he was later revealed in the press as chief of counterintelligence on the covert side of the CIA. He would be grateful for a few minutes of my time.

I called Sherman Kent to ask if he had any idea why Angleton was interested in me. He didn't, but warned, "Be cagey with Jim. He's the kind of fellow who, when his wife says 'good morning' to him at the breakfast table, spends the whole day trying to figure out what she was getting at!" I got a clue when I discovered that Angleton was also responsible for the Vatican. Talking over the day's activities with Edith that night, she suggested that Angleton's Vatican brief might be the result of people thinking that his unusual middle name made him especially qualified to defend American interests against the popish plots some feared Kennedy's election would bring to the United States.

It turned out that Angleton wanted to convey Mr. McCone's thanks for my memorandum. There wasn't going to be a U.S. ambassador to the Vatican under a Catholic president, he said, but McCone wanted to have his own special representative there. I could be the man. He, Angleton, didn't think I was right about the new pope and these priests. He believed that a lot of them were indeed Marxists and that some were deep-cover Soviet agents. But that didn't matter. I had my "ins," and we needed all the information we could get on them. How about it?

I went home and told Edith about the offer. Personal envoy to a pope we had come to admire without ever having met him! A few years in the center of the cultural universe for us and the children! A likely promotion, fine free housing, generous allowances, and additional income from the house we would vacate and rent in Washington!

Then we looked at each other and shook our heads simultaneously. "No," she said. "You've wanted to get out of that place for a long time, and now you're finally going back to State. Maybe you can be a real ambassador someday. You'd prefer Afghanistan or Yemen anyway." The next day I called Angleton and said, "Thanks, but no thanks. I already have a new job." That ended the matter.

For the next few years in Washington, we took what comfort we could from what was going on in the American church. Pope John's encyclicals, "Mater et Magistra" and "Pacem in Terris" were brilliant beacons probing the future. His successor Paul VI's "Humanae Vitae," devoted almost entirely to birth control, was a dim light poking under old furniture. It polarized the church in America into liberal and conservative wings, and Washington resounded with the results.

Senator Eugene McCarthy, a fellow parishioner, led dissident hymns at Mayflower Hotel meetings. We and a minority of the congregation walked out of St. Thomas Apostle Church during the reading of a harsh call for conformity from Patrick, Cardinal O'Boyle, our strongly conservative archbishop. We had to admit the situation was not as bad as it might have been. The urbane new pastor of St. Thomas arranged to have the ushers notify the dissidents on the church steps when the reading of the episcopal letter was finished and Mass was about to resume.

7

Back in the Department

When I returned to State in 1962, it still had the distinction of being known (often grudgingly) as "the Department." In most other ways, however, it was a very different place from the one I left in 1953. The quarter-square-block it occupied in those days, at 21st Street and Virginia Avenue Northwest, had housed the War Department before the Pentagon came into being. Things had marched to the easy cadence of the Eisenhower administration. Now the old building had been given to AID (the Agency for International Development), and State occupied new construction on the other three-quarters of the block. It all pulsed to the vigorous tempo set by John F. Kennedy, a president insatiable in the business of foreign affairs—and in other things too, although few knew so at the time.

Kennedy called desk officers direct. Assistant secretaries took them along for White House conferences. The only man at State who did not appear constantly excited was Secretary Dean Rusk. The old Ivy League dominance had given way to graduates of a variety of universities. I was pleased to note that the largest group were from the University of Chicago. Two things were the same: Almost all at the "policy level" were men, and women Foreign Service officers still had to resign when they got married.

The Policy Planning Council to which I reported had just had its name changed from Policy Planning Staff. The new nomenclature was supposed to represent the difference between a purely supportive role and a consultative and participatory one. It consisted of a dozen men, about half career Foreign Service Officers and half newly recruited academic luminaries. Its leadership had also changed. George C. McGhee, chairman at the beginning of the Kennedy administration, had gone off to Bonn as ambassador to West Germany.

Walt Whitman Rostow, famous for his "takeoff" theory for underdeveloped countries while at the Massachusetts Institute of Technology, moved from the National Security Council to take over Policy Planning. At that point, Walt was not yet caught up in Vietnam, as he became a few years later when he returned to the White House as Lyndon Johnson's national security adviser. Walt's sparkling mind and universal interests brought out the best in everyone.

One of our members devised a plan for "an opening to China." Word came back from the president that it looked good. Send it back to him in his second term when he would have a real mandate from the American people. Another figured out an approach to the Arab-Israeli dispute, not unlike that put forward by Jimmy Carter at Camp David sixteen years later. This time, according to White House gossip, the reaction was, "Bring it back in Bobby's administration." Yet another on our staff devoted years of his life to a fanciful plan for an "MLF," a multilateral nuclear force, designed to end Allied gripes over U.S. unilateral control of nuclear weapons in NATO. Nothing at all came back on that.

We didn't mind the rebuffs. We knew that Kennedy's 1960 electoral victory had been narrow and, in the minds of some, doubtful. We realized that a president could not do everything at once, and, liberal internationalists that we were, we were happy to see the administration giving time and attention to domestic desegregation. The important thing was that the president heard our voice.

We were even proud of the one thing our chairman did that irritated us. Most of our time was spent on individual projects, but in accordance with the "council" concept, Friday afternoons were sacred to group deliberation. At 2:00 P.M. Walt would take his place at the head of the table and announce, "I want us to produce some real collective wisdom this afternoon, but before we start I'll just catch you up on a few things I've been doing." At 5:30 or 6:00, he'd still be going on when his secretary appeared to drag him away for another meeting.

The assassination of President Kennedy cast a deep pall over the Department of State. For many it was he who made their ten- and twelve-hour days worthwhile. The brilliant, before-their-time ideas stored up for the second Kennedy administration seemed as dead as he was.

Yet, after a surprisingly few days, things picked up again. Lyndon Johnson was not the State Department's favorite character, but he made himself felt immediately and colorfully. Unlike the cool, detached Kennedy, who viewed all foreign leaders through the same skeptical lens, Johnson had intense likes and dislikes. Two of these were relevant to the part of the world with which I was concerned. LBJ was fond of Pakistan's President Ayub Khan and distrustful of India's Prime Minister Jawaharlal Nehru.

The most important project I was involved in was a policy-and-programs study on India and Pakistan, one of a series on areas deemed important to the United States. India was attacked by China in 1962. Under the vigorous and adroit leadership of John Kenneth Galbraith, the Harvard professor Kennedy sent as ambassador to India, a U.S. military assistance program was hastily concocted for hitherto neutralist New Delhi. Pakistan urged that it be made contingent on India's agreeing to a settlement of the Kashmir dispute, but the Kennedy administration deemed the stakes too high to permit such a complication. A mini–U.S. military mission was established in New Delhi, and the program went ahead.

It did not work out very well. The Chinese undertook a unilateral ceasefire after achieving their limited objectives in contested territory. The dispute between India and Pakistan over Kashmir remained as bitter as ever. Massive military aid continued to flow to America's established ally, Pakistan, which India pointed out was not under threat from anyone. The Soviet Union, acutely aware of China's breakaway from what not long before had been the Sino-Soviet bloc, promised Nehru more and bigger arms than the United States was ever likely to supply.

Galbraith tried to salvage something by focusing on economic and technical aid to India. He got administration approval for what was one of the biggest AID programs to date, a $500-million soft loan for construction of a state-owned steel mill at Bokaro. I caught a worm's-eye view of what followed.

Having wangled an invitation to lunch in the White House Mess from erstwhile ONE colleague Robert Komer, I was eating and chatting when Galbraith strode in. Back in Washington at the end of his term in India to rally support for the Bokaro mill, he had spent the morning before congressional committees and had to go back in the afternoon. It was hard going, he told us. The Republicans were aghast at the idea of American financing of a state-owned steel mill. A lot of Democrats shared their sentiments. He was waiting to see the president to get him on the phone to change the Democrats' minds. The call to the Oval Office came before he had finished his sandwich.

Fifteen minutes later, he returned, glassy-eyed (if anyone can imagine John Kenneth Galbraith in that condition). Kennedy had refused. He did not have enough clout to spend any of it on this issue, the president had said. He would support the Bokaro project as long as it was alive, but it would have to stand or fall on whether or not Galbraith could convince a majority in Congress of the merits of the case. Good luck! Galbraith bravely trudged back to the Hill, but that was the end of that. Not surprisingly, the Soviet Union built the mill a few years later.

Against this background Howard Wriggins (a university professor in real life) and I undertook our India-Pakistan study. We researched our subject in depth. We visited both countries and consulted extensively with their leadership. We talked to every U.S. official who had anything to do with them. We charted a wide variety of possibilities and options. We produced a paper that Walt acclaimed a model of long-term policy planning. Then, within a year came something we had not considered at all, the India-Pakistan War of 1965. It opened a whole new range of unanticipated policy and program decisions. All over the government our model paper went into newly fashionable shredders.

Oddly, the project I remember most fondly from my time on the Policy Planning Council was almost trivial. Walt called me into his office one day for an eloquent lecture on American history. Its gist was that the broad-based U.S. economic and industrial takeoff in the second half of the nineteenth century rested heavily on two things: the extension of a cheap national postal system all over the country and the establishment of the great mail-order houses, Sears Roebuck and Montgomery Ward. Now the farm wife had a motive to produce eggs and dairy products beyond the family needs. The few dollars she made from selling them could promptly bring her a new dress or cooking pot.

"The British left a good postal system in India and Pakistan," he said. "Go design a mail-order catalog for the villagers there. We'll get AID to supply the merchandise they want until they can make it themselves."

I chose East Pakistan as a pilot area and badgered the consulate in Dacca into sending me consumer goods advertisements from the local newspapers. I compiled all the per capita income and disposable cash figures I could find. I got USIS, the United States Information Service, to do a survey on consumer preferences. I consulted with Edith on housewifely desires. The result was a pasted-over Montgomery Ward catalog full of cloth, flashlights, cooking pots, soap, and the like, plus, at Edith's insistence, insect spray, underwear, children's medicines, and simple toys. About that time, however, Walt was called back to the White House, and I went on to other things in the State Department. For all I know, there may still be a copy of this policy effort somewhere in the State Department's files. Anyway, it was fun.

During my fifteen months on the Policy Planning Council, I remained on the CIA payroll. The Agency was eager to place someone else into the exchange program, and the council was up to its full complement on the State Department rolls. Roger Hilsman, director of State's Intelligence and Research Bureau (INR), asked if I would like to head up the Near East and South Asia Office in his bureau. The office was a mix of Civil Service specialists permanently stationed in Washington and career Foreign Service officers temporarily at home on what they considered "slow-track" assignments. The two groups did not get along. Maybe I was enough of a hermaphrodite to make them work together. There was a five-year Foreign Service Reserve (FSR) commission in it for me, with a salary slightly higher than that of my Agency GS-15.

By the time I got to INR, Hilsman had gone on to become assistant secretary for the Far East. He was succeeded by his deputy, Thomas Hughes, an intellectual protégé of Vice President Hubert Humphrey who subsequently became president of the Carnegie Endowment for International Peace. The purpose of INR/RNA (said to stand for "Intelligence and

Research/Regional Near East and South Asia") was the same as that of intelligence anywhere. It was supposed to give the top of the department comprehensive, objective information free of the bias that might creep into the views of those actually responsible for policy and its implementation. Despite the images projected by popular novelists, there was no "spooky side" of the State Department intelligence house.

INR produced a daily *Digest* and RNA usually had something in it. The *Digest,* because it was their own, was read by the "Seventh Floor," where the secretary and under secretaries dwelt; but there was only occasional evidence that they were influenced by it. The demands of deciding among the options for action that flowed up from the regional policy bureaus left little time for that. Besides, the State Department had its own ways.

I discovered them one day when I went to see an office director in the Near East policy bureau. One of my analysts wanted some queries for information to be cabled to a particular embassy. The office director refused to clear it. Why? The response was simple: "It's insulting. If the embassy had anything relevant to say on those subjects, it would send the material in on its own."

The big event of my two-and-a-half years in RNA was the 1965 India-Pakistan War. My colleague on the Policy Planning Council and I had failed to rate it as a possibility. My staff in INR and I failed to predict it until a few days before it happened. Once it did, however, we woke the department of Defense up fast with an exciting and perfectly accurate piece on the defeat of U.S. state-of-the-art Patton tanks, supplied to Pakistan, by ancient U.S. Sherman tanks long ago given to India. (The Shermans had been thoroughly dug in for an ambush of an unwary Pakistani commander.)

The only significant reorganization of the Department of State in the thirty-eight years that I knew it took place in 1966. The story—or myth—runs like this. Dean Rusk, badgered by an impatient Lyndon Johnson for a firsthand description of the official residence at an embassy he wanted to confer on a political friend, called the relevant assistant secretary for the information. The man had thirty countries in his jurisdiction. He'd never been to this particular capital and didn't know. The deputy assistant secretary responsible for that part of the bureau didn't know either. Neither did the office director, who had visited or served in four of the five countries under his direction, all except this one. Appalled at the uninformed "layering," Rusk decreed that, as of July 1, policy responsibility for any given country would flow directly from him through the assistant secretary to a newly created "ambassador-like" country director, responsible for at most three countries, in which he or she must have served.

Raymond A. Hare, a classic, old-time career FSO who had been ambassador in several Middle Eastern countries and under secretary for political affairs, asked me to become country director for Pakistan and Afghanistan. Finally, I had made it to policy management—and for the two countries I knew best! To make things even more appealing, Lucius Battle, the new assistant secretary for NEA, made no bones about his limited knowledge of South Asia. "You two run it!" he told me and Douglas Heck, the country director for India. "If you need help, let me know."

The new system was an improvement. Cables that formerly had to carry five or six clearances now moved with one or two. The implications of action in a foreign country were judged by someone who knew that country rather than someone whose main interest was getting along with Washington colleagues. Rusk's bestowal of "ambassador-like" authority on the country directors encouraged cooperation from representatives of the other foreign affairs agencies. So did proposals by the country director for Saturday or Sunday interagency meetings to clear up threatened disagreements.

The one defect in the new system was classic. U.S. relations with such countries as Greece and Turkey, Israel and Egypt, or India and Pakistan were dominated by their quarrels with each other. Country directors responsible for each country tended to share their "client's" conflicting ideas of what the United States should do. Deadlocks had to be decided by the assistant secretary. Foreign ambassadors resident in Washington promptly became aware of this and focused their attentions on him also. What was the point in dealing with your country director if he couldn't deliver the department?

Despite the fact that Heck's experience had been in India and Nepal and mine in Pakistan and Afghanistan, we shared a common view of the subcontinent. We were aware that our two signatures on a proposal for either country usually breezed through higher echelons simply because we were in agreement. We agreed that, except for matters of absolute conscience, when we differed we would take turns giving in or flip a coin on the decision.

Afghanistan required little time. Terrible as its travails were to be a dozen years later, in those days it was a self-sufficient little country with a patient and sturdy people. The monarchy had ceased to be absolute, and a popular modernist prime minister, Hashim Maiwandwal, had just taken office. The United States and the Soviet Union had even managed to establish coordinated, if not cooperative, road-building projects in the country.

The only serious threat to U.S.-Afghan relations developed during an official visit by Maiwandwal to the United States. On a long airplane trip to the West Coast, the prime minister pressed me into service as a bridge partner to take on a couple of his cabinet colleagues. The Afghans were superb at the game. I am not. After two successive four-spade defeats, the State Department protocol chief, who was also aboard, averted a diplomatic crisis by bringing back the Air Force copilot and consigning me to his seat in the cockpit.

The India-Pakistan War had ended in a stalemate. It left in its wake a congressional ban, endorsed by the State Department, on military assistance of any kind to either country. Pakistan, almost exclusively dependent on U.S. arms, was rapidly losing its military capabilities. India, only peripherally benefited by U.S. arms, was expanding its military capabilities with large-scale Soviet military aid. The United States did not want to see an out-and-out Soviet-Indian military alliance, but it was in Pakistan, not India, that we had intercept facilities whose Pentagon proprietors insisted were vital to national security. An executive branch instruction came down: devise a military supply policy for South Asia that takes all these things into account and we'll try to sell it to Congress.

I spent most of my three years in NEA on the project without achieving anything. The flexible Heck-Spain partnership was inhibited by ambassadors in India and Pakistan who had strong and contradictory feelings. Chester Bowles was back in New Delhi as ambassador, again. He was not prepared to give an inch. We'd finally gotten out of our arms relationship with Pakistan, and as long as we stayed out he would take care of India's drift toward alliance with the Soviet Union. Eugene Murphy Locke, a brilliant, hard-boiled, Yale-educated Texas lawyer, businessman, and politician, newly appointed to Islamabad, took seriously his instructions from his friend Lyndon Johnson: "Keep President Ayub happy!"

When Locke returned for a brief consultation in Washington, he stayed at the White House. Gene and I got along very well and with a politician's knack for personal relations, he confided to me that he had told the president what a good country director he had (something a career ambassador would be unlikely to think of). They'd talked about "doing something" for Ayub and concluded that overhaul of an antique submarine Pakistan had on lease from the United States and fifty more Patton tanks with spare parts would have to do for the moment. "Tell that fellow at the State Department you're so high on to go get 'em!" Johnson directed. "Tell him to keep it quiet, and if we can't do it ourselves to find someone else who will!" With that Locke went back to Islamabad.

It was a strange way to get instructions. I confided in my colleague Douglas Heck. We sure did "need help" with this one, so we took the story to Assistant Secretary Luke Battle. He received it skeptically but said he'd check it out with the Seventh Floor. An hour later he called back to report. "By God, it's for real! The secretary says the president is mad because it isn't already taken care of." To Doug Heck's uneasy conscience, we were told not to inform Chet Bowles. Another politician, not one of Lyndon Johnson's or Dean Rusk's favorites, there was no telling what he might do.

Arranging the submarine overhaul was easy. Turkey had several of the same kind of boat on lease from the United States and had developed its own dry dock and maintenance facility for them. Happy to provide help to a CENTO (Central Treaty Organization) ally and to do a favor for its principal arms supplier, Turkey took the boat in. The only problem was that it was so badly in need of repair that it tied up the Turkish dockyard for more than a year. When I was later stationed in Turkey, I was treated to frequent complaints by the Turkish Navy about "that crazy business when the United States got us to tie up our facilities fixing a broken-down Pakistan sub."

The tanks were a more difficult proposition. I got INR to extract from the Pentagon a highly classified list of "U.S. Weapons in Foreign Inventories." Those with Patton (M-48) tanks included, if I remember correctly, West Germany, Belgium, Italy, Turkey, Jordan, Iran, and Korea. Rich Iran, Pakistan's Muslim neighbor and another CENTO ally, with a shah known for his ability to make decisions unencumbered by local institutions or public opinion, seemed a likely place to start. We got a prompt answer. His Imperial Majesty welcomed the opportunity to assist his friend, President Ayub; but, in the common interest, he couldn't reduce his own order-of-battle. If the United States would provide him fifty of its new T-60 tanks, he'd pass on the same number of M-48s to Pakistan. At the time, the T-60 was brand new, not yet even in the hands of U.S. armored divisions. Clearly, the Iranian approach was a flop.

Turkey simply said no. It had NATO as well as CENTO responsibilities, and there were already hundreds more Soviet tanks on its border than it possessed. Besides, it was doing its part with the submarine overhaul.

King Hussein was worried that another Palestine war was heating up and he would need everything he had, not to attack Israel but to defend his borders. He could promise no more than to take the matter under advisement.

Italy wanted to help. It had a nearly shut-down production facility for the soon-to-be-NATO-obsolete T-48s. It could be started up again, but it would be expensive and take a long time. Also, Rome did not want to get involved in anything illegal. The United States had a lot of surplus T-48s of its own. Why not just give them to Pakistan?

Belgium had such a small defense force and such a tight budget that every tracked vehicle counted. Things might become more flexible if Brussels got the contract it was seeking for a new NATO aircraft. Action would have to wait on that decision. And the day we drafted a "top secret" message to Seoul asking the embassy there to take on our problem, skirmishing broke out in the DMZ (Demilitarized Zone) on the North Korea–South Korea border. Foreseeing the obvious, we never sent the cable.

This is not a suspense story, and it will hardly surprise anyone familiar with the ways of foreign affairs that we never got the tanks for Pakistan. Neither did it make any difference at all in the long-range scheme of things. By 1967, Lyndon Johnson was preoccupied by Vietnam. He pulled Locke out of Islamabad and sent him to Saigon as "deputy ambassador" to keep an eye on things there. After a short time, Locke resigned to run for governor of Texas to replace John Connally. He came in fifth in a field of nine and died of a brain tumor not long after.

In 1968 Johnson announced that he would not run for president again. The congenial Luke Battle left the NEA assistant secretaryship and was replaced by competent career FSO Parker Hart. Doug Heck went off to Istanbul (where he had been born) as consul general. A few months later Nixon's election victory brought Joseph Sisco to the NEA job. A civil servant for most of his career, Sisco was bright and energetic but had never served overseas and knew nothing of South Asia. His purpose in life was to please new Secretary of State William Rogers and to take personal credit for everything that happened.

The message to old NEA warhorses like me was clear: it was time to move on. The pill was sugar-coated. President Nixon had appointed Kenneth Keating as ambassador to India but was having trouble finding the man he wanted for Pakistan. Why didn't I go out and run the embassy for a few months as that rare thing, a true chargé d'affaires *ad interim,* until a good Republican could be found?

The bureaucratic process that made this possible had been completed earlier. Looking over the NEA Table of Organization one day, Luke Battle had discovered that, alone among his country directors, I was a reserve officer and had only a year and a half to go on my commission. "Why don't you apply for reintegration as an FSO?" he asked.

"I'm not sure they'd take me back in," I said. "And how do I answer the question of why I left in the first place?"

"Why did you?"

"I wanted to get some more education on the part of the world I was interested in."

"It might do. Try it."

I shot the necessary paper arrows into the air. Word came back that I would be exempted from the written examination because I had already passed it. The three elderly FSOs who conducted the oral examination never asked the damning question. We chatted for an hour about the needs and objectives of the Foreign Service officer corps and about South Asia. They said they thought the Foreign Service would welcome me back. They'd so recommend to the chairman of the Board of the Foreign Service–Assistant Secretary Battle! If I'd known, I'd have sweated less.

The family was enthusiastic about going overseas. God knew, said Edith, that she was ready for a change. Maybe the temporary assignment in Pakistan would lead to other foreign postings. Patrick, seventeen, a senior at Gonzaga, the Jesuit high school in Washington, could live with her brother in Chevy Chase and finish at Gonzaga. He volunteered to take care of the family car.

Despite her mother's tales of the fun she'd had at a boarding school in Montana after the Helena earthquake, Sikandra, fifteen and a sophomore at Visitation Convent, was not overjoyed at the prospect of joining the boarders there just when she was getting ready to swing. "They make you go to bed at 9:00 P.M." I suspect that, in her tough ladylike way, she privately swore that one day she would have her revenge.

Stephen and Bill, both in the lower grades, would come with us. Typical small boys, they were overjoyed at the prospect of getting out of their present school, St. Thomas Apostle, where they had to wear uniforms and say "Yes, Sister" to the nuns. When word got around the State Department that we'd be gone for four to six months, people home on temporary assignments began telephoning to rent the house on Cathedral Avenue.

All in all, it was a good move. We had been in Washington fourteen years. The people at the top of the department who considered me "bright" were no longer there—and I was no longer all that "young." In our personal lives, the exciting days when we'd waited eagerly for "Good" Pope John's pronouncements, sent a telegram saying "Resign!" to Pope Paul after his birth control encyclical, walked out of church during the reading of Archbishop Patrick Cardinal O'Boyle's antediluvian pastoral letters, and sung folk hymns at the Mayflower Hotel with fellow parishioner Senator Eugene McCarthy—those days were past.

Gone, too, were the days of careless unstructured protest on Vietnam, when we had walked through crowds of gentle demonstrators on the Mall in the company of Ellsworth Bunker, our ambassador in Saigon, and seen him cheered as one who was seeking peace in his own way. Now letters of dissent from young Foreign Service officers gave way to resignations and to the leaking of damaging documents. Lyndon Johnson was gone—and his Great Society with him. Public protest hardened into destroying draft records and applauding the stridency of Jane Fonda.

I had come home to Washington from a trip abroad in 1968 a few days after the assassination of Martin Luther King, Jr., to a city I hardly recognized. A curfew was in effect. Military searchlights beamed up and down Rock Creek Park in front of our house. Neighborhood housewives served coffee to National Guardsmen manning machine gun posts on quiet street corners. Edith and the boys had sat in the window of our third floor bedroom and watched Washington burning across the park.

Few trusted President Nixon and his "sinister" adviser, Henry Kissinger, who seemed to be drawing the United States deeper into the Southeast Asian morass. The mindlessness that cost four young lives at Kent State

University was just around the corner. It was far from clear which side was right, but it was unmistakable that America had become divided in a particularly ugly way. For a little while at least, it promised to be more satisfying to represent our country abroad than to live in it at home.

8

Practicing Diplomacy

BY TRADITION, THE PRINCIPAL officer of an American diplomatic or consular post abroad flies the flag. Old Glory flaps over his office, his residence, and on the fender of his car. It decorated the black Cadillac limousine that met us when we landed at Rawalpindi in July 1969. It had been Deputy Chief of Mission Jordan "Tom" Rogers's flag on the way to the airport. It was mine on the way back. Such first times are remembered. An aging FSO may be uncertain of the exact years he served in Lima or in Kathmandu and of whether Marge was his secretary in one and Ellen in the other or vice versa. But just ask him when and where he first flew the flag!

The embassy's greeting was kindly. White House politics about ambassadors had given Tom Rogers a chance at several months of being chargé. State Department politics had cut that role to a few weeks. Yet Rogers showed no resentment. Neither did the dozen counselors and agency chiefs who made up the senior staff. To the hundred or so other staff the arrival of a new boss meant little. They did not even have to come to the airport to greet him.

The Chancery (or office) part of the embassy was in an old apartment building in Rawalpindi. We were taken first to the Residence in the new city of Islamabad, a forty-minute drive away. There we were greeted with pomp and ceremony by the legendary Maqbool, since 1948 head bearer at the American Residence. He introduced another ten turbaned, white-clad servants. To our joy one was the son of Izat Khan, who had taken such good care of a young couple on their first assignment in Karachi eighteen years earlier. In those days such transgenerational relationships involved a devotion and loyalty beyond anything comprehensible in the United States.

To Steve's and Bill's delight, each was assigned his own bearer and taken off to the side yard to the biggest aboveground swimming pool either had ever seen. (It had been bought and abandoned by Lyndon Johnson's appointee, who had gone home on his own after the election.) Impressed by all their perquisites, they took to introducing themselves as "the sons of the chargé" when they entered the American International School. This provoked scorn and scuffles from their democratically minded classmates, and it didn't take them long to give it up.

After only a few days, Edith remarked on the service. "I like this. Washing, cleaning, cooking, and things like that don't have to be very well done for me to prefer this to doing them myself, but they are superbly done in this house. I like that even more!"

Day-to-day work in the Chancery was as it might have been anywhere: getting a U.S. senator's nephew held on a drug charge out of prison; arbitrating a dispute between the consul general in Lahore and the consul in Peshawar about which end of the Indus River Attock Bridge each should take down his flag in deference to the other; or trying to convince a newly assigned agricultural attaché from Kansas that in Pakistan, as in the United Kingdom, "corn" meant wheat, barley, and oats, not the yellow ears so familiar to him.

President Ayub had given way to President Yahya Khan a few months before I arrived, but the U.S. ban on military supply to Pakistan remained in force. The Pakistanis, still friendly and polite, had settled on their response. Our ten-year no-rent lease on a large U.S. Air Force intercept and communications station at Budabar near Peshawar would not be renewed.

While still in my former job in Washington, I had concluded that this would not be a catastrophe. After months of outcry from the Pentagon that U.S. national survival depended on Budabar, I asked how much the Department of Defense would be prepared to pay in rent if that was the only way we could hold on to the base. After numerous meetings the answer came back: "Up to $200,000 a year."

The problem, now that I was on the ground, was how to arrange the liquidation with minimal scars to the overall relationship. The lease provided that the land and everything permanently established on it went to Pakistan. The United States was entitled to remove furniture, recreational equipment, air conditioners, generators, and the like. "Of course," said the amiable general from the Interservices Intelligence (ISI) directorate with whom I was negotiating, "our Air Force plans to use the place for headquarters. We'd be happy to have the moveable stuff too, if the U.S. were inclined to be so kind." He did not need to point out that it would cost more to airlift the matériel out than it was worth. We both knew it.

The U.S. Air Force was not inclined to be kind. It demanded $2 million. Unhappy at such a petty approach, I sent a strong personal message to Philip Hilbert, under secretary of the Air Force. Didn't the idiotic USAF have any regard for the future? We might want to do something with Pakistan again some day. The answer said, in effect: Don't worry about the future. Congress is threatening to cut off all our appropriations now because we are illegally expanding the military aid program by buying things out of our own support appropriations and giving them to our friends. You call yourself a diplomat. Get us something for that junk!

The bargaining got underway in earnest. I knew Pakistan was short on foreign exchange. What about $2 million in rupees? The general laughed. One million U.S. dollars? One million U.S. dollars in rupees? Five hundred thousand dollars in dollars or rupees? No! No! No! No! A break came when I met the Pakistan Air Force commander-in-chief at a social event. We had been friends when he was a flight lieutenant in Karachi and I a vice consul. I warned in apocryphal terms what Budabar would be like stripped of all its comforts. He shot off to complain to President Yahya.

When I next sat down with the ISI general, he was cold and businesslike. We both knew that the United States was never going to take that stuff away, he said, but he would give $250,000 worth of Pakistani handicrafts in return for clear title to it. The offer was final. For the next year or so, the best bargains in USAF PXs all over the world were copper pots, onyx bowls, and cotton rugs.

The following months were crammed with activity. President Nixon arrived for an official visit—about which I'll have more to say later when I tell of my occasional dealings with the great men of those days. In the way of FSO rotation, Sidney Sober, another experienced career FSO, came to replace Tom Rogers as DCM. A new Republican ambassador, Joseph Farland, was appointed. A former FBI agent married to a West Virginia coal heiress, Farland and his family were due to arrive in Islamabad in October on the night of the Marine Ball, the premier social event in every embassy. Assuming that he would be tired, I cautioned the security guard detachment that the new ambassador would probably not be present at their ball.

I gave Sid Sober the draft of a brief speech I'd promised to deliver in case the ambassador did not attend. Sid flew down to Karachi in the embassy airplane to meet Farland and discovered on the way to Rawalpindi that Farland was a former Marine. Outraged at the mildness of my proposed plaudits to the corps, he came straight from the airport to the ball, where we quickly rearranged the head table. The new ambassador gave a rousing hour-long paean that covered not only the halls of Montezuma and the shores of Tripoli but every other engagement the Marines had ever fought.

Next morning, while the Farlands caught up on their sleep, the Spains departed for Washington. Once there, we repossessed our elder children, our house, and our car and reinserted Steve and Bill with the nuns at the parish school.

My next, again temporary, assignment was to head an interagency group doing a "program analysis" of Turkey, under the auspices of Henry Kissinger's National Security Council staff. In the Old Executive Office Building, I met my first Republican "egghead," a wan young man who had been an instructor at Cornell (or maybe it was Williams or Amherst). His kind were virtually unknown in Washington in those days, when incubators like the Heritage Foundation were themselves unborn. He was unconcerned by my lack of experience in, and small knowledge of, Turkey but seriously disturbed by my computer illiteracy.

Fortunately, the Air Force colonel assigned to the team had completed a year's course in the new electronic marvels *and* had access to one in the Pentagon. (In those days the things took up whole rooms.) He quantified anything we wanted. I began to realize dimly what the world of the future was going to be like.

We divided the costs of our intercept facilities in Turkey by the units of intelligence collected. It was cheap. We went on to assess the value of the units by counting those deemed worthy of publication in intelligence community bulletins. Taken this way, per-unit costs skyrocketed. We compared support costs and firepower for U.S. troops on the communist border in Europe with those for Turkish troops on their border with the Soviet Union. If I remember correctly, American firepower was three-to-four times greater and cost thirty-to-forty times more.

We found out that it cost much more per kilo for the Bureau of Narcotics and Dangerous Drugs (predecessor of the Drug Enforcement Agency) to cut off a kilo of heroin "at the source" in Turkey than to seize and destroy it on the streets of New York. We discovered and charted that over the twenty years of the Turkish-U.S. alliance, USIS's opinion polls showed that Turkish disillusion with the United States had grown in direct proportion to USIS's budget. We found that the more USAID's program decreased, the more personnel were assigned to Turkey.

The first six months of 1970 in Washington provided a classic example of the "broken-field running" that constituted the senior Foreign Service appointments process in those days. Almost every night at the dinner table, Steve and Bill asked: "Where are we gonna go next, huh? And when?" My exploration of the subject led in a dozen different directions. Under Secretary for Management William B. Macomber, in an unguarded moment, allowed as how I might, just might, be somewhere around the ambassadorial threshold, "say, Jordan"—a real tribute, since he had been ambassador there himself. I no longer had any official claim on NEA, but I still had friends there. They thought Cyprus might be right.

The Senior Assignments Office under the director general of the Foreign Service pursued the matter in its own systematic way. Having demonstrated reasonable competence as a chargé d'affaires, I should now prove myself as a DCM. Without a word to anyone, I was "paneled" as DCM, Tehran, and travel, household effects shipping, and medical inoculation orders began to pour forth. It was a good job officially, but the ambassador in Iran was Douglas MacArthur II, by acclamation the most difficult supervisor in the career Foreign Service. Combining the least appealing traits of his famous uncle and those of the curmudgeon who was my first ambassador in Karachi, MacArthur blew a whistle to convene meetings. Even in private he called his DCM "DCM"! Neither I nor Edith had ever met MacArthur or his wife, "Wowie," former vice president Alban Barkley's daughter, whose reputation was equally ferocious. We concluded we were a little old for the experience, and I undertook a campaign of escape and evasion.

Spring came. Others went to Jordan and Cyprus. Increasingly conscious of upcoming indentured servitude in Tehran, I ran into Carol Laise in the hallway. One of the few senior women FSOs in those days, she had briefly been my colleague as the first country director for India in 1966. While ambassador in Nepal the following year she had married Ellsworth Bunker, once ambassador to India and at the time ambassador to Vietnam. Lyndon Johnson, fond of both of the ambassadorial couple, gave them an airplane to go back and forth between Kathmandu and Saigon. In those days, press and Congress thought that cute rather than corrupt.

"Hi, Carol," I said. "Good to see you! Finished in Nepal?"

"No! Back on consultation. Why do you ask?"

"Well, I'm finished in NEA and I'm looking for a nice little embassy to go after. Just thought Kathmandu might be fun if you were finished."

"Well, be careful. I'm not finished!"

"OK. See you."

A few days later Rodger Davies, NEA's kindly acting assistant secretary (later to be killed while ambassador to Cyprus), called me in. "Look. I know you're beating the bushes for an embassy, but I'm not going to be able to keep you out of DCM Tehran much longer. I have an out for you. Your old pal, Doug Heck, called from Istanbul today. His marriage is breaking up, and he wants to go somewhere else. Without a family, he says, he can put up with MacArthur. We can probably pull off a switch—he goes as DCM Tehran and you replace him as consul general Istanbul."

"Well, that's interesting, but—"

"Let me read you something else that just came in from Saigon," Rodger interrupted. "I don't need to tell you that, these days, what Saigon wants, Saigon gets!" He excerpted the cable: Ambassador Bunker was reorganizing all U.S. civilian and military information elements in Vietnam into a single unit to be headed by a minister-counselor for public affairs. He understood Jim Spain was looking for a job. He'd be ideal. Confirm assignment ASAP. "Your family can stay in Washington or live in Bangkok," Rodger explained. "You have until six o'clock to give me an answer."

I made a phone call to Edith and went back to tell Rodger how delighted we were to be going to Istanbul. He said we should be there by July 4, 1970. Some predated papers were shuffled, cables sent, and the deed done. "Incidentally," he added, "I wonder how Ellsworth knew you were looking for a job?"

The distinction between diplomatic and consular posts was less sharp than it had been before World War II. Still, there was a difference. The former were responsible for U.S. relations with foreign governments, the latter for day-to-day matters involving U.S. citizens in all or part of a foreign country.

Within living memory, Istanbul had been the capital of both the Turkish Republic and the Ottoman Empire. It was still by far the country's largest city, its financial, industrial, educational, cultural, and communications center. The U.S. consulate general had some concern with these things, but its main business was consular.

The way of life was pleasant. The consul general worked in the lavish, ghost-haunted, nineteenth-century Palazzo Corpi, overlooking the Golden Horn. He and his family lived in a big house at the edge of the Bosphorus at Emirgan, a third of the way to the Black Sea. Sikandra, who had come with us under a hastily constructed "junior year abroad" program at Georgetown Visitation, attended the Kiz Kolegi, the American-founded Girls' College at Arnavutkoy, two towns down the Bosphorus from Emirgan. Steve and Bill went to the Community School in Rumeli Hissar, intended for children of the faculty of another venerable American institution, Robert College.

The *Hiawatha*, last of the diplomatic yachts that had once made Istanbul famous, provided access to all parts of the great city by water. Fifty feet of gleaming mahogany and brass, it dated to 1934. Long afterward Edith and

I agreed that the most glamorous night in our diplomatic life was one in 1971 when, in dinner jacket and long dress, we went up the Bosphorus on the *Hiawatha* to Anadolu Kavak, headquarters of the Turkish commander of the Straits, to attend a party celebrating the 881st anniversary of the Turkish Navy. With our captain and crew in white turtleneck sweaters and blue blazers and a spotlight on the flag flying at the prow, we swung up to the dock ("just a little whitewater, sir, not too much," Naci Kaptan explained) to be piped ashore and greeted by the Hollywood-handsome Turkish Circassian admiral and his wife. Small wonder that the principal task of the principal officer in Istanbul was the preservation of the *Hiawatha*.

Istanbul was a particular joy for a family interested in history and archaeology but whose previous residences abroad had been largely beyond the geographic boundaries of their own civilization. Here, where Asia and Europe met along the shores of the Dardanelles and the Bosphorus, dozens of cultures—Trojan, Greek, Roman, Byzantine, Turkish, and West European imperial—had left their footprints. We spent the Sundays and holidays of our first months tracing out ancient aqueducts, some still working, in the countryside beyond the city walls. We chose the sixth century A.D., when the Roman Empire was turning from Latin to Greek, as our special interest. Books in hand, we followed Justinian the Great and his circus-girl empress Theodora through their great Church of the Holy Wisdom and in and around the Hippodrome, where her courage saved their thrones during the "Nika" riots of 532 A.D.

The consulate general's most famous client, Billy Hayes, turned up in October 1970. A young Long Islander, typical of the "hippie" generation, he arrived in Istanbul one night and tried to leave the next morning—with five kilos of hashish taped to his body. In Pakistan I had sometimes been able to handle drug cases by private dialogue "between the sahibs," that is, reasonable senior officials on both sides. In the usual arrangement, the government handed the offender over to a consular officer with the proviso that he or she be out of the country the same day. It saved trouble and expense for everyone.

I suggested to the head of the consular section that I try this technique with the governor of Istanbul, on whom I'd recently called. He was aghast. "You'll get us all thrown out of here! Once a case gets into the Turkish judicial system, even to talk about it constitutes criminal interference."

The peculiarities of the Turkish judicial system surfaced in the course of the trial. The roles of prosecuting and defense attorneys are not very different from those in an American court. But there is no jury. A decision is reached by a majority vote of a panel of three judges. The prosecution, as well as the defense, can appeal. The first argument to the court is usually on the charge itself. The prosecutor wanted the charge to be narcotics smuggling, penalty thirty years. The defense wanted possession, penalty five years.

In what was clearly an act of mercy, the judges held for trial on possession. Hayes received five years. With the usual one-third off for good behavior, he was within a few months of release when the full bench of the Court of Appeals upheld a challenge by the prosecutor. The accused had already cleared customs and emigration when he was caught. Five kilos were more than could be justified for personal use. The case must be retried as smuggling. It was. The prisoner was left with something like twenty-five years to serve.

Long Island's *Newsday* made the case a sensation. One of their best muckrakers came to interview Hayes and everyone else connected with the case. Congressmen and civil rights organizations took an interest. The more pressure for leniency from the American side, the more Turkish public and official opinion dug in. What kind of an ally had Turkey bound itself to? The U.S. government was threatening Turkey with all kinds of penalties if it didn't ban its centuries-old opium crop. At the same time, it was demanding special privileges for its national convicted of narcotics abuse.

Hayes's father, a decent and appealing man, mortgaged the family house to raise money to enable him to spend long periods in Istanbul and to pay for lawyers. Edith visited Billy regularly while he was in Samalcilar Prison, bringing candy, magazines, and books of yoga. (In later years she reminded me, "I always told you Billy wasn't a bad kid. He never mentioned me at all in his book!")

Eventually Hayes was transferred to a "half-open" (minimum security) island prison in the Sea of Marmara. One night a fisherman took him off and smuggled him into Greece, whence he went quickly back to Long Island. The outcry over his escape was modest. There were rumors that Turkish officials, eager to get a nuisance off their hands, had actually known about the plans in advance. Before long, *Midnight Express*, an exaggerated but not altogether misleading book about his experiences, appeared. Behind it came the movie, dramatically stirring but, in its "documentary" portrayal of all Turks as brutal and bestial, viciously inaccurate.

Terrorism came to Istanbul in the fall of 1970. Violence, begun by ill-organized radical youth groups with names like "Dev Genc" (Left Youth) and "Dev Yol" (Left Road), spread quickly. Conservative groups reacted in kind. Mustaches became symbols—those of the left turned down à la Fu Manchu; those of the right turned up. Young men lost their lives by presenting the wrong face in unknown company. Both sides had shoot-outs with the police and with each other.

Steve and Bill returned hours late from school one day to report how their bus had to pull off the Bosphorus Road and wait while one such event played itself out. They were excited but disappointed because they couldn't find out which side had won. Sixteen-year-old Sikandra wandered at will throughout the city with her Turkish friends from the Kiz Kolegi. We knew that even now rigid Turkish mores made for little danger of robbery or molestation, but we asked her how she handled the strong anti-American feeling among many young people. "Oh, I just tell them I'm Canadian. Steve and Bill usually say they're Irish."

We initiated new precautions when a bomb was thrown over the wall of the Palazzo Corpi and staff members' cars were burned. The main security problem, however, centered on port calls by the U.S. Sixth Fleet, permanently stationed in the Mediterranean. Istanbul was a favorite U.S. Navy liberty port. Turkish Navy policy was to welcome any and all port calls. Its commanders were looking for an opportunity to smoke out the leftists and crush them. Rightist groups added to the volatile situation by announcing that they would carry on communal prayers at the dock to thank God for the noble Americans.

The usual lineup on a decision about a port call was: for, Turkish Navy, U.S. Navy, and Department of Defense in Washington; against, Turkish Foreign Ministry and Turkish 1st Army Commander (responsible for security in Istanbul). Ambassador William Handley at our embassy in Ankara tended to be in favor but deferred to his consul general in Istanbul. ("If someone gets killed, you're responsible, so you get to call the shots.")

In 1970–72 we waved off a good number of ship visits, but we also got a lot in. We skewed schedules to bring them when the university was closed. We got captains to settle for two rather than four days. We had ships tie up at obscure moorings. We sent consulate people to sea to brief the sailors on how to minimize the chances of trouble. No one died.

Personal security became a major strain as the violence escalated. At one point we had twenty-four Turkish soldiers at the house in Emirgan, manning four machine-gun posts and playing soccer with Steve and Bill. Two police bodyguards accompanied Edith to the hairdresser and sat between us in the movie theater we attended on our twentieth wedding anniversary. Deputy Robert Dillon and I developed a routine we followed before parties, each making sure the other's jacket was draped properly over the .38 magnums we carried.

When authorities captured the men who kidnapped and murdered the Israeli consul general, the killers revealed that he had been a target of opportunity. They had been practicing for weeks to get the "arch-imperialist," but the Israeli had come along where they had been expecting the American, so they took the Israeli instead.

In 1972 it was proposed that I go to Embassy Ankara as deputy chief of mission to replace David Cuthell, an old Turkish hand whose four-year assignment was up. Despite the attractions of Istanbul, I was more than willing. Ankara was where government-to-government business was done.

The family's reaction was different. Edith mumbled something about "Whither thou goest, I shall go, I guess," but her heart wasn't in it. Sikandra had already headed back to Washington to board at Visitation for her senior year. Steve took up an admission to Phillips Exeter in Massachusetts, about which he had hitherto been unenthusiastic. Bill, after extracting a promise that he could spend all his vacations in Istanbul, reluctantly consented to be enrolled in the Department of Defense's George C. Marshall School at Balgat, a suburb of Ankara.

My two years in Ankara gave me all the diplomatic challenges I could want. One of the most sensitive was internal to the American community. There were more than ten thousand U.S. military personnel in Turkey, and, in the early 1970s, racial and class tensions within their ranks were high. Malingering and insubordination were not uncommon.

There was division, too, between American military and civilians. I got a vivid glimpse of this just after arrival in Ankara when I went out to Balgat, the small military base in Ankara, to play tennis. The court was next to the school. When the embassy political counselor's ten-year-old son came scuttling out of the building in a way that suggested he was up to no good, an aging sergeant stood in the doorway shaking a fist. The dialogue went like this: "Dirty little hippie!" "Rotten old lifer!"

Eventually, the embassy became a court of appeal for soldierly complaints. Privates and sergeants charged that U.S. commanders, rather than trying those accused by court martial, turned them over to the Turkish courts, where the rights of defendants were minimal. The provost marshal refused to notify the embassy of Turkish arrests of uniformed personnel—in order to avoid a consular officer's being present to look after their interests. Complaints were numerous, confused, and sometimes silly. Political-military counselor Richard Boehm and I spent hours talking to privates and sergeants, colonels and generals. All displayed a reasonable amount of good will, and a crisis of discontent was avoided. "Fragging," so popular in Vietnam at the time, never came to Turkey.

The opium problem was still very much with us. Ambassador Handley had convinced Turkish "caretaker" prime minister Nihat Erim to ban all production after the 1973 crop. The menace should have ended once and forever in the summer of 1973, but in October a general election gave the premiership to Bulent Ecevit, leader of the opposition Republican Peoples Party. To nationwide acclaim, he rescinded the ban.

Washington exploded. One congressman proposed solemnly that B-52s be sent "to destroy the poppy fields which were destroying America's youth." A Turkish parliamentarian pointed out that the chief cause of death in Turkey was automobile accidents. He demanded that Detroit be shut down.

William B. Macomber had replaced Handley as ambassador in the summer of 1973. Now that the Turks were out of the opium business, we old "Turkey hands" had assured Macomber, they would stay out of it. He disagreed. He had listened to the election campaign speeches with an acute political ear and correctly predicted that Ecevit would go back to it if he won.

Macomber then wisely set us on another tack. "Get technical! Find a way that they can grow the stuff but can't let it leak!" It turned out that there was such a way. A new method, called the "straw process," had been developed in Germany. It eliminated incising the poppy pod, which put the raw opium gum directly in the hands of thousands of peasant producers. It fed the entire plant into a sophisticated multiprocess factory before the gum flowed and recovered more opium from it than from the pod alone. The extraction took place within the confines of a factory where tight control was easy. The United States financed the factory. More than twenty years later, the illegal opium flow from Turkish production is still minimal.

The Montreux Convention took up a lot of my time in Ankara. Signed in 1936, the convention gave control of the Bosphorus and Dardanelles to Turkey and detailed the kinds of ships allowed to pass through. For instance, the riparian countries, Turkey, Bulgaria, and Russia, could send cruisers with fourteen-inch guns, while nonriparian states were limited to destroyers with ten-inch guns. But we were now dealing with ships undreamt of in 1936.

In the U.S. Navy old-fashioned destroyers with six-inch, eight-inch, and ten-inch guns had given way to missile frigates, comparable in size and tonnage but with greatly increased firepower. The Soviet Union built its first aircraft carrier in Kiev on the Black Sea and then assigned it to the Baltic fleet. It argued that the carrier could come out because it was not prohibited in the Montreux Convention. The U.S. missile frigates could not go in because they were not mentioned. We pressed for a different position, of course: The Soviet carrier could not come out because it was bigger than a cruiser with fourteen-inch guns. The U.S. missile frigates could go in because they were no bigger than a destroyer with ten-inch guns.

Our batting average came out at .500. The Turkish Foreign Ministry decreed that the Soviet carrier could come out and the U.S. missile frigates could go in. Under instructions from an irate Department of Defense in Washington, I indicated to a Turkish official that we would appeal based on some obscure letters that had been exchanged at the time of the convention. I got a down-to-earth answer. "We're not running a class in international law. Montreux lends itself to any interpretation we choose to put on it. We want your frigates in the Black Sea to show you are our powerful ally. We want that damn Soviet carrier out of there so it can't dominate our northern border."

The Montreux Convention came up again in October 1973, when the Yom Kippur War broke out between Israelis and Arabs. Soviet arms flowed to the Arabs by ship through the Straits and by air over eastern Turkey. The convention provided for the closure of the Straits in time of war, but neither Turkey, the Soviet Union, nor the United States was at war. National Security Adviser Henry Kissinger called a worldwide alert of U.S. forces on the basis of a report that one of the Soviet ships passing through the Straits carried a nuclear weapon (not mentioned in Montreux either). Furthermore, the air corridor over eastern Turkey provided for in the convention was for use by civilian aircraft only; transport of weapons was prohibited.

The United States decided to concentrate its efforts on stopping the airlift in the east. We had hard intelligence that Soviet arms were being unloaded at airports in Syria and Egypt. I brought it to the Foreign Ministry, citing the Montreux Convention. The Turks responded with a list of all Soviet aircraft overflying Turkey. They were all giving Aeroflot (civilian) call signs and declaring their cargo as medical supplies.

"But we—and you—know different!" I insisted.

"Yes," the Turkish official agreed, "but when we ask them to land for inspection, they say that there is nothing in the convention that requires them to do so. What do you want us to do, shoot them down?" Henry didn't.

For a decade NATO had been haunted by the prospect of war over Cyprus between two members, Greece and Turkey. There were no "good guys" in the situation. Ankara, Athens, and Greeks and Turks on the island were all equally truculent and intransigent. Under the London-Zurich Accords of 1960, which gave Cyprus independence, the Turks had rights of intervention. They were eager to assert them.

In 1964 a crisis had been warded off only by a brutal letter from President Johnson to Prime Minister Inonu, warning that if the Soviet Union acted against Turkey in response to an invasion of Cyprus, U.S. and NATO guarantees to protect Turkey would not apply. "The Johnson Letter" prevented the invasion but left an indelible mark on U.S.-Turkish relations. In 1967 another brink-of-war Cyprus crisis was defused by the skillful mediation of U.S. special envoy Cyrus Vance.

In 1974 a coup on the island sponsored by the colonel's regime in Athens threatened to unite Cyprus with Greece. Turkey again prepared to invade. This time no one in the embassy or the State Department thought we could stop it. Our aim was to get the Turks to limit themselves to a beachhead, minimize the chances of war between the two NATO partners, and encourage Athens and Ankara to negotiate a permanent solution.

The night before the invasion took place, a "Nixon letter" to Prime Minister Ecevit appeared in a cable to the embassy. Highly classified, it was even harsher than the Johnson letter and was to be delivered immediately. Though we didn't like it, that was the way the president wanted to play it. Ambassador Macomber got a midnight appointment, and we made our way through tumultuous crowds to see the prime minister.

An aide waved us into Ecevit's office. We stopped at the door. He was on the telephone. He gestured us to sit. "Henry," he explained. We knew he had once been a member of Kissinger's Harvard seminar and were not surprised at the first-name approach that seemed to characterize the conversation, of which we could hear only one side. The substance, however, was surprising. "Henry" was telling "Bulent" that the United States would rather Turkey did not invade but accepted the fact that it might have to. In return the Turkish prime minister promised restraint and negotiation.

Ecevit hung up, greeted us, said he was very pleased with his friend Henry's understanding, and asked what he could do for us. Macomber made a courageous decision. He looked at me and shook his head. "The Nixon letter" remained buried in my pocket. We said that we'd just stopped by to see how things were going.

Back at the Embassy, we called the Operations Center in the department to say that we were not going to deliver the letter unless reinstructed to do so. The man on duty opined that we could expect that. Secretary Kissinger had drafted the letter himself just a couple of hours earlier after coming back from the White House, where he had "prayed" with President Nixon. (Washington had its own crisis; Watergate was near its climax.)

The night passed. The Turks invaded the next morning. The colonels' junta in Athens fell shortly afterward. It was a sticky situation, but there was no Greek-Turkish war. Three or four days later, a one-line "Official Use Only" cable appeared on my desk. It said simply "Disregard State 1212345" (or whatever the number of the presidential message had been). I wonder what future historians pursuing official records will make of the exchange.

9

First Anointings

THE ELEMENTS OF POMP AND power associated with diplomacy grow out of the fact that the ambassador is the accredited and acknowledged representative of his sovereign. Like that sovereign, he has plenipotentiary powers and is not subject to the laws of the foreign state in which he carries on his master's business. This immunity extends by courtesy to others "in his train," that is, to those who accompany and serve him, his embassy.

The otherwise self-consciously democratic United States reinforces this feudal concept by the way it selects and treats its ambassadors. The envoy is appointed by the president and confirmed by the Senate. Called "Mister [or Madam] Ambassador" by Americans and "Excellency" by foreigners, he or she has the right to preface his or her name with "The Honorable" for the rest of life. Crested china, silver, glassware, and a personal flag with a circle of stars surrounding the Great Seal of the United States go with the job. At the same time, the selection process is as haphazard as a schoolyard basketball game.

In 1951, when I came to my first Foreign Service job in Karachi, the embassy was literally built around the ambassador. In those days, challenges to his word on anything having to do with U.S-Pakistan relations were inconceivable. In any event, the only non–State Department people present were army, navy, air force, and agricultural attachés, whose very titles acknowledge their subordination. The ambassador-centered embassy was still a reality fifteen years later, when officials in Washington refused to put questions to the embassy because it would be "insulting."

Anyone who is in contact with an American embassy knows how artificial this concept has become in the last decades of the twentieth century. For one thing, the ambassador might find that his sovereign has taken advantage of the marvels of modern communications to have a personal conversation (about which the ambassador might or might not be made aware) with his opposite number.

In the wide variety of countries in which the United States Information Service (USIS) and the Agency for International Development (AID) are represented, these agencies usually have more program funds than the State Department and more and higher paid personnel, with equivocal titles, such as "director." The Department of Commerce now has a separate Foreign Service. The Drug Enforcement Agency (DEA) and the Federal Bureau of Investigation (FBI) have their own representatives in many capitals. They see their roles as law enforcement rather than support of ambassadorial diplomacy. The CIA has long encouraged its people in the field to evade ambassadorial knowledge and authority. In the Agency's "internal culture," there sometimes seems little difference between lying to an ambassador (or Congress or the public) and lying to a KGB opposite number.

Other factors also loom large in the ambassadorial life. One sage old career man used to advise neophytes to remember two basic principles. "Always locate USIS between the university and the chancery. That way, when the student rioters come out they hit USIS first, and you have time to get police protection for the chancery." His second rule: "When considering a post, remember that your popularity and degree of satisfaction in your work will be in inverse proportion to the number of U.S. nationals in the country."

I've never been sure how sound the advice is. In Pakistan, in my early days when Dacca was part of East Pakistan, students from the University of Dacca did hit USIS first. Then they burned down the police station on their way to the consulate, so no help was forthcoming. In Tanzania, in my later days, that government had given "political refuge" to a number of American blacks wanted in the United States on criminal charges. Most of these avoided the embassy, but one called me regularly on the telephone to inquire about "making a deal" with the FBI. That was fine, part of our work; but he wouldn't come in to the Chancery to talk because he feared (erroneously) that "if I do, the Marines will beat me up and throw me on a plane for home." So I had to meet him on street corners instead.

Still, everyone wants to be an ambassador. Corporate lions throw money at political parties to that end. Academics write books and hire flacks to call them to the right peoples' attention. Senior military officers agree to retire early without making waves in return for the promise of an embassy. Defeated senators and representatives and unsuccessful high-level bureaucrats find honorable consolation in the job. Staid senior career Foreign Service officers scheme and maneuver among themselves for precedence. In President Johnson's day, one of the most effective tricks was to leak to the press that a rival was going to be appointed to this or that embassy. That ended whatever chance he or she might have had.

However theoretical the power has become, the pomp is still there. John Kenneth Galbraith, who once enjoyed both in New Delhi, had a comment on the State Department's constant complaining about the influx of political appointees. "Take away all the perks and privileges," he said, "and you won't be bothered by outsiders wanting in."

Returning from Ankara in the summer of 1974, it had been four years since I had been actively engaged in the rat race. Before I could reenter, word came that I was assigned as "diplomat in residence" for one year at Florida State University in Tallahassee. "Be happy with it!" the Senior Assignments Office advised. "There is absolutely no chance of a mission now, and this ties you down for only a year."

It was a happy year. Young Bill, the essential "Foreign Service brat," went into the seventh grade in his seventh school. Steve proposed (successfully) that if we were "the kind of family that puts a premium on having a graduate of Phillips Exeter," he'd stay there, but he'd really like to be with us and do his twelfth year at Ponce de Leon (pronounced "Ponki dee Leeon") Public High School in Tallahassee. At Christmas, Sikandra came down from her freshman year at Beloit College in Wisconsin, Patrick from law school in Boston. To complete the holiday, both Edith's mother and mine showed up, too.

The south is the south, but the friendly, urbane Florida state capital was a far cry from the backcountry Louisiana of my Camp Polk army days. In the Capitol building for a seminar, I was taken casually and without appointment for a chat with Governor Reuben Askew. My academic duties were light, principally sharing the teaching of "U.S. Foreign Policy since World War II." Friday night pep rallies and Saturday afternoon football games opened an unfamiliar vista of American life. Frequent speaking engagements from Jacksonville to Montgomery brought home that foreign policy issues were not the most important element in the lives of most Americans.

In April 1975 the half-dozen diplomats in residence scattered around the country were called into Washington for a conference. Some useful talk on how to improve the program resulted, but no one could offer any information on upcoming assignments. Setting off on my own to see the director general of the Foreign Service, now Carol Laise, returned from Kathmandu, I got a friendly but unencouraging "No one can get anything out of the secretary's office on assignments. Enjoy yourself down there. Don't worry. We haven't forgotten you. Don't call me. I'll call you."

Wandering down the seventh floor corridor, I popped into the little cubicle behind the secretary's office where Special Assistant Lawrence Eagleburger held forth. "Hello, Larry. I'm up from Florida State. I'm finishing there soon."

"Yeah, and you want to be an ambassador."

"Well, that would be nice. It seems to me that my time has more or less come."

He pulled over a pile of loose-leaf notebooks. "How's your Spanish?"

"Not a word."

A book was pushed aside. "French?"

"I read it well enough, but to speak decently I'll need a refresher course."

He shoved aside another book. "Here! Africa! We need someone in Tanzania. The secretary is pulling Beverly Carter out for negotiating with terrorists [the allegation later proved untrue]. It's an interesting place. Julius Nyerere. *Ujaama* and all that."

"Well . . . I'm a Near East/South Asia type, and—"

"That's the point. The secretary has instituted GLOP [the Global Outlook Program]. People are getting too narrow. Everyone has to have an assignment outside his area."

"Well, OK."

"Henry have anything against you?"

"I'm not sure. He wrote me a nasty letter when I was in Pakistan. He thought I'd breached security on his trip to China."

"Let me find out." He disappeared into Kissinger's office to return a minute later. "Nah. He doesn't have anything against you. It'll take a few months, but you can count on it."

As I left reasonably elated, he added. "Stop in and tell Carol, will you?"

We arrived in Dar es Salaam in December 1975. It was a dozen years since the great burst of new countries on the continent, but East Africa still had a flavor of the old days. A leopard lived in the garden of a house a block from ours. Snakes crawled into bedrooms. The most comprehensive guide to travel in the bush was Teddy Roosevelt's *African Game Trails,* published in 1909. Nationalism was rampant, anti-Western propaganda shrill, but the pace of life was slow and personal relations friendly.

Witty, literate, always accessible, President Nyerere fascinated us throughout our three and a half years in Tanzania. As devoted a socialist as I ever met, he had little regard for the Nixon-Ford administration. Tanzania was a leading world voice in favor of Puerto Rican independence. It had expelled the Peace Corps. It was supporting revolutionary movements in Rhodesia and Namibia. Relations with the United States were at an ebb, and no one in Washington seemed to care.

After several conversations with Nyerere, I concluded that his views and ours on the problems of Southern Africa were not, in fact, incompatible. This was important because, as chairman of the "Frontline States" (Tanzania, Zambia, Mozambique, Kenya, and Botswana), he set African policy on the subject.

DCM Herbert Levin and I set out to catch the secretary's attention (Levin had worked on Kissinger's staff in the White House). We reported voluminously and truthfully (if selectively), and soon a cable came back "From the Secretary: You will see President Nyerere, repeat President Nyerere, not Foreign Minister or Prime Minister, and you will say: . . ." There followed three and a half pages of global exegesis and Southern African admonitions. I delivered the message—selectively—to Nyerere and reported back what looked like common ground.

The next thing we knew another cable announced that the secretary was going to travel to Southern Africa. First stop Dar es Salaam! In ten days! There followed the usual Secretariat logistics. A Secret Service detail would accompany him. An armored Cadillac would be flown in. There would be two working sessions. Nyerere would give a dinner for Kissinger. Kissinger would give a lunch for Nyerere, and so forth. Aware that no invitation had been issued and that the usually good-humored Nyerere was sensitive about being ordered about, I trotted off to see him again.

"Mr. President, I've been reporting to Secretary Kissinger about Rhodesia and Namibia, and I think the United States might be able to help out in a solution. It seems to me, though, that he ought to talk to you directly. Suppose he were to visit here?"

"Oh, that would be fine! I've heard so much and read so much about Henry Kissinger, but I've never seen him."

"How about a week from Saturday?"

Nyerere flashed his pixieish grin. "Fine. I extend a warm invitation."

Kissinger made three visits to Dar in 1976, on one of which British Foreign Secretary David Owen joined him. On the first occasion, I was not impressed with Henry's diplomatic technique. He led an obviously puzzled Nyerere through a long dialogue on the state of the world. When I tried to turn the discussion to Southern African issues, I got a kick under the table from the assistant secretary sitting next to me. Then he passed a note: "Be careful! The Secretary doesn't like to be interrupted when he's playing games!"

Progress was nonetheless made. The outlines of an "Anglo-American" proposal for the independence of Zimbabwe began to emerge. Henry himself came up with a plan for a Zimbabwe Development Fund and somehow got Sweden to commit the first sixty million dollars.

I was given the task of explaining the Development Fund to Robert Mugabe, the powerful Marxist (and Catholic) Rhodesian rebel leader, who was residing in Dar es Salaam. I found him at the local hotel, pulled out a cable summarizing the concept, and began to talk.

"Wait a minute!" Mugabe ordered. "Give me the paper!"

I recalled that the cable also contained some of Henry's uncomplimentary comments on Mugabe. There was nothing to give him, I explained. I was just looking at some notes to help me brief him orally.

"Give me the paper or we don't talk! You people are always coming along, telling me something, and then reneging on it!"

The stalemate went on for an hour, during which he gave me tea and showed me pictures of South African incursions into Rhodesia but refused to be informed on the Development Fund. Eventually, I got up to leave, saying I was sorry I had failed in my mission. I didn't know how to explain it to him or to Washington.

He let me get my hand on the door before calling me back. "Let's go over this thing again." This time he listened, nodding at some points and scowling at others. At the end, he cautioned me—he had not agreed to anything, but he would be willing to receive and study a paper along the lines I indicated. For some years afterward I got Christmas cards from him.

U.S. Ambassador to Tanzania Spain (*center*) with Secretary of State Henry A. Kissinger (*right*) and Kissinger's bodyguard (*left*) at a 1976 press conference in Dar es Salaam. *Courtesy USIS/Dar es Salaam*

Facing Zimbabwean rebel leaders (not shown) at a meeting in Dar es Salaam, 1977. *From left:* Ambassador Spain, U.S. Representative to the United Nations Andrew Young, Secretary of State Cyrus Vance, and British Foreign Secretary David Owen. *Courtesy USIS/Dar es Salaam*

Toward the middle of 1977, Cyrus Vance, Andrew Young, and Assistant Secretary for Africa Richard Moose took over the negotiations, and things opened up even more. Nyerere was adamant on one point: "The armed forces of an independent Zimbabwe must be made up primarily of the independence fighters." David Owen flatly rejected this when Vance put it to him at a meeting in Dar. He refused even to listen to me when I tried to argue the point. I went home and cried on Edith's shoulder.

The next morning, as the high-level visitors were about to depart for other capitals in Africa, she pointed to Owen standing dourly in the door of the airplane while Tanzanian officials clustered around Vance and Young on the ground. "He looks lonely. You could try him again," she suggested.

Owen turned the idea over in his mind as if he had never heard it before. "Well, it might work," he said, "but I can't sign a paper on that. They wouldn't stand for it at home."

"Could you maybe say something to that effect in a speech at one of your upcoming stops?"

"Well, maybe. Who are you anyhow?"

"I'm the American ambassador here."

"Oh. I thought you were one of my advisers."

I passed word of the exchange to Vance, who tied it down on the airplane, and Owen made a pretty good gesture toward what we wanted in Lusaka, Zambia. We were over the hump.

Not long afterward, I got a demonstration of how important sheer accident can be in the Foreign Service. A cable from Washington to the five U.S. ambassadors in the Frontline States reported that British and American drafters had completed work on an Anglo-American plan for Zimbabwe. Secretary Vance was meeting in London the next day to finalize it. It shouldn't be exposed to the Africans yet, but the ambassadors should cable their judgments as to probable reaction.

I trotted off to see Nyerere. There were so many points that were important in a Rhodesian solution, I said. I wasn't sure about some of them. What did he think about a, b, c, d, e, and f (the Anglo-American Plan)? He expounded in detail. I went back and sent the information to Washington, info London. It was handed to Vance in London, on his way into town. Things went smoothly. Owen remarked at the end that the United Kingdom and the United States were in agreement, but he wondered what the Frontline States would think. Vance pulled out my cable and told him. I'm pretty sure the incident had an effect on my subsequent onward and upward assignments—and on my later down and out ones!

In August President Carter invited Nyerere for an official visit to the United States. They understood and appreciated each other instantly. To push ahead to a solution, Stephen Low, our ambassador to Zambia, was designated U.S. representative on the Anglo-American negotiating committee with British ambassador John Graham. The framework for an independent Zimbabwe was set, although it took another three years to bring it to reality.

In 1977 or 1978, when the Labour government of Prime Minister James Callaghan was still in power in London, I got to wondering if perhaps Foreign Secretary David Owen and the Whitehall professionals were not being more stubborn over concessions on Zimbabwe than party opinion would have permitted. Back in Washington on consultation, I mentioned my theory to Thomas Farmer, a lawyer and onetime general counsel of USAID. Why didn't I find out, he suggested. Thomas McNally, Callaghan's parliamentary secretary, was a friend of his. He'd call and see if Tom and the prime minister could see me when I transited London on the way back to Dar the next day. Soon I got word. I should appear at 10 Downing Street at 7:00 P.M. McNally would give me a drink. Callaghan would join us if he could get away from Parliament.

Crossing the Atlantic that night it occurred to me that I was playing rather fast and loose. Kingman Brewster, former president of Yale, was the one charged with dealing with HMG (Her Majesty's Government.) Ambassadors (especially, I fear, professional ones) are sensitive about poaching. In the morning I went straight from Heathrow to Grosvenor Square to mend my fences. "King" Brewster couldn't have been more amiable. He knew President Carter's policy on southern Africa. All the luck in the world on getting HMG to be more flexible! But he didn't think I would accomplish much. In his view, Owen and the Foreign Ministry were a lot more liberal on the issue than the Labour Party.

McNally, a delightful intellectual, fed me whiskey, remarking that the occasion justified raiding the prime minister's private stock. As soon as I mentioned the word "Zimbabwe," he denounced Owen for wanting "to give everything away." He was trying to stretch far beyond what the British electorate would put up with. Several other Labour Party stalwarts wandered in and out to share the whiskey and denounce the Foreign Office even more strongly. The striped pants boys were going to cost Labour the next election. They couldn't understand why Jim Callaghan put up with them. At midnight, we had finished two bottles. Callaghan still hadn't shown up. But I had my answer—and my night at 10 Downing Street.

The years in Tanzania were good ones for the Spains. Nyerere's magnetic personality drew a wide variety of American visitors, most of whom stayed in the Residence at 3 Kenyatta Drive. On one day, we had Sergeant Shriver and his family, George McGovern, Charles Diggs, and Andy Young (the last a particularly frequent and welcome visitor) all in the house at the same time.

Our own Patrick, now a fledgling lawyer with an electronic transnational in Chicago, visited regularly. Sikandra came from Beloit to climb Mt. Kilimanjaro and dived to recover souvenirs from the historic wreck of HMS *Pegasus,* sunk in Zanzibar Harbor by the Germans in World War I. Steve, punishing himself for having quit the University of Florida by laboring on a construction job in Atlanta, showed up to work on his novel and to labor on construction of a new embassy. Bill, in the ninth grade at the Tanganyika

International School, confessed that he liked it better than any of his eight other schools.

Edith got Nancy Kissinger to persuade her husband that the embassy needed a recreational beach house that was available for a bargain but hitherto denied by State's accountants. When the sole, East German–supplied commercial meatpacking house in the country closed down for lack of spare parts, the USIS cultural affairs officer and I spent a weekend in the bush each month, bringing back a thousand pounds or so of venison to our embassy families.

In 1978 the witches' brew stirred by the gross and brutal Idi Amin in neighboring Uganda boiled over. Returning one day from seeing a friend off on the one 707 that usually took off each day from the Dar airport, Edith reported that suddenly a whole fleet of 747s had materialized before her eyes. They had been diverted from Kampala at the time of the Israeli hostage rescue operation against Entebbe (Kampala's airport). Not long afterward, Amin invaded Tanzania, and full-scale war broke out. "Mwalimu" (Teacher) Nyerere turned into "Simba" (Lion). The veranda of his little house at Msasani became littered with maps as he directed the battle down to the company level.

In Nairobi, Kenya's leadership was as distrustful of socialist Nyerere as of barbarous Amin. The United States undertook to try to keep the Kenyans from supporting Uganda, and Nyerere appreciated this. But it became embarrassing professionally for me when I was ordered by Washington to stop in Nairobi, on my way back from consultation, to get the political appointee who was our ambassador there to be a little more enthusiastic in the cause. (Poaching again!)

State's other concern was intelligence reporting that the erratic Libyan leader, Muammar Qaddafi, a pal of Amin's, had sent numerous Libyan troops to Uganda. Could I confirm that? I went to see Nyerere and put the question. "Yes," he said with a twinkle. "There was a whole battalion of them on the road below Kampala. We wiped them out!" In April 1979 the Tanzanians took Kampala. Amin fled. The war was over.

By that summer we were overdue for transfer. So much had been going on that we hardly thought about what might come next. It was a phone call from a high official in Washington: "Is it true that you are the only career

Foreign Service officer whom Andy Young likes?" I mumbled and said Ambassador Young would be in a better position to answer that. "Well, what about this? Is it true that you're the only FSO who likes Andy?" Again I evaded. I couldn't speak for my colleagues, but I certainly liked the U.S. permanent representative to the United Nations. "Good! He'll be calling you in an hour to ask you to be his principal deputy in New York. We want you to do it!"

There was just time for consultation with Edith. We agreed that we could think of any number of other assignments we'd prefer. Being Number Twos again was not particularly appealing to the aging couple. And New York, for God's sake! But we did like Andy. It was an important assignment. And maybe it was about time for us to start going where we were needed rather than where we wanted.

When the call came, we said yes, and events proceeded apace. I flew to Washington for confirmation by the Senate, while Edith packed and despatched household effects and air freight from Dar to New York. I stopped for a week at USUN in New York to sample my new job.

I sat next to Princess Radziwill at a formal dinner on the twelfth floor of the USUN Building. I had an informal lunch, arranged by Andy Young, with the Kuwaiti ambassador. We discussed how, when I got back, I should get to know the Arab representatives at the United Nations. If peace was ever to come to the Middle East, somehow a dialogue must be established. I put down the first month's rent on a tiny two-bedroom apartment on the East Side, an incredible $2,200.

Back in Dar I made my formal farewells. The diplomatic corps gave me a silver tray. The foreign minister gave me an official dinner. President Nyerere gave me a private one.

Two days before we were scheduled to fly out for New York, the embassy administrative officer reported that there was a little problem. Under our permanent-change-of-station orders, he had authority to purchase one-way tickets for Edith and Bill, but I had already used my ticket when I went back to Washington for confirmation. Indeed, I owed the government a good deal of money for my return trip to Dar. Yes, it was silly wasn't it? He had been on the phone twice to the travel people in the department who controlled such things, but they said nothing could be done.

In a fine fury, I called the Operations Center and informed the duty officer that I wanted to speak to the director general of the Foreign Service, or the under secretary for management, or the deputy secretary of state—in that order. Ordinarily such a demand from an ambassador in a small post would have been fobbed off, but word had gotten around that important people were talking to me these days. In a typical State Department reaction to that, a voice announced that the acting secretary was coming on.

Then I heard Warren Christopher. "S/S says you have a problem, Jim. What can I do for you?" Aghast at what I had gotten myself into, I told him. He took a few notes and said he'd try to fix things up. A half-hour later the administrative officer was back with a "Flash" telegram authorizing my travel.

My travel problems were minuscule compared to what happened the next day. First the BBC and then a telegram from the department reported that President Carter had fired Andy Young from his job at the UN. Young had violated U.S. policy by meeting with a representative of the Palestine Liberation Organization. As I discovered later, the story wasn't quite that simple. Andy had met with the PLO man in the apartment of the Kuwaiti ambassador but told Carter it was by accident. The Israelis had the apartment bugged and sent the White House a transcript that indicated the meeting was far from an accident. That was when the president exploded.

Warren Christopher was promptly on the line again. Could I stay on in Tanzania for a while? The department had no idea whom the president was going to appoint and didn't want to present the new permanent representative with a preselected deputy. I replied that my good-byes had already been said. The protocol chief was going to be waiting at the airport in the morning to see me off. I'd better get out.

We agreed that it would be useful if the Spains took their time getting to New York. We managed to twist our itinerary en route by way of Australia and then Fiji, where we spent ten days with Sikandra, then a Peace Corps volunteer in Suva. By the time we got home, Carter had decided to replace Young with Donald McHenry, who had ranked third among the five ambassadors at USUN.

McHenry very decently invited me to stay on in the deputy's job, but we both knew things had changed. He had plenty of government experience of his own. He knew a great deal more about the United Nations than I did. (Just before his appointment he had become a national figure due to television coverage of his successful efforts at Kennedy Airport to block an

Aeroflot plane from taking off, because the United States believed a defecting Soviet ballerina on board was being removed against her will.)

I took two days to try to redirect our household effects and air freight to Washington and to recover some of the money I had put down on the New York apartment. Then Don and I shook hands, and I headed for Washington, where Edith had already found a two-bedroom rental for us at Columbia Plaza in Foggy Bottom, Foreign Service families' perennial "home away from home."

A hint of things to come came at President Carter's swearing-in of McHenry at the White House. Vance said he wanted to talk to me, but the conversation was interrupted.

A few days later a great shadow fell across our lives. Almost immediately after arriving in Washington, Edith asked when our regular medical examinations at State were scheduled. They turned out to be several weeks

Peace Corps Volunteer Sikandra Spain at the University of the South Pacific, Suva, Fiji, 1979.

off so, unknown to me, she took herself to the medics. When we were in Fiji with Sikandra, she had noticed a lump in her breast. The same thing had happened years earlier, but biopsies had revealed no malignancy. This time her instincts told her that the problem was serious.

The doctors agreed. Her operation was on October 4, her birthday. The lump was malignant, and a modified mastectomy was performed. Pathology would not be complete until Monday, October 8. Until it was, we would not know if the cancer had spread or what kind of therapy would be needed.

On October 6, while Edith was still in the hospital, Harry Barnes, now director general of the Foreign Service, called to tell me that I had been promoted to career minister. By the way, he added, the president and the secretary wanted me to go to Turkey as ambassador. Expecting instant and jubilant acceptance, he was surprised when I asked to wait until Monday to give an answer.

Edith and I spent the weekend in the hospital chatting of this and that—while the pathologists presumably relaxed on golf course or tennis court. When she had discovered the lump in Fiji, she said, nothing could be done about it so there had been no point in telling me. I told her about the promotion. I didn't tell her about Turkey. If the pathology report was negative, we weren't going anywhere.

On Monday morning the surgeon called. Pathology indicated (incorrectly as we were later to find out) that the cancer had not spread. No further therapy was needed. He would clear her for overseas after a month of recuperation. This time we rejoiced together over Turkey, and I called Harry Barnes to say that, yes, we would be happy to go to Ankara.

10

Camelot, Catastrophe, & a Coda

COMING BACK AS AMBASSADOR to an embassy in which one has served in a lesser capacity must surely be the greatest pleasure in the Foreign Service. Old friends appear. Most of them have also risen in estate. For once the boss is likely to know as much as or more about what is going on as his political and economic experts do. Not long after I arrived in Turkey, I was showing off with tales of my talks ten years before with Ismet Inonu, Ataturk's partner and contemporary. "You actually knew Ismet Pasha, sir?" a young political officer exclaimed with awe in his voice. When, as a result of previous service, you speak something of the language, you are another step ahead.

The assignment in Ankara brought a bittersweet experience that descends upon aging Foreign Service families. The children were all off at school or work. For the first time since we had gone to Karachi thirty years before, Edith and I were alone. The Embassy Residence is one of the largest and most luxurious possessed by the U.S. government abroad. Situated on twelve acres next to the President's House on the top of Cankaya Hill, it has

Edith and James with Acting Secretary of State Warren Christopher after Spain's swearing in as ambassador to Turkey, January 1980. *Courtesy State Department*

more than thirty rooms. It is surrounded by swimming pool, tennis court, plantings of fruit trees, patches of woods, and exquisite flower gardens. Exploring the house and grounds together was an exciting experience. Like children, two people well into their fifties played pool in the recreation room, took tea in the orangery, splashed each other in the pool, and held hands in front of the fire in a private second floor sitting room with a magnificent view over the snow-covered hills.

Terrorism was still endemic in Turkey. In the fifteen months between June 1979 and September 1980, we lost nine Americans to violent death. One day our Turkish police bodyguards came in a delegation to ask why I did not carry a gun. They were willing to fight and die to protect me, they said, but they couldn't understand why I didn't carry a weapon to help them. I drew a .357 magnum from the security office and went back to old Istanbul custom. That led to both Spains joining periodic target practices at the police range. Here there was confirmation of unity and determination—and some embarrassment. Edith shot better than I and outscored all but one of the bodyguards.

Diplomatic business went on as usual. Shortly before we arrived, the U.S. Congress had lifted the military aid embargo it had slapped on Turkey after its 1974 invasion of Cyprus. On March 29, 1980, I signed a Defense and Economic Cooperation Agreement (DECA) that restored alliance relationships. About the same time, an Enforcement of Judicial Judgments Treaty went into effect. It provided that convicted American prisoners in Turkish jails and Turkish ones in American jails could be turned over to their own countries for completion of their sentences. This got the last of the American narcotics offenders back home.

In my eighteen months in Ankara a lot of money changed hands. We disbursed and supervised the implementation of a half-billion dollars in economic aid and three-quarters of a billion in security assistance, and we rescheduled about two billion in previous debts. Dozens of specific agreements on these matters were negotiated and signed, mostly with economic czar Turgut Ozal, who was later to become prime minister and then president of Turkey. The count of U.S. military personnel in Turkey had dropped to somewhere around five thousand, but their presence required almost daily decisions. When and where should they stop wearing uniforms to reduce their vulnerability to terrorists? How many of what kind of USAF airplanes were permitted to use the NATO field at Incirlik? Should Turkish or American contractors have priority on a $90-million housing program for U.S. military personnel?

In late 1980, Turkey and Greece, still angry at each other over the Cyprus situation, got into another confrontation over control of the Aegean Sea. That two-hundred-mile-wide stretch of water was dotted with three thousand islands, mostly Greek. Potentially valuable oil and mineral deposits lay under the sea surface. Turkey claimed those on its continental shelf, which extended halfway into the sea. Greece declared a twelve-mile limit for territorial waters around each island.

Such a limit would cut off access through international waters to Turkey's ports of Istanbul and Izmir. It would also mean that all shipping between the Black and Mediterranean Seas would have to pass through Greek territorial waters. Warships would have to get prior permission; submarines would have to surface. Thus, the United States and the Soviet Union had major stakes in the issue. It was back to the international law books for the embassy—which couldn't find an answer. The problem found no solution in the then ongoing Law of the Sea Conference either. As far as I know, there is still none.

Terrorism mounted throughout the summer of 1980. Scarcely a week went by without the assassination of a prominent political figure, including former prime minister Nihat Erim. From our sitting room looking out over Ankara, we listened night after night to gun battles in the city. The elected government of Prime Minister Suleyman Demirel was unable to control the situation.

Early on the morning of September 12, the military, led by General Kenan Evren, chief of the Turkish General Staff, took over in a bloodless coup. Later that morning the embassy sent a cable to Washington emphasizing two principles. The first concern of the United States should be the attitude of the new government toward the alliance. There seemed no reason to worry about that. The second point, deliberately phrased in reverse diplomatic language, was that the United States should take care to do nothing that could delay or inhibit a prompt and complete return to representative government.

In the days and weeks that followed, with bakeries shut down by curfew, soldiers distributed bread. Graffiti, a hallmark of radical politics, was scrubbed off the walls. A mixed military-civilian cabinet was appointed. Terrorists—and suspected terrorists—were rounded up, and restrictions put on the press and universities. Law and order was reestablished all over the country. Often this was done in a brutal manner, but most Turks seemed to welcome it. Liberals in the Carter administration, European governments, and human rights groups clamored for punitive measures against the military regime. Hard pressed to hold to our two principles, I went off to see General Evren.

"Are you going to return the country to democracy? I need to know!" I said in not very diplomatic language.

Kenan Pasha stared at me coldly. "Yes, as soon as we get it cleaned up. We are doing what Ataturk told us to do. We restored democracy twice before. It hurts me that the United States feels that it has to ask the question."

I went back to Washington with that, and we managed to hold to a noninterference policy. It took three years, but the pledge was fulfilled. Since then Turkey has enjoyed more than a dozen years of uninterrupted representative government. The Turkish-American relationship continues strong. I remain convinced that both countries are better off than would have been the case if the United States had attempted to impose harsh sanctions on the proud Turks.

Patrick, Stephen, and William came for Christmas 1980. (Sikandra was still in the Peace Corps in the South Pacific.) Edith and I discovered the other side of that happy coin of being alone together. Family holidays are especially poignant when the members have been separated for the rest of the year. Parents and children take pleasure in letting each other know of their achievements. Patrick, the successful young lawyer, arrived in the middle of a formal dinner we were giving in honor of the foreign minister at a long table gleaming with china, silver, and glass. Beribboned aides stood in the hallway. Flagged limousines waited on the driveway. He peeked in and went upstairs to his room. When it was over, we settled down to talk.

"You never considered joining the Foreign Service, did you, Pat?"

"Nope."

"Well, you saw things tonight. It's not a bad life."

"I never said I didn't want to be an ambassador. But I'm damned if I'll go through what you did to be one!"

I suspect that other Foreign Service parents have heard something similar from their sons and daughters.

January brought a different sort of coin altogether. Like American ambassadors all over the world, I had submitted my resignation to President Reagan after his election in November 1980. There was no way to tell whether it would be accepted, but I took some comfort from the fact that more than half of my predecessors since World War II had been career diplomats (as opposed to political appointees) and that I had been in Ankara less than a year. Just before the inauguration, a private message came from a high military officer in Europe with whom I had long been friendly. He had talked to Alexander Haig, newly designated secretary of state. Haig had said that all U.S. ambassadors in Europe were going to be turned over—except Todman in Spain and Spain in Turkey. On the basis of that, Edith and I placed an order for more wine.

A week after Inauguration, an "Eyes Only" message from the department arrived. I was being "rotated." Prepare to ask for *agrément* for Robert

Strausz-Hupé, a venerable University of Pennsylvania professor of conservative views who had served as ambassador in the Nixon administration. I was told on the telephone that I need not hurry to leave. It would be summer before he would come. The several months that followed were full of interesting and satisfying work; but an ambassador's effectiveness inevitably declines when it is known that the end of his term is near.

Without a pang of conscience, we spent more time than we otherwise would have in visiting favorite places in Turkey—Van, Gordium, Cappadocia, Aphrodisias, Side, Bodrum, and Marmaris—taking advantage of accumulated leave. In February we went off to Egypt for a week's cruise up the Nile to celebrate our thirtieth wedding anniversary at the Old Cataract Hotel in Aswan, where Agatha Christie's *Death on the Nile* begins. In June the boys came to visit again, and we built a family yacht cruise from Knidos to Fethiya on the Mediterranean coast around Sikandra's arrival on her way home from the Peace Corps in Fiji.

Then we dispersed, as we had so often over the years. Edith and Sikandra headed for Washington to take back the house on Cathedral Avenue and get ready for we knew not what. I said my official goodbyes in Ankara and stopped for a final farewell in Istanbul.

Archbishop Salvatore Asta, the papal nuncio, a favorite friend in the Ankara diplomatic corps who was summering in his palace on one of the Princes Islands in the Sea of Marmara, gave me lunch. Other guests were Monsignor Asta's sister and niece visiting from Italy and Monsignor Bata, French-speaking Chaldean archbishop of Beirut. We debated the authenticity of Meryemana, the site near Ephesus that many believe to be the final home of the Virgin Mary. Salvatore regaled us with details of the latest rounds of negotiations between the Vatican and Turkey over ownership of St. Peter's Church in Antakya (ancient Antioch). History confirms that the first Apostle lived and preached in the cave church, but the first documented claim to it in Vatican archives dates only to the twelfth century, when a Crusader count confirmed title. The earliest Turkish document is a Seljuk *firman* of the fourteenth century. Monsignor Asta was confident that the Vatican would prevail but thought it might take another generation or two.

From his table I went to the airport for my flight to the United States. My special adventure was over.

* * *

When I checked in at the State Department, I met with Secretary Haig. He talked mostly of the NATO he had once headed and the people we both knew there. He muttered about having more fine senior FSOs than he could place and told me that I would be on a "Foreign Affairs Fellowship" for a year.

I spent 1981–82 at the Carnegie Endowment for International Peace on Dupont Circle, working on a book, *American Diplomacy in Turkey*, writing for the international affairs quarterlies, and attending seminars. By the time the year was up, Edith's cancer had appeared again. It had recurred once when we were in Turkey. That time radiation was supposed to have eliminated it. Now it had metastasized further. More radiation drove it into remission, but the long-term prognosis was not encouraging.

The Foreign Service bureaucracy, with surprising humanity, suggested that I extend my fellowship for another year. Carnegie had already promised my office to someone else, so I moved over to the Rand Corporation on M Street. A year later the cancer was back. This time the doctors recommended massive, intensely painful chemotherapy as the only possible answer. Take another semester and see how things come out, the State Department told me.

By Thanksgiving 1983, the malignancy had been driven back once more. The weekend after that holiday was when catastrophe struck in the automobile accident that killed Sikandra and left Edith an invalid. She was out of the hospital by Christmas, frail but able to move about. The boys came to the house on Cathedral Avenue. For the first time in many years they slept in their old rooms among familiar things. We went to the garden store on Wisconsin Avenue to get the tree as we had so often in the past. We reminisced about memorable events, like the night in a long-gone January when I had burned the tree in the fireplace, set the chimney on fire, and inspired the arrival of a half-dozen fire trucks. Not for a moment was anyone unaware of a missing presence.

In January 1984 the State Department rediscovered me. The inspection required by law for all State Department missions every five years was long overdue at the U.S. mission to the United Nations in New York. Ambassador Jeane Kirkpatrick, Ronald Reagan's appointee to USUN, distrusted the Washington foreign policy establishment, suspecting that it was out to get her. She had repeatedly refused to permit an inspection, on the grounds that her cabinet rank meant that she was not subject to supervision by

Secretary of State George Shultz. I was called in and instructed to see if I could organize an inspection. Maybe as a former ambassador without connections to the new administration and not on the Inspector General's staff, I could work something out.

After several telephone calls, I managed to get an appointment with Kirkpatrick in New York. I emphasized the congressional origins and authority of the law. I pointed out my present lowly status in the State Department. I chatted of how I had disregarded inspector's recommendations in my own days as an ambassador, and I got permission to spend time at USUN. During two weeks of periodic visits, I managed to insinuate the usual inspection team into the building—political, economic, and administrative experts, and auditors. Then a still fragile Edith and I, not sure whether she should come or not, moved up to a residential hotel on the East Side for the normal month's work of an inspection.

Knowing that Jeane Kirkpatrick and I disagreed on every conceivable point of American foreign policy, I avoided substantive discussion and concentrated on organization and technique. Here she was responsive. Accessible and willing to delve in detail into alternative ways of doing things, she could always be caught by an idea. We had almost daily confrontations when I was called in to her office to try to explain why I talked to people from other UN missions and from the UN Secretariat, why my auditors were asking to see her household accounts at the Waldorf Towers, and why I listened to the complaints of her "idiot" security staff. By the time it was all over, however, we were on a first-name basis and I had developed considerable respect for the intellectual prowess of our ambassador to the United Nations. I doubt much good came out of the inspection, but the law had been complied with.

Our month in New York was quiet. Edith spent most of her time reading in our hotel room, occasionally picking up the makings of a gourmet meal in the specialty food shops that abounded in the neighborhood and cooking it in our tiny kitchen. We visited a museum or gallery now and then, saw a few old friends, and tried out different restaurants. Once we went up to Morningside Heights to look again at the places around Columbia University we had known thirty years earlier. We had a drink at the neighborhood bar where we had watched the McCarthy hearings on television, strolled through the playground next to Grant's Tomb where Patrick had learned to walk, and stopped in to say a prayer at Corpus Christi Church, where Sikandra had been baptized—and been mistakenly entered into the marriage register by a non-English-speaking priest.

As the Metroliner taking us back to Washington emerged from the Hudson River tunnel onto the Jersey flats, Edith looked back at the New York skyline. "I'm glad I came," she said. "It can't be much fun to have a sick woman as a wife, but we did have some fun over there, the kind of fun we'll have to get used to now, I guess." We sat silently during a sixty-second stop at the 30th Street Station in Philadelphia, staring out at the platform where Sikandra used to meet us during her years at the University of Pennsylvania. Near Wilmington she took my arm and said softly, "I think there's something wrong with my left leg. I can hardly move it." I had to help her through Union Station in Washington and to bed at home. By the next morning, both legs were paralyzed and she was taken to Georgetown Hospital.

She never came home again. The oncologists could find no evidence of a return of the cancer, but clearly they feared it. The orthopedists focused on the accident injuries and held out the hope of a spontaneous recovery. But it didn't happen. As Washington's glorious spring came and went, she grew weaker and weaker. The awfulness of not being able to comprehend what was happening hung heavily about us. In April she asked for a wheelchair and ambulance so she could go to Rock Creek Cemetery to publicly mourn for Sikandra "while I still can."

In early June the doctors drained a buildup of fluid in Edith's chest. It was full of malignant cells. The long argument between oncologists and orthopedists was over. They asked for a meeting with me. With that peculiar reluctance doctors have to say outright that someone is dying, they spoke of "treatment focused on encouraging vital signs and maximizing the patient's comfort." That night when I went to visit her, she let me know with a wan smile that they had told her of the new development. "They have me doped up to the gills."

After thirty-three years of gay repartee, anxious consultation about the children, ruminations about the state of the world, and just plain talk, that was our last conversation. At ten o'clock that evening, as Bill and I were brooding at home, James Kane, our family doctor, called. "She's gone," he said. "The nurses were preparing her for the night. She had trouble breathing for thirty seconds and then her heart stopped." With a touch of poetry rare for his profession, he added, "Even that great heart could stand only so much."

The four Spain men tried to pick up their lives without the two women who had to an extraordinary degree gentled and inspired them. The trauma was worst for the youngest. Bill, silent, somber, and not sleeping at night, helped clean out and sell the Cathedral Avenue house, the only home he had ever known. He moved me into an apartment near Dupont Circle, then went back to the University of Massachusetts at Amherst. The Foreign Service gave me undemanding jobs, writing performance reviews and sitting on senior officer promotion boards.

A substantial insurance settlement for Edith's and Sikandra's deaths came through. Because I was involved in the accident, the settlement was in the boys' names. I have never been prouder than when I watched them, seated around a dining room table at a friend's house, give much of it to their mother's favorite charities—in Washington to the House of Ruth, a refuge for battered women, and Martha's Table, a meal provider for street children, and in Turkey to the Aphrodisias Archaeological Excavation. Their sister was remembered in a bequest to Beloit College in Wisconsin, for an annual award to a student who shares Sikandra's devotion to international peace and cooperation.

Then in January 1985 the State Department came up with something to stir me from my lethargy. The embassy in New Delhi was open. The White House had offered it to Illinois Senator Charles Percy, former chairman of the Foreign Relations Committee, defeated in the November 1984 election, but he declined. The department saw a chance. Largely, I think, because of Under Secretary Ronald Spiers's advocacy, I was recommended to George Shultz for the job. Shultz concurred, perhaps with my accomplishment at USUN in mind. He had just signed the papers to be sent to the White House when a telephone call came from Presidential Assistant Michael Deaver: Never mind sending over any names for New Delhi. He and the president had already decided on the new ambassador there.

The only post left in the department's hands was Sri Lanka, which in the usual horse trading over smaller posts the White House had swapped for a political appointee to Nepal. "You need to get out of here. Go off there," I was told. "It's an interesting little country and a great place to live. By the way, you get two interesting little countries. You are also accredited to the Maldives."

* * *

Sri Lanka, the pearl-shaped island in the Indian Ocean below the Indian subcontinent, is an ancient land. Called *Lanka* by its early Buddhist inhabitants, *Tabrobane* by the Romans, *Serendip* by the Arabs, and *Ceylão* by the Portuguese when they came in 1505, its history is a tangle of tales of great and small people that has fallen into a pattern and taken on a logic over the millennia. If after thirty years of seeing places and people through two sets of eyes, I was now to look at things alone, it was good that it was in a land encrusted by time and one where I had not lived before. It made it a little easier to understand how and why human beings come and go with the years.

For a place halfway around the world from North America, the island has remarkably enduring connections with the United States. The first Protestant missionaries arrived in 1814, just as the War of 1812 was ending. Suspicious British authorities in Colombo and Galle sent them up to the remote area around Jaffna in the north, where they established the first modern schools and hospitals, giving the minority Tamil population an advantage over the majority Sinhalese elsewhere on the island. One of them, Harriet Winslow, Secretary of State John Foster Dulles's great-great-grandmother, is buried there. In the 1840s and '50s, whalers sailing out of New England swarmed about the great harbor of Trincomalee on the east coast. Their journals, on display in the museums of New Bedford, Salem, and Nantucket, tell of the gems they bought—some of which turned out to be cut and polished fragments of medicine bottles left by their predecessors.

In 1880 another American showed up in the southern port of Galle. Colonel Henry Steele Olcott, born in 1832 in Orange, New Jersey, had served in the Civil War. With his scandalous Russian "friend," the mystic seeress Helena Petrovna Blavatsky, he founded the Theosophical Society in New York in 1875 and came to Ceylon to encourage the quiescent majority of Sinhalese Buddhists to an outburst of religious nationalism. His statue stands opposite the railroad station on a street named after him in downtown Colombo today. Unknown to most of his fellow countrymen, he is still the most acclaimed and revered American in Sri Lanka.

Sri Lanka is indeed "a great place to live." Buddhist, Hindu, Muslim, and Christian had long since learned to coexist. Each community is rich in its own traditions and manners and eager to explain them to others, but without expecting outsiders to observe them. It is difficult to give offense. Xenophobia does not exist.

Spain at the ambassadorial desk in Colombo, 1988. *Courtesy USIS/Colombo*

Still, the country is troubled. In colonial days the minorities were favored by the British. After independence in 1948, the Buddhist majority asserted itself. Christians and Muslims readily found a way to fit into the new order. Tamils (mostly Hindu, but some Christian) did not. Tamil-Sinhalese tension grew and broke out in 1983 into large-scale anti-Tamil rioting. In response, the Tamil-dominated north and parts of the east slipped out of government control. "Serendip," the "fortuitously harmonious" country, became the bitterly divided one the world knows today.

Until 1987 the question before the government was whether to seek a "military" or a "political" solution to the problem. President J. R. Jayawardene at first leaned toward the former, but it was clear that with his ill-equipped token twenty-thousand-man armed forces, he could not simply suppress the insurrection. He hoped for financial and military assistance from the United States and Sri Lanka's other Western friends to put down what he saw simply as "Marxist" (they were not) "terrorists" (they were). To keep the problem at fever heat, the Tamils were actively supported by India, which has its own fifty million Tamils just across the Palk Straits. In 1987, after Jayawardene made major concessions to Tamil grievances, India sent the IPKF (Indian Peace-Keeping Force) to restore normalcy.

Indo–Sri Lankan relations have been cordial ever since, but the IPKF did not work out. In some two years sixty thousand Indian troops took heavy casualties trying unsuccessfully to disarm the militant LTTE (Liberation Tigers of Tamil Eelam), who by now were committed to an independent Tamil state. The IPKF presence also provoked another insurrection by militant Sinhalese youth in the south, which the government was able to put down only by brutal measures. Eventually, a new Sri Lankan President, Ranasinghe Premadasa, sent the IPKF home. Sri Lanka's ethnic conflict was left deeper and more bitter than ever.

Routine business continued. We did not have the problem of American narcotics offenders that we had in Turkey, but we were plagued with more and more young Sri Lankans disappearing forever into the United States, in violation of their educational and business visas. There were constant squabbles over American import quotas for Sri Lanka's rapidly growing garment industry. Although we had agreement in principle on a new Voice of America station, years went by while we tried to find a mutually acceptable location, moving from one site to another and then back again in the face of local objections.

Ambassador Spain introduces U.S. Representative Stephen Solarz (*right*) to Sri Lankan President J. R. Jayawardene, Colombo, 1988. *Courtesy USIS/Colombo*

To liven up relations with Washington, I had a skirmish with CIA Director William Casey. He conceived a scheme for shipping arms covertly through Sri Lanka to Afghan and Angolan rebels. I managed to deflect it, but bickering went on. When home on consultation, I asked the head of the Intelligence and Research Bureau in the department for support on this and on some minor problems I had with an amiable but not overly bright station chief. Irangate had not yet happened, but his reply reflected the atmosphere building up in Washington: "No! I don't think you're right on this one, but that's not the point. I can't afford to have any trouble with CIA."

There were also routine pleasures in Sri Lanka. Arthur C. Clarke, the famous science-fiction writer, has long lived on the island. We became friends, lunching and talking frequently. When my sons visited they were more impressed by my ability to take them to see Arthur than by anything else I did. The ancient cities of Anuradhapura, Pollonaruwa, and Sigiriya never pall. Anuradhapura was bigger than Augustus's Rome in the first century A.D. The British planters are gone from the tea estates in the hills, but the nineteenth century lives on, with clouds floating around the estate bun-

Futurist Arthur C. Clarke (*left*) and Spain, U.S. Ambassador to Sri Lanka, at a USIS exhibition on Charles Lindbergh in Colombo, Sri Lanka, 1987. *Courtesy USIS/Colombo*

galows and wild boar running through the tea bushes. The white sand beaches encircling two-thirds of the island entice throughout the year. Everywhere the smiling, courteous, handsome people, despite the terrible things they sometimes do to each other, are a foreigner's delight.

In the spring of 1989, when I was going to the Maldives for a few days, I advised DCM Edward Marks that if a particularly idiotic instruction we had been warned was coming arrived, he should tell "those people in Washington to go to hell." "No," he said, "I'll just stall until you get back. Chargés don't tell Washington to go to hell. Most ambassadors don't any more either. Folks back there just put up with you because they know what you're like."

That set me to thinking. It was almost forty years since I first joined the Foreign Service. I had been in Colombo more than three years. No replacement had been named, but my assignment would certainly end soon. I called Larry Eagleburger, then deputy secretary of state in the new Bush administration. I did not want to mark time in some routine job, I said. I was ready to retire but would be happy for one more good post. Was New Delhi or something like it open? He said he'd check. When he called back, the response was as direct as it had been fifteen years earlier when we talked of Tanzania. "It would be best if you retired." It was apparent that my reputation with the Republicans in Washington was no better in 1989 than it had been in 1981.

My sons, two now with wives, had called a few days earlier to ask me to join them on a vacation in Turkey. They were all coming together in Istanbul on June 16. I had said no, I couldn't. I would be leaving Colombo soon, but no replacement was in the works. I really should stay put. Now I called back and said that I would meet them in Istanbul on the 16th.

Bereft of all responsibilities, I had already decided that Sri Lanka offered a more appealing place in the sun for me than any I was likely to find between Miami and La Jolla. I sent a cable to Washington saying I was retiring, went off to Turkey, and came right back for my "golden years" in a country I had grown to love.

11

Foreign Face Cards

FOR MANY AMERICANS, CElebrities are movie stars, rock and roll singers, or athletes. In my life they were military and political leaders, whose fame may be only slightly more lasting. Even in those early days I found observing them more interesting than standing outside Grauman's Chinese Theater to catch a glimpse of Ava Gardner (which I had also done), and I may now have a footnote or two to contribute to history. Appropriately for a life spent in diplomacy, where the principals are like the face cards in a game of bridge or poker, I begin by noting the foreign face cards with whom I have played.

The first distinguished foreign personage of whom I can remember being aware was the Prince of Wales, later King Edward VIII of England and, after his abdication to marry Mrs. Wallis Simpson of Baltimore, the Duke of Windsor. During a visit to what was still the Dominion of Canada in the early 1930s, he announced he was extending the royal train trip to the United States. The mayor of Chicago, William Thompson, was an English-descended Republican not beloved of Irish Catholic Democrats, who normally dominated the political life of the city.

An election was coming up, and Thompson recognized an opportunity. He loudly refused freedom of the city to the prince and announced that if the "disgusting degenerate" (we forget that the current young royals are not the only ones in our time to have a reputation for promiscuity) showed his face in Chicago, he, "Big Bill," would be on the railroad platform to greet him with a punch in the nose. When "Big Bill" was reelected, I recognized that politics was more complicated than simple Democratic-Republican rivalry.

My first encounter with a notable foreigner was with Indian prime minister Jawaharlal Nehru. The only time I ever saw him face-to-face was in the brief meeting under the auspices of Chester Bowles described in chapter 1. But when I came back to Columbia University in 1953 from my first Foreign Service tour, stories of Nehru's visit there were still fresh, and I drank them in. After all, I had met the man not long before! Two of these stories had repercussions in Indian-American relations.

One is widely known. At a dinner given by New York's business leaders, the speaker who introduced Nehru looked up and down the table, counted off on his fingers, and proudly announced that the importance the United States attached to India was reflected in the men around the table. He calculated that together they were worth more than $10 billion. Nehru, disgusted, recounted the incident in New Delhi for a dozen years.

The other story I got from an eyewitness in 1953 but have never heard or read anywhere else. The prime minister came to Columbia to receive an honorary degree not long before General Dwight D. Eisenhower left the presidency of the university for the presidency of the United States. Amidst the usual academic pomp and ceremony, Nehru walked up the steps of Low Memorial Library to be met by Eisenhower and a couple of deans at the top. The citation was read, the degree granted, and the blue and white hood bestowed. Nehru turned to walk down the steps.

Eisenhower, staring at his back, began counting *sotto voce:* "One, two, three, four, five . . ." He turned to one of the deans and remarked, "That's exactly how far I'd trust that fellow!"

Nehru heard. He paused for a moment, turned and looked back at Eisenhower, then silently continued his downward progress. "You're interested in India," my informant told me. "That's when U.S.-Indian relations started to go to hell!"

In my time (1951–53) in the U.S. embassy in Karachi, I began to realize that the great men of the world were a mixed bag. Too obscure to have anything to do with Prime Minister Liaquat Ali Khan or Governor General Khwaja Nazimuddin, Edith and I did become friends with Shahid Suhrawardy, the brilliant lawyer and last chief minister of undivided Bengal who eventually became prime minister of Pakistan.

Suhrawardy had delayed coming from Bengal to Pakistan but then started a political party in opposition to the ruling Muslim League. He was not highly regarded by the government. Senior diplomats avoided him, so he used to come to our house for a drink and to dance with Edith to phonograph records. I, who didn't like to dance, and Suhrawardy's conservative aide, Mujibur-ur-Rahman, later the first prime minister of Bangladesh, sat in a corner and talked politics.

One day I told my crusty ambassador about our new friend. He exploded. "Just the kind of thing an idiot like you would do! Don't you know that he's poison to the government. If the governor general finds out about this . . . !" Then he checked himself. "Well, it looks good at home when we have contact with everyone. I suppose you can go ahead. But don't ever try to get me to have anything to do with him. You're just a vice consul. If the governor general ever calls me on it, I'll disown you and send you home."

Nothing happened. Although "just a vice consul," I was emboldened to seek other contacts. One was Khan Abdul Qaiyum Khan, chief minister of the volatile North West Frontier Province and chancellor of the University of Peshawar, with whom I arranged our first Fulbright program. Qaiyum was an enormous man with a flamboyant personality, given to embroidered ankle-length overcoats and heavily armed bodyguards. He had just won a provincial election in which there were widespread charges of fraud. "Find out from your friend Qaiyum how and why he stole the election," my ambassador instructed.

The next time I was in Peshawar, I tried to ease in to the subject. Having congratulated Qaiyum on his victory and listened to his plans for the future, I mentioned the fraud charges. Some people said the election wasn't fair. Perhaps this was "sour grapes" from the opposition?

"Listen, son," he replied. "That was a fair election. Those bastards had just as much chance to rig things as I did!" Having grown up in Chicago, I could hardly disagree.

Another great man in Pakistan in those days was the minister of education, an amicable but indecisive Bengali. He said or did something that provoked the students, and Karachi broke out in riots. On my way to see him, I found a student mob fighting the police in front of his office. Taking refuge in a side street, I felt a tugging at my pants leg. I looked down to see an immaculate twelve-year-old dressed in the usual jacket, shirt, and tie of an upper-class schoolboy. "Please, sir," he said, "would you be so good as to move your leg?" I did. He picked up the cobblestone on which I was standing, said "Thank you, sir!" and flung it at a policeman.

Later in the day, I decided to try to get to the minister at his home. Across the front of the house was a solid phalanx of police armed with *lathis,* the iron-ringed bamboo staves used for riot control in the subcontinent. The roar of an approaching mob of students could be heard in the distance. A young Pathan police superintendent suggested I wait until tomorrow to pursue my business.

"Things are pretty tense," he explained. "I have a rifle platoon behind the house. I hope I don't have to use it." Then, exasperated, he blurted out, "That fat idiot inside just called me in and reminded me that he had ordered up men with guns. Where were they? I took him out back and showed him. Do you know what he said? He didn't mean that kind of guns. He wanted the big kind, the ones on wheels! Artillery, for God's sake!"

The student mob arrived. There was no sign of the minister, but his wife came out on the verandah and tongue-lashed the mob. It promptly dispersed. There was no need for guns of either kind.

In 1954, while studying the Pathans in Kabul, Afghanistan, I asked the press office official who was vaguely overseeing my activities if I could meet a government official who could tell me something about "Pushtunistan," the movement for an independent Pathan state that Afghanistan was supporting. The next day I was led off to Prime Minister Sardar Mohammad Daud. In two hours the tough, articulate Daud told me more than I ever wanted to know. He ordered that I be taken to the Khushal Khan Khattak School and given a complete briefing there. He authorized me to go anywhere I wanted in Afghan tribal areas. Thenceforth, I was known in Afghanistan as "Sardar Daud's American." Nothing was too good for me. I got a whole chapter for my first Pathan book out of the experience. I also learned that, often, "all you have to do is ask."

* * *

For the decade that bridged the fifties and sixties we were on the remote fringes of official social life in Washington. Except for a few top officials, CIA people had no protocol status and were not invited to embassy and State Department events. To compensate, the Agency bought tickets for all luncheon presentations by foreign dignitaries at the National Press Club and passed them out to selected employees. We were warned not to participate in question periods.

Being a Middle-Eastern type, I got to eat and drink with such visitors as the Israeli and Afghan prime ministers, the presidents of Turkey and Pakistan, the shah of Iran, and the kings of Saudi Arabia and Jordan. And, oh yes, once Edith and I were invited to a dinner at the Iranian Embassy honoring General Hassan Pakravan, who later became chief of SAVAK (the shah's infamous intelligence organization). He had been Iranian military attaché in the Karachi of our youth.

There was one other social experience during my CIA days that has its small connection with history. One day a call came from Allen Dulles's office. Would I come upstairs and take a nice lady out to lunch? The director would pay. I mustn't say anything to her, and I shouldn't listen to anything she might say. But I should try to cheer her up. The "nice lady" turned out to be Mrs. Francis Gary Powers, whose husband had been shot down in a U-2 plane over the Soviet Union and was still in Russian hands. The plane had taken off from Peshawar. I suppose that's why Dulles thought of me.

In addition to banging his shoe on the table at the UN, Nikita Khrushchev trumpeted that he had drawn "a red circle" around my favorite city. I made the most of the director's offer to pay. We both had two martinis and a very good lunch. Neither of us had much to say to the other.

Things opened up when I moved back to State. During my days at the Policy Planning Council, we began to be invited to the Soviet Embassy and came to know Ambassador Anatoly Dobrynin, dean of the Washington diplomatic corps and of the Soviet Union's professional diplomats. I had never had anything to do with Soviet affairs and the reason for the attention was unclear. In those days of constant Cold War spy scares, I waited for a recruiting pitch, but none came. We invited Dobrynin to our own small occasional cocktail parties for South Asian types. To our amazement, he came. Soon we found ourselves pressed for invitations from State Department colleagues, who wanted an opportunity to collect quotes from the formidable Russian that they could use in their cables.

As often in the Foreign Service, the connection paid off years later, when I was ambassador in Sri Lanka. By then Dobrynin was the top party foreign affairs official in Moscow. When the Soviet ambassador in Colombo, a "political appointee" from Kazakhstan, was going home on consultation, I asked him to say hello to Dobrynin for me. Following his return my diplomatic colleague looked upon me with added respect. "Ambassador Dobrynin conveys his respects to you. He says you are a very honest and competent diplomat. I should not fight with you but rather learn from you!" Belatedly, I realized why Dobrynin had been such a hit in the United States.

One of our little parties took place while my mother, then in her seventies, was visiting us. She came downstairs for a half-hour and said a few hellos. Afterward, as the family dined off the leftovers, I asked her how she liked the party. The devout old Irish Catholic, Democratic lady replied that the party was fine, but she didn't like the way I behaved. I spent all my time talking to other women and paid no attention to Edith at all. She refused to accept my explanation that that was the way things were at Washington cocktail parties. Trying to get my own back, I began talking of Teddy Kennedy. It was a few months after Chappaquiddick. What did she think of his behavior? He didn't report the accident to the police. His wife wasn't even there. A girl had died. . . . She cut me off coldly. "Lies! All lies!"

When I was in INR, I encountered my only opportunity ever to take a "bribe" from a foreign power. On the last Friday of every month the minister of the Israeli embassy and I ate eggs Benedict together at the Madison Hotel. It was an exciting experience for both of us. His wife kept a strict Kosher household. In those days Catholics weren't supposed to eat meat on Fridays. We discussed my forthcoming visit to Israel, where he intended to join me for a trip along the volatile Israel-Lebanon border. I mentioned casually that Edith was going to meet me in Rome on the way home for a vacation in Europe. He insisted that she must come to Israel, too. That would not be possible, I said. The U.S. government was paying for my trip to Israel, but I was paying for hers and our resources didn't stretch beyond Europe.

When I got back to my office, my secretary told me that the local manager of El Al Airlines had called twice in the last ten minutes. When I called back, he said that he wanted to provide a complimentary round-trip passage on El Al from Rome to Tel Aviv for my "lady wife." It took only seconds to realize that I must decline. The "bribe" was a pretty innocent one, but I kept my fingers clean—and Edith never saw the Holy Land.

While on the subject of temptations that beset Foreign Service officers, I should add that I met many beautiful foreign women in my long diplomatic career. Not one of them ever showed the slightest interest in seducing me for nefarious (or other) purposes. I suspect that most of my Foreign Service colleagues can make the same claim.

During my tenure as country director for Pakistan and Afghanistan, I was able to renew an acquaintanceship with President Ayub Khan of Pakistan, begun back in 1954 during my stay in his country as a Ford Foundation Fellow. Ayub was then Army chief of staff and used to visit every other evening at the house of Major General and Begum Shahid Hamid, who were friends of friends and put me up in Rawalpindi for several days. We talked of the days before Partition and of Pakistan's future, but mostly I sat silently sipping whiskey while the two generals spoke of horses and polo.

In Washington a dozen years later, I didn't have enough rank to be invited to the White House events in Ayub's honor, but I was designated to help the chief of protocol select and acquire the official gift. I thought an American-made shotgun would be nice. I located a beautiful over-and-under gun in Virginia. It was within the specified price range, and an assistant protocol officer went over to procure it. Just as she returned, word came that the "Seventh Floor" of the State Department objected. A gun was not a proper gift from peace-loving Americans. The splendid sporting weapon was returned, and the visitor got a glass vase instead. Nothing stays secret in Washington. At a Pakistan embassy reception to which I was invited, Ayub greeted me with a gesture of lifting a shotgun to his shoulder, shrugged ruefully, and said "Thanks for the thought."

I was to see Ayub once again a year or so later when I visited Pakistan with an American delegation, led by Averell Harriman, to the dedication of the Mangla Dam in the Punjab. This time Ayub made sure I was invited to the festive lunch, and I thanked him for it. We joked about how soldiers had to fling into the air the recalcitrant doves that were supposed to take off from their baskets the moment the water flowed into the spillway at the dam. By then, Ayub was tired and troubled. His "Basic Democracies"

Spain (*left*), the State Department's director for Pakistan and Afghanistan, meets Afghan King Zahir Shah (*right*), with U.S. Ambassador Robert Neumann (*center*), Kabul, 1968. *Courtesy Royal Afghan Government*

approach to representative government in Pakistan had failed. Popular discontent was evident everywhere. By the time I came to Islamabad in 1969, he had been ousted from office. An honest and energetic man who had accomplished much, he had held on to power too long.

On the same trip our delegation stopped in Kabul, Afghanistan. At a royal lunch the shy and gentle King Zahir Shah, who had just removed his autocratic cousin, Prince Daud, as prime minister, talked of his plans for further democratization of his country. (Daud was later to oust the king and be brutally slaughtered in the events that led up to the Soviet invasion in 1979.) My knowledge of Afghan customs came in handy when Harriman, the wealthy connoisseur of fine food and drink, asked me afterward about the fine wine that the king had served. Where did it come from? Was it Afghan? I had a laugh while telling him yes, it was Afghan—pomegranate juice.

* * *

Once the family and I went overseas again, the "rubbing of shoulders" with the Great began in earnest. General Yahya Khan had replaced General Ayub Khan as president a few months before we arrived in troubled Pakistan in 1969. I had been friends with Yahya during my earlier incarnation in Karachi. That he liked a drink was known even then. Indeed, I had occasionally supplied a bottle of whiskey from our rationed diplomatic stock. I don't suppose that the difference in rank was much greater in those days when he had been a colonel and I a vice consul than that between a president and a chargé d'affaires. I observed that now he never had anything more than a glass of sherry with lunch or dinner.

In any event, in Pakistan old friendships run deep. To the annoyance of my anointed ambassadorial colleagues in Islamabad (including old friend General Pakravan, who was back in Pakistan as Iranian ambassador), Yahya took to calling the American chargé to sit next to him on public occasions. We talked of the long-standing U.S.-Pakistan alliance and how to preserve it. He got me off the hook with the U.S. Air Force on the matter of compensation for the movables left at Budabar. I escorted to him a long line of visiting senior U.S. officials, culminating in President Nixon's visit on August 1, 1969. Lasting good came out of that. Henry Kissinger's subsequent secret visit to Beijing from Pakistan, the first step in U.S. recognition of Communist China, was arranged.

By the time of the breakup of Pakistan in 1970–71, the Spains were in far-off Turkey. Yahya emerged in the world press as the bloody but incompetent "Butcher of Bengal." Word came from old friends that he was drinking again. That might have explained some of the brutality and inefficiency of Islamabad's performance in what soon became the independent country of Bangladesh.

In my mind even now, however, the real reasons for the breakup were different. Aspiring prime minister Zulfikhar Ali Bhutto, fearing rejection by an East Pakistani majority, enraged the people of East Pakistan by forcing a delay in the national elections Yahya had promised to restore democracy. An always suspicious India seized the opportunity to undermine Pakistani unity and supported Bangladesh independence by war. In my experience Yahya was a decent and honorable man. His intentions were good, and his sins were human. May peace be upon him.

In Istanbul in 1970–72, as befitted a consul general, my main contacts among the great were the *Vali* (governor), whom I relied upon to get admission to the then closed *haram* part of Topkapi Palace for visiting American dignitaries; the Turkish First Army commander who helped me fight off Turkish and U.S. Navy demands for frequent port calls; and the chief of police, an always smiling Yaz (a Turk from the Black Sea coast) who could never hear enough about how the Chicago Police coped with their turbulent citizens. After Prime Minister Suleyman Demirel was ousted from office by the military in March 1971, I renewed acquaintances with the man I had met years before as the first Turkish Eisenhower Fellow in the United States. I also got to know Bulent Ecevit, the poet and scholar from the Am-erican Robert College who two years later was to become prime minister.

The truly "big" celebrity we encountered in Istanbul, however, was from outside Turkey. Queen Elizabeth II, accompanied by Prince Philip, Princess Anne, and Prince Andrew, came on a state visit. The consuls general

U.S. Minister Spain (*center*) and Bulent Ecevit (*right*), soon to be prime minister of Turkey, with a European ambassador (*left*), Ankara, Turkey, July 4, 1973.
Courtesy USIS/Ankara

and their spouses were invited to a gala late evening reception for them. The Turks know how to do a state occasion. Fireworks laced the sky and guns boomed a salute from the harbor as we made our way up to the Ottoman Yildiz Palace on a hill above the Bosphorus. Turkish soldiers in ancient janissary costume held torches aloft along the drive. Inside, Turkish protocol officers in white tie and tails lined up men in black tie (with exotic "decorations" I couldn't begin to identify on their jackets) and women in long dresses in a long narrow hall. Edith and I were near the front.

An orchestra at the far end of the hall struck up. Massive double doors a few feet from where we stood swung open, revealing a royal party obviously taken by surprise. The queen was standing in front, head turned speaking to the children at the rear. She was addressing herself to Anne, who must have been about sixteen at the time and had a teenage scowl on her face. We couldn't hear the words but the meaning was clear: "I don't care what you want. You're going to go out there and act like a young lady!" Andrew, perhaps ten, conscientiously stared at the floor. Philip, poised between mother and children, studied the ceiling with his hands behind his back. Edith nudged me. "Remind you of our house?" she asked, as the doors swung shut again.

They soon opened once more, and a smiling royal family sallied forth. Anne and Andrew immediately shot to the other end of the hall, where some young people from the local British community had been organized for them. I found myself making small talk with the queen, while my rebel Irish ancestors whirled like dervishes in their graves. Philip chatted with Edith for what was later described by an annoyed protocol officer as "rather too long a time for HRH to spend with one person." I asked her what they were "gabbing" about. "Horses and mountains," replied the Montana girl. "He knows a lot about them."

Five years later I was to meet the queen again when she came on a state visit to Tanzania. The ambassadors greeted her at a "diplomatic circle" given by President Nyerere. She pretended to remember the Istanbul encounter. After exchanging small talk, I gave way to the next colleague in order of precedence. Then I cut back to the other side of the room. An angry English equerry upbraided me for "walking in front of the Queen." Nyerere, leaning against a wall, observed the incident. Grinning, he strolled over to join me—walking in front of the queen. The equerry did not reprimand him, I guess because he was a sovereign too.

When in Ankara as DCM in 1972–74, I saw something more of Demirel and Ecevit, but successive ambassadors William Handley and William Macomber handled most of our business with president and prime minister. Ismet Inonu, however, became my special contact, and Edith started having tea with his wife and daughter. Long in retirement at his modest "Pembe Kiosk" ("Pink House") near the center of Ankara, Inonu dated back to the days of the Young Turks who had first attempted to liberalize Ottoman rule. He had distinguished himself in World War I and won lasting fame when he defeated an invading Greek army closing in on Ankara at the Battle of the Sakarya River in 1921. Partner of Ataturk and several times president and prime minister, he was known fondly to all classes of Turks as "Ismet Pasha."

I first met him when he visited Washington as prime minister during the Johnson administration. At a reception in the Turkish Embassy, I said a few complimentary words when he offered his hand in the reception line. Smiling whimsically he shook his head and pointed at his old-fashioned hearing aid, indicating that it was turned off. Then he gestured at the long line of well-wishers and shrugged, but didn't let go of my hand. I muttered a few more words. He nodded approvingly and let me go. When Bill Handley took me to see him in Ankara, he claimed to remember all this. "You were the only one I explained to that I couldn't hear. The rest never knew. It was like Lausanne." The reference was to the Lausanne negotiations in 1922 during which the Republic of Turkey was established. Inonu won diplomatic fame there by turning off his hearing aid whenever Lloyd George or Clemenceau insisted on something he didn't want to accept.

Handley had introduced me (not altogether accurately) as a Middle East expert, someone who "knew all about Arabs." It was not an ideal note, as Inonu had led the Ottoman effort to put down the Arab revolt in World War I. As we were standing in the door to leave, Ismet Pasha called me back. Somewhat to the annoyance of my ambassador, he gestured for me to lean over so that he could whisper in my ear. "It's all right to know about Arabs, young man," he said, "but never trust them!"

Despite his impaired hearing, Inonu had a passion for Western classical music. He insisted on being invited whenever USIS brought in a singer or instrumental ensemble. Edith and I were asked to sit next to him and his wife in the front row of the auditorium. I responded enthusiastically to his sometimes complimentary, sometimes critical comments on the music. That was part of being a diplomat. But I wasn't as frank with him as he had been with me. I never confessed to being tone deaf.

Ismet Pasha died while we were in Ankara. His wife of more than fifty years threw herself on his coffin at the funeral. "Ismet! Ismet!" she cried, "Why do you leave me? We had such good times together!" Edith said it was the most touching eulogy she had ever heard.

As is already evident in this narrative, the same people keep turning up again in the Foreign Service business. For example, Iranian Major Pakravan and Pakistani Colonel Yahya in 1951 Karachi were Ambassador Pakravan and President Yahya in 1969 Islamabad. In Washington in 1975, Larry Eagleburger was one of several FSO-2 assistants in Secretary Kissinger's office. In 1992 he was himself secretary of state. Indian diplomat J. N. Dixit, whom I met as economic minister in the embassy in Washington while I was a country director, was an ambassadorial colleague in Colombo and subsequently foreign secretary of India. Indian ambassador N. N. Jha, a colleague in Ankara in 1980, was again a colleague in Colombo in 1990.

Something else is worth noting. When I started to return regularly to Pakistan in the mid-1980s, I was surprised that so many friends of my youth were dead. The explanation was simple. They had all been twenty years older than I when I met them. In Washington a junior FSO has small chance of extended personal contact with an assistant secretary in his own or any other agency. As a diplomat abroad, he inevitably finds himself dealing with senior officials. It is in the nature of representing his country.

The ultimate achievement in this official social climbing comes when you are an ambassador, the anointed representative of your sovereign. Even chiefs of state and heads of government accept you as an equal—something they do not do with their own ambassadors and cabinet ministers. In most countries in the world, the American ambassador is "more equal" than his colleagues from other states. It can be a heady draught. More than one inexperienced envoy has imbibed too liberally and embarrassed and antagonized everyone around him. These phenomena explain why, other things being equal, career diplomats are usually better at their job than those who are seeing an embassy for the first time.

12

More Foreign Face Cards

I WAS LUCKY WITH THE first chief of state I came to as an AEP (Ambassador Extraordinary and Plenipotentiary) in 1975. Julius K. Nyerere, president of Tanzania, popularly called *Mwalimu* (Teacher), was a mixture of radical socialist ("No man should have an automobile until every man has a bicycle"), African chief ("If a capitalist tomato is better than a socialist one, eat it first"), and Christian humanist ("God created us all to live on this earth together, but He left up to us how to do it"). In those Cold War days, another favorite saying of his was, "Whether the elephants are fighting or making love, the grass gets trampled. We are the grass."

I presented my credentials in a white suit of the kind favored by old-fashioned Southern senators, which I had bought at a bargain before leaving Washington. He received them in a dark-colored "Kaunda suit," a long-sleeved, v-necked "bush suit." He commented that the next time we talked he would be in shirt sleeves. I could be too. "In East Africa we dress for work and the weather."

In the next three and a half years, I came to him dozens of times at his modest private house in Msasani, a village suburb of Dar es Salaam. The first time I brought a note-taker from the embassy, a usual practice for calls on high officials. It allows the ambassador to concentrate on what he wants to say without at the same time having to strive to remember exactly what his interlocutor says. It is also satisfying, and good training, for the young diplomat. Nyerere was alone.

The next time I came, I left the note-taker at home, and the president had one. We grinned at each other. After that it was just the two of us. The practice makes for greater frankness and understanding and ensures that what goes into the record is what each of the parties says the other said.

One night when the US-UK-Frontline States negotiations on Rhodesia were at a critical stage, Nyerere sent for me. I reread the latest instructions from Washington and went. He offered a glass of rosé wine and leaned forward. "Mr. Ambassador, can you remember from your school days what is the 'ultimate sin'?"

I thought back on my time with the Jesuits. "Let me see, Mr. President. Is it 'final impenitence'?"

"Yes. That's it. It means that you are dying and you refuse to be sorry before God for your sins. But," he continued, "isn't there another sin even worse than that?"

"I'm not sure, Mr. President. Could it be despair?"

"Exactly! Despair means that you are dying. You have committed a great sin and you won't be sorry for it, because you don't believe God will forgive you anyway. Right?"

"Yes, Mr. President. Something like that."

"Well, please tell President Carter that I and the Frontline States are on the verge of despair over Ian Smith [the white rebel hard-liner in Rhodesia]. We're all going to be damned unless your president and the British do something about Smith."

He went on to list exactly what should be done. I reported the conversation, though without the introduction—I doubted it would have much meaning to Carter, whose Baptist educational beginnings had been different from my own.

When Nyerere was not teasing me with Latin tag lines I often failed to cap, he quoted liberally from Shakespeare, whose *Julius Caesar* and *Merchant of Venice* he had translated into Kiswahili. One night while on the usual subject of Rhodesia, he complained of the unhelpful activities of two of the independence leaders, the Reverend Sithole and Bishop Muzorewa.

Trying to top his act, I remarked. "It sounds as if you see them as 'turbulent priests,' Mr. President."

Nyerere looked puzzled for a moment. Then he caught the allusion to Henry II's remark about Thomas Becket. He laughed, slapped his knee, and then turned sober. "No. Not that. I certainly wouldn't kill them. *Mzees* [elders] may do that sort of thing. *Mwalimus* [teachers] don't." (The reference was to a recent mysterious death of a cabinet minister in Kenya.)

Midway in my stay in Tanzania, I found that I had taken on the dim view of white South Africans held by the Tanzanians, who usually referred to them derisively as "the Boers." "Clientitis" is a deadly disease for diplomats, and I got Washington's permission to visit Capetown, Pretoria, and Johannesburg to see how "the other half" lived. In a staff meeting at the Embassy, I sought advice about telling the Tanzanian government of my upcoming trip. All were against it. I'd lose my good name if our hosts knew I was seeing the enemy. Just say I was going to Nairobi or Cairo. I decided to play things straight and told Nyerere at our next meeting. "How interesting!" he responded." I've never been there either. When you get back, you must come and tell me what you saw."

Nyerere had strong views on the role of expatriates. Diplomats could import food, liquor, and fancy cars. Foreigners who came to aid in Tanzania's development, however, should live as close to the people as possible—without access to diplomatic privileges. As Thanksgiving and Christmas approached one year, Tanzania's food supplies were scant. Even sugar and flour were absent from the local markets. I faced an angry group of American USAID contractors demanding access to the embassy commissary.

I went to see Nyerere. In principle he was not sympathetic. However, my suggestion that it was hard to deprive people of a little holiday comfort won a concession. "If you feel it's an emergency, Mr. Ambassador, do what you think best—but only as long as the emergency lasts."

The advent of the Carter administration brought a flood of American visitors to Dar es Salaam. Nyerere often liked to deal with them in a pixieish way. One was the black chairman of a congressional committee. The visitor spoke eloquently of his support for the Frontline States' positions on Rhodesia and Namibia. Nyerere thanked him. The congressman went on to a long and violent denunciation of South Africa. The "Night of the

Long Knives" was coming, and the white man was going, alive or dead!

"No, Mr. Chairman," Nyerere responded, "we can't handle it that way. The Boers are Africans, bad Africans, but Africans. They have no place to go home to—just like some people in your country." I didn't report that part of the conversation, unsure how it would sit in Washington. I didn't know if the visitor had caught the allusion—and besides, he was a nice man.

Governor Jerry Brown of California, who had won President Jimmy Carter's enmity by declaring his intention to contest for the Democratic nomination for president in 1980, was treated to another example of the Tanzanian president's sense of humor. In Nairobi for a vacation with girlfriend Linda Ronstadt, he decided suddenly to visit Dar on the Saturday before Easter 1979. The Uganda-Tanzania war had climaxed with the fall of Kampala, and the international press were flocking to Tanzania. The candidate undoubtedly figured he could benefit from a little publicity.

I took him to see Nyerere. Brown began by saying he was in Africa to learn. What did President Nyerere think about the state of the world? Mwalimu said no, the governor should be fair. California, never mind the

Visiting California governor Jerry Brown (*left*) with Ambassador Spain and President Nyerere, Easter, 1979. *Courtesy USIS/Dar es Salaam*

United States, was much bigger and more important than his little country. He wanted to hear what Brown thought about the world.

The governor obliged with a long dissertation on the "greenhouse effect." Then he got to his point. Would Nyerere give him an airplane to go to Kampala so he could tell the world about the good thing Tanzania was doing there? The president replied that he had only one airplane that was working, and he'd given it to the international press the day before. Sorry.

Brown came back to the subject twice. Surely, something could be found. With a wink at me, Nyerere closed him off. "Governor, I'd certainly like you to see Kampala, but it's still dangerous up there. You could get killed. Then my friend President Carter would never forgive me!"

As with Ismet Inonu and his wife, I had "good times together" with Nyerere. His doctrinaire socialism did little for the economy of his country. He instituted collective farming. Food production fell. He allowed a reversion to private plots. After production rose again, he decreed a return to "*Ujaama,* the right way to do things." But he never thought for a moment of "liquidating the kulaks." Of all Africa's leaders, he was the only one to relinquish power voluntarily and to allow his country to turn to a different economic system. Meanwhile, he devoted himself to the pursuit of North-South equality in the world. Through it all, he loved to laugh.

I was not at the United Nations long enough to meet any great men, albeit I was told that on occasion one or two of them had been heard to laugh also. The Turks, whom I was to mingle with next, despite their reputation for dourness and formality, did laugh. They were easy to talk to. Their language permits alternate forms of address. "Bay" is the equivalent of "Mr." One uses it with a surname, as in "Bay Demirel." But one can also take the given name and attach "Bey" (or "Pasha" if the person is military) to it, as in "Suleyman Bey." The convention is very useful in diplomacy.

Prime Minister Suleyman Demirel welcomed me back by suggesting it had taken me a long time to come as ambassador. *He'd* first become prime minister fifteen years before. Saying nothing of the violence and terror that was now endemic in Turkey, Suleyman Bey told me of the devotion and suffering of the Turkish people and his determination to help them to a good life.

New U.S. Ambassador to Turkey Spain calls on Prime Minister Suleyman Demirel, Ankara, 1980. *Courtesy USIS/Ankara*

He spoke eloquently of one "Corporal Hussain," a typical Turk of the Republic. In the 1920s, during the War of Independence, Hussain was a poor peasant. He joined Ataturk's forces. Unable to obtain a gun, he joined the women in carrying artillery shells by hand to the Battle of Sakarya. He returned a corporal and cultivated his few acres in Isparta. He educated his children and lived a happy life. "And there," Suleyman Bey said, gesturing at a picture on his wall of a grizzled old man with a nub of a cigarette in the corner of his mouth, "is Corporal Hussain! My father!" It was easy to see how Suleyman Bey became prime minister of Turkey seven times (second only to Ismet Inonu who held the office ten times).

Removed by the military in September 1980, he gave me lunch as a private citizen in Istanbul when I was leaving Turkey in the summer of 1981. "What they've done to us is ridiculous," he said. "I don't know if you intend to come back, but I do!" He is president of the Turkish Republic as I write.

The poet from Robert College did not fare so well. Bulent Ecevit, head of Ataturk's Republican Peoples Party, swept into the prime minister's office on a tide of popular sentiment after the military intervention of 1971. In 1974 Kara Ogulu (Black Son), as the diminutive Ecevit was affectionately called, had added to his luster with repeal of the unpopular ban on poppy cultivation and the invasion of Cyprus. But his administration lasted less than a year. The shrewd Demirel, head of the opposition Democratic Party, maneuvered away Ecevit's majority in Parliament and returned to power in March 1975. Two years later, Bulent Bey played the same trick on him but this time held office for only a month before Demirel overturned him again.

Bulent Bey, widely admired in international socialist circles, was more of an etatist in the Ataturk tradition than a proper socialist. He believed that the state had an obligation to control the economy to benefit the mass of the people. We argued the relative merits of this versus a private-sector approach to popular prosperity. I told him of the horrors that heroin (made from illegal Turkish opium) was wreaking on our youth. He told me of the hardships the ban on poppy production caused his people. Unlike the big, bluff Demirel, he was small and soft-spoken. He was also kindly. I never heard him say a bad word about anyone. When I left Ankara in 1974, he came out of his house to say good-bye.

In 1981 before our departure, Edith and I went to have tea with him and his more radical wife in their modest apartment in a suburb of Ankara. He was pale and did not look well. An ulcer kept recurring, he said. He gave me a beautiful cased meerschaum pipe. It was, he said wryly, a carryover from his days as prime minister when he handed out official gifts.

I asked if he had any plans to travel abroad. He replied that the military government had just denied him permission to attend a socialist conference in Europe. "To keep you away from bad companions?" I joked. "Yes," he said, "Willy Brandt, Helmut Schmidt, Indira Gandhi. A real bad lot!"

Unlike Tanzania, where brilliant and experienced politicians were scarce, the Turks had a plethora of leadership. I name here only a few whose paths I crossed between 1970 and 1981. Qassim Gulick was a feudal lord from the Cilician Gates (southeastern Turkey) whose "name and fame" (a popular Turkish phrase) were known all over the country. Senator and secretary general of the Republican Peoples Party, he came within an ace of being prime minister. Having missed, he settled down in his small house crowded with antique treasures in an older section of Ankara to be kind to an American couple and to offer advice to anyone who wanted it. In his seventies, he mastered Chinese.

Nihat Erim, the gentle professor, served as prime minister after the 1971 military takeover. He tried hard to ensure a return to representative government while fighting opium production and terrorism, for which he later paid with his life. Still, he found time to keep track of our children and write a laudatory review of a piece on the Turkish opium problem that I published in an obscure journal while at Florida State University in 1974.

Hasan Isak was Ecevit's defense minister during the 1974 Cyprus invasion. He and I went through a stressful forty-eight hours of constant contact. The Turkish Air Force spotted two destroyers moving toward Cyprus, the vanguard, it assumed, of a Greek counterinvasion. "Get them to pull back!" Hasan Bey pleaded. "Otherwise, it's war!"

In close communication with our embassy in Athens, I became convinced that the warships were not Greek. Hasan Bey refused to believe it. What else could they be? I was in his office when the dots on the map that represented the ships crossed into Cypriot territorial waters. "It's too late," he said. "We are sinking them!" Hours later we discovered that they were Turkish destroyers. Going through an experience like that together makes men friends for life.

Ilter Turkmen, a professional diplomat, was foreign minister under the military regime in 1981. He cautioned me about American preoccupation with "radical Islam," as personified by the Khomeini regime, which held our embassy people hostage. "You should understand," he said, "that, unlike us, the Iranians never had a real revolution. They needed one. The only person who had consistently opposed the shah was a priest. So now they're all running around saying their prayers and covering their faces."

Throughout 1980 I negotiated interest rates on the refinancing of Turkey's debts with Turgut Ozal. A roly-poly, chain-smoking economist of international caliber, he would spend two hours dickering over a quarter-point. The only one of Demirel's advisers to survive the transfer to military rule, he became deputy prime minister for economic affairs. He founded his own Motherland Party and, after the restoration of civilian rule in 1983, was chosen prime minister and, later, president. A relatively conservative Muslim, he didn't drink but took pleasure from outrageous jokes.

Ismael Dokuzoglu I first knew in 1970 as governor of Sinop on the Black Sea coast. He kept a benign eye on the large U.S. electronic installation there. I accompanied him into the bowels of the Roman-built prison to watch the one American narcotics prisoner weaving rugs. It turned out that the governor visited him every week. In 1974 Ismael Bey became director general of the National Police with authority over the dozens of minor run-ins U.S. military personnel have with the police all over the country. As DCM I was on the phone with him constantly. If our offenders had a shred of right on their side, they could expect leniency; if they did not, then justice tempered with mercy.

Then, of course, there were the *pashas,* the generals and admirals. They came from a different stratum of society than the civilians, often being educated in military schools from extreme youth. They were a sober and disciplined lot. Devoted above all to Ataturk's ideals, by the time they got to the top they were as urbane as the civilians.

General Kenan Evren, president of Turkey after the intervention of September 12, 1980, answered questions tersely and truthfully but could be loquacious on family matters. He obliged me by giving interviews to the American correspondents who poured in after the takeover. He agreed with me that visits by high-level U.S. Defense Department officials were not desirable because of the implication that the United States might have been involved in the coup. (It was not.) By personal messages, he helped me wave off visits pressed by Defense Department Under Secretary Robert Komer and Chairman of the Joint Chiefs of Staff David Jones.

When I paid a farewell call on him at the premature ending of my assignment, he said, "I don't understand why your country wants to replace someone who knows our people and speaks our language with someone who does neither. But soldiers do what they're told. Diplomats should also." There was sense in that, too. And Kenan Pasha did give the country back to representative government.

Admiral Bulent Ulusu had been commander of the Northern Seas in Istanbul when we were there. He came to Ankara to serve as Prime Minister under Kenan Pasha, and our family intimacy continued. It was the only time that I saw a prime minister more often in his house than in his office.

In the spring of 1980, another leading *pasha* gave a touching farewell party for us in his house. Explaining privately that he did not want to set a precedent that would require him to do the same for other ambassadors and that the Foreign Ministry wouldn't let him do anything official for a foreign civilian anyway, he asked me to give him a guest list. In addition to Turks, I noted some diplomats who were special friends.

At the party, still working at diplomacy, I could imagine the latter composing morning telegrams to their capitals: "Last night, while at a rare private dinner with General . . . , I told him of our high regard for Turkey and our willingness to offer it arms sales . . . [or kumquats or whatever]. The general in turn said . . ." One ambassador from a small country caught me as the party was breaking up. "Thanks," he said. "If it wasn't for your going, I would never have made it to this house, no matter how long I stayed in Ankara." I modestly said that it was nothing, but he should remember that he "owed one" to the American embassy.

The Turks—civilians of all parties and professions and the military of all ranks and color of uniform—are an impressive lot. They held on to representative government through terrorism and military intervention. They changed economic ideology and sustained development. They nurtured the only really secular state in the Islamic world. They make a major contribution to the NATO alliance while maintaining an independence that has made them the most influential power in the Middle East. They tell the truth and keep their word. Halfway around the world and fifteen years after I last lived among them, I remember and cherish them.

Sri Lanka, like Turkey, has no dearth of leadership. Of its two major political parties, the United National Party (UNP) is roughly the equivalent of the Republicans in the United States. The Sri Lanka Freedom Party (SLFP) parallels the Democrats. There is a real choice of economic policy as free elections bring first one and then the other party to power. In continuing cycles, the country has seen nationalization, denationalization, renationalization, and then denationalization again. The people who run the two parties are all from the same social class—the wealthy, educated, high-caste elite of "Colombo 7," the capital's Georgetown. This is true even of the "radical left," Communists and assorted varieties of Trotskyites, who align with the SLFP.

When I arrived in 1985, the UNP was in power. Its leader, Junius Richard ("J. R.") Jayawardene, in his seventies, had dominated politics since 1977, when his party had come back in a landslide election victory. Known variously to his opponents as "Yankee Dickie" because of his pro-Western policies and the "Old Fox" because no one ever outsmarted him, he was soft-spoken, decisive, always accessible, but often enigmatic, with a talent for making people feel at ease.

Shortly after my credentials presentation I found myself sitting with other diplomats a table away from J.R. at a wedding reception at a local hotel. He seemed to intend to remain indefinitely, sipping tea and chatting with guests. I had a dinner engagement and hoped to leave early. I mentioned to an ambassador sitting next to me, "It looks as if it is going to be quite a while before we can get away."

"Why do you say that?"

"The president seems to be settling in for the night. We can hardly leave before he does."

"Look!" replied my colleague, getting up. Cabinet members, other high Sri Lankan officials, and half the diplomatic corps were walking out. I joined them. To have done so under similar circumstances in Turkey would have gotten me declared *persona non grata*. Here J. R. waved a cheery good-bye.

J. R. demonstrated his quixotic side at the first state dinner I attended in Colombo for a visiting head of state. It was given for President Mohammad Zia ul Haq of Pakistan, little Sri Lanka's natural ally against Indian domination of the subcontinent. The presidential residence, an eighteenth century colonial mansion adorned with dark time-worn beams and venerable oil paintings of bewigged and beribboned former rulers, glittered with silver and glass. A flourish of trumpets greeted the arrival of the two presidents. Elaborately printed copies of their speeches and toasts lay at each place. Neither Ataturk nor Elizabeth II, both expert practitioners of pomp and ceremony, would have asked for anything more.

At the proper time, J. R. ambled over to the microphone. As everyone had a copy of his speech, he remarked, he saw no reason to give it. He wanted instead to apologize to Great Britain and say thanks to Israel. Sri Lanka had recently voted in favor of a UN resolution condemning British action in the Falkland Islands. The United Kingdom was Sri Lanka's friend, and Sri Lanka should have stood by it. The foreign minister sitting at the head table looked as if he wished he could crawl under it.

J. R. went on. Israel had given medical care and prostheses to soldiers injured in Sri Lanka's ethnic conflict. His government had limited relations with Israel and disapproved of many of its policies. But no public expression of gratitude for the medical aid had yet been offered, and he wanted to do so now. Sri Lanka knew a friend when it saw one. The intensely anti-Israel Zia looked as if he wanted to crawl under the table, but he gamely went to the microphone and read his speech.

I saw J. R. frequently as our two governments sought to implement an agreement for expansion of our Voice of America (VOA) relay station on the island. The problem was a new site. One day we pored over maps for an hour. J. R. knew his country like the back of his hand. We finally settled on land near Chillaw and had a cup of tea while awaiting the arrival of the chairman of the Sri Lanka Broadcasting Company (SLBC) to confirm our choice. We thought the matter was settled. (It wasn't. The site has since been shifted twice.) J. R. called after me on my way out, "Oh, next time you see my foreign minister, will you tell him what we agreed?"

As the ethnic struggle intensified, some of the most painful démarches I ever delivered were designed to convince J. R. that Western military assistance was not going to be forthcoming, that he should seek a "political solution" with the insurgent Tamils, and that the United States was troubled by the violations of human rights that were taking place. On specific instructions from Washington (drafted no doubt by the Human Rights Bureau), I complained about the lack of autopsies, as required by law, on those killed in the fighting.

"Did you do autopsies on the people you killed in Vietnam?" he demanded angrily. Then, in a cry from the heart, he said "I am a Buddhist. I am revolted by the taking of any life. I am trained in your Anglo-Saxon law. My career has been in democratic politics. Do you think I am proud of what we are doing?"

Tension between Sri Lanka and India grew until July 29, 1987, when Indian Prime Minister Rajiv Gandhi came to Colombo, at Jayawardene's invitation, to seek an agreed solution to the ethnic problem. He undertook not only to cease supporting the insurrection but to send troops, the Indian Peace-keeping Force (IPKF), to disarm the Tamil fighters and "establish normalcy."

Sri Lanka promised substantial concessions to Tamil "grievances" through devolution of power to local areas. It also promised to undertake development of the Trincomalee oil tank farm (left over from British days) only as a joint venture with India, not to make Trincomalee or any other port in Sri Lanka available for military use by any country in a manner prejudicial to India's interests, and to review its agreement with foreign broadcasting organizations to ensure that their facilities were used only for public broadcasting and not for military or intelligence purposes.

Suddenly, I found myself plunged into diplomatic action. Every capital from Moscow to Washington welcomed the prospect of improved India–Sri Lanka relations and the ending of a brutal civil war. The problem was that the last three clauses seemed aimed at the United States. The latest proposal for restoration of the Trincomalee tank farm had been by an American-led consortium. It had been defunct for some time, so that didn't matter much. Colombo was a favorite leave port for U.S. Navy ships moving back and forth from the Gulf to the Far East. That could hardly be prejudicial to India, but the matter had to be clarified. We knew VOA didn't engage in military or intelligence work, but was a claim going to be made that it did?

J. R. gave me assurances on all points and invited me to the tea party celebrating the accord. The embassy had been exchanging thoughts with Washington on a special "reconstruction and rehabilitation" aid package, if ever a settlement was reached. Overnight, I asked for and got a seventy-five-million-dollar commitment—and letters from President Reagan to both Jayawardene and Gandhi congratulating them on their achievement. I delivered these at the tea party.

That night J. R. called me back to State House. While the Indian prime minister slept a few rooms away, J. R. said he also needed "token" U.S. military assistance to show his people that he was not solely dependent on India. We settled on three million dollars worth of Foreign Military Sales (FMS) credits for spare parts for his U.S.-built helicopters. Not wanting to risk the accord that had just been signed, I insisted that the deal had to be cleared with India.

I don't think J. R. ever forgave me for extracting that concession, but he undertook to meet it. "I'll ask Rajiv in the morning," he said. "If the matter gets to New Delhi for decision, the bureaucrats in South Block will sabotage it." State and the Pentagon had a busy day, but a cable came in during the small hours confirming the FMS deal. I told J. R. He got Gandhi's agreement—with the condition that J. N. Dixit, the Indian ambassador in Colombo, monitor it with the American ambassador. "Dixit says he trusts him," Gandhi remarked.

A few minutes later Gandhi reviewed an honor guard prior to departure. As I stood gaping fifty feet away, a disgruntled Sri Lankan sailor tried to bash in Gandhi's head with a rifle butt. He escaped with minor injuries. The deal held.

J. R.'s associates in the UNP were a varied and competent lot. Ranasinghe Premadasa, his prime minister, was from a lower caste, outside the Colombo 7 circle. A self-made man, he had attracted a substantial following through his *Gam Udawa* (Village Renewal) program. When I arrived, it was generally agreed that his caste would prevent his ever becoming president. Four years later he was elected president—only to be assassinated in the violence surrounding the Tamil-Singhalese conflict. Two other relatively young competitors to succeed J. R., both Oxford-Cambridge-Harvard graduates, Lalith Athulathmudali and Gamini Dassayanake, met the same fate. Ranjan Wijeratne, a former tea planter, who served alternatively as foreign and defense minister, was blown up too. Finally, a young relative of J. R., Ranil Wickremasinghe, inherited the old man's mantle—only to lose the premiership in the 1994 elections that brought the SLFP to power after seventeen years.

There is no xenophobia in Sri Lanka. Through all the turmoil not a single foreigner was ever targeted. But the island paradise has a different way with its own. In the course of a few years four of the five top leaders to whom I was closest were killed.

Former and future Sri Lankan prime minister Sirimavo Bandaranaike with Spain, Colombo 1988. *Courtesy Prasanna Hennayake*

The SLFP, which now dominates Sri Lankan politics, also had an ample supply of leadership, much of it concentrated in the family of Solomon West Ridgeway Dias Bandaranaike, its founder. He too fell to an assassin's bullet, in 1959. His wife, Sirimavo, succeeded him as the first ever woman prime minister. Ousted by J. R. in the 1977 elections, she and son Anura kept the party alive and led the opposition for seventeen years. Now she is back as prime minister, while daughter Chandrika serves as president. Anura meanwhile went over to the UNP and finds himself still in the opposition.

SLFP Bandaranaike rule in the 1990s is much less radical and experimental than it was the first time around. Each of the sprightly family is a unique personality. "Madam," Prime Minister Sirimavo, in her seventies, presides over cabinet and parliament with a strong hand, criticizing the constant tardiness of the president, her daughter. President Chandrika, popular throughout the country, gets away with it. When Anura rises as he has for so many years from the opposition benches, the house fills up to listen to its most entrancing orator.

Maumoon Abdul Gayoom is president of the 200,000-person, 3,000-island Republic of the Maldives. It straddles the Equator some five hundred miles south of Colombo. Its people are all Muslims of an orthodox gentle and tolerant kind. There is no room for farming on the tiny coral islands. The only money-earners are tourism, a dried fish considered a delicacy in Asia, and in recent years garments sewn in factories on Gan, the southernmost atoll. I visited my "other country" three or four times a year during my time as U.S. Ambassador in Colombo. A diminutive, soft-spoken man, Gayoom is an alumnus of the American University of Cairo. He is understandably a dedicated environmentalist. "If, as the scientists say," he told me when I presented my credentials, "the world's oceans are going to rise two meters in the next fifty years, you will lose a few beaches in California. We will lose our entire country."

In a state as small as the Maldives, the president is involved in everything. He telephoned me in Colombo once to report that U.S. Customs had impounded a half-year's production of garments in New York. Loss of the foreign exchange would wreck the national budget. What had been done wrong? I discovered that the Chinese-run factory on Gan, desperate to fill an order, had imported sewn blouses and collars in two parts from its branch in Macao. It assembled and labeled them in the Maldives and then sent the whole order to the United States under the Maldive quota.

Ambassador Spain (*center*), in Male, Republic of the Maldives, with President Maumoon Abdul Gayoom (*right*) and embassy political counselor Ernestine Heck (*left*), 1980. *Courtesy Government of the Islamic Republic of the Maldives*

We got a customs man out and eventually got the garments released with a promise from the factory owners never to do it again.

Not long afterward, the United States got a return. As USAF traffic between the Persian Gulf and the Far East increased, requests for landing rights at Colombo were near to overloading the circuit. I asked about the possibility of stops at Male in the Maldives. The response: "Why not? Anytime! You are friends and we make money selling fuel. Your planes are very big, aren't they? They will need much fuel."

My last significant bit of diplomatic business with Gayoom was in the fall of 1988. He woke me from sleep at 6:00 A.M. in Colombo with a telephone call announcing, "We are being invaded by somebody. I don't know who. They came in a ship and are besieging the government compound. I am calling you from a friend's house nearby. Can you send help from Diego Garcia [the U.S.-U.K. base in the center of the Indian Ocean]?"

In midmorning he called to report that he was still alive. His security forces, all hundred of them, were holding out. He had asked India for help. The invaders had been identified as Sri Lankan Tamil mercenaries led by a dissident Maldivian businessman in Singapore. When I reported all this, Washington, sensitive about the Diego Garcia base, would have nothing to do with the request. (There were no troops there anyway.)

I knew a couple of American destroyers were due in Colombo the next day for shore leave and suggested that they be diverted. To add weight to the argument I added that I might have to arrange evacuation of U.S. nationals. It was a shot in the dark, because I didn't know whether there were any Americans in Male. However, it got reluctant agreement. The ships would stay out of sight, and I mustn't tell Gayoom or anyone else about them. The matter was Top Secret, known only to the White House, the secretaries of state and defense, and the chief of staff of the Navy. There was a U.S. election coming up in a week, and no one was about to open himself to accusations of military intervention.

By late afternoon, an Indian peace-keeping force arrived in Male and ended the invasion. The next morning Gayoom called again. "Having your destroyers out there is very comforting. Thank you! The United States is a true friend!"

"Um, yes, Mr. President. We try to be. Um, how do you know about the destroyers? Can you see them?"

"Oh, no. But our radio station and the Indian Navy captains are in touch with them. In addition to everything else, it is thoughtful of such a great power to be so modest."

"Um, we try to be. You are very welcome, Mr. President."

13

American Jokers

PLAYING WITH JOKERS IN THE pack is exciting. They can fill a straight or turn a mess of pottage into a royal flush. They are a very American institution. In government, presidents, vice presidents, cabinet secretaries, congressional committee chairmen, and their associates are the jokers in the pack. They make and break careers and decide national issues, usually on the basis of much less experience and knowledge than that of people in the civil, military, and foreign services.

In the early days of the Republic, our jokers were very accessible. Citizens called to see them with casual abandon: to promote a son's appointment to the military academy, to get a postmastership for themselves, or just because they were in Washington and wanted to say hello. Even when the lofty personages couldn't stand their constituents any more, they used courtesy and indirection to get rid of them. Andy Jackson moved the whiskey barrels onto the White House lawn at his Inauguration.

This now-lost accessibility lasted a long time. In the 1930s, Edith's father, first as state engineer of Montana and then as an upper-middle-level federal civil servant, put on his white tie and cutaway coat and took her mother off to FDR's White House ball for the Department of Agriculture. Edith was invited to Eleanor Roosevelt's teas for the daughters of government servants. As Joseph Alsop said in his great memorial book, when FDR came in the United States was Anglo-Saxon; by the time he died it was American. When I first came to Washington in the years after World War II, many of its citizens were able to regale newcomers with stories of how they'd shared an evening walk on Pennsylvania Avenue with Harry Truman.

This kind of openness no longer exists. I don't like to think of myself as a bush league Clark Clifford or a Buckingham Palace footman trying to make a few quid from a Fleet Street tabloid. The best a worm's-eye view can expect is a footnote from some future historian or biographer. Nevertheless, I learned from my occasional glimpses of the great. Most of them are what they seem to be—perhaps because the media, which sets their images, gets the same fleeting looks at them that I did. We could have done worse with our leaders in the twentieth century. I find it encouraging that our country is likely to see their likes again.

Douglas MacArthur was brilliant and theatrical; Harry Truman, tough and indomitable; Dwight Eisenhower, shrewd and paternal; John Kennedy, rash and dynamic; Dean Rusk, glacial but kindly; Richard Nixon, tricky but competent; Henry Kissinger, brilliant, naive, and not altogether to be trusted; and so on for Jimmy Carter and Cyrus Vance, Ronald Reagan and Alexander Haig, George Bush and James Baker, Warren Christopher and Bill Clinton, and a lot more "greats" I brushed against in those days.

Putting aside my boyhood spectator views of Al Capone and Franklin Roosevelt, my adolescent "Peeping Tom" activities with Clare Boothe Luce, and my "gofer" services to Jim Farley and Harry Truman at the 1944 conventions, the first notable American with whom I truly "shared a situation" was Douglas MacArthur. The occasion was confusing but illuminating. By the first big military holiday of 1946—I can't remember whether it was Memorial Day or Armistice Day (now Veterans's Day)—the wives of the senior officers had arrived in Occupied Japan and social activity recommenced.

The MacArthurs gave a reception at their American embassy Residence in Tokyo. I was called up from Yokohama to take pictures and early on placed myself in a far corner of the deserted ballroom. Soon the Supreme Commander's fellow members of the Allied Control Council arrived, British, French, Dutch, Australian, and Chinese, all gorgeously uniformed and bemedaled field marshals, with their wives in long dresses. They formed a reception line with Mrs. MacArthur at the other end of the room. There was no sign of the General of the Armies himself. Lesser guests arrived and clustered near the reception line chatting loudly.

A small door opened in the obscure corner near me. General MacArthur entered and sat down in a chair. He was wearing neatly pressed but laundry-worn "sun tans"—khaki pants and open shirt— with no adornment save the circle of five small stars on his collar. Only the corncob pipe was missing. He did not even glance at the brilliant group fifty feet down the room. Perplexed, I asked hesitantly "Is there anything I can do, sir?"

"No thank you, Sergeant."

The strange two-part tableau went on for several minutes. Then someone up front saw him. The whole crowd of splendid people raced down the room to their host. He greeted everyone graciously. As the mob thundered up, he glanced at me again and said. "Thank you anyway, Sergeant." If I could have conceived such a thing, I would have thought he winked. I asked myself how could a man like that not have won a war!

In Washington in 1950 waiting to get into the Foreign Service, I had to watch my pennies. I had run out of my GI Bill benefits and could no longer live simply by going to school. My normal procedure was to sleep late in my thirty-four-dollars-a-month hall bedroom in a rooming house in Georgetown, then have the twenty-nine-cent special breakfast (two eggs to taste, toast, and coffee) at People's Drug Store, and skip lunch. For variety, I used different outlets of the large chain. Having finished indulging myself at the long-gone store on the southwest corner of 17th Street and Pennsylvania Avenue Northwest, I came out onto the street one day to have the plate-glass window a few feet away shatter. Shooting was going on just down Pennsylvania Avenue in front of Blair House, the state guest house across from the White House where Harry Truman was staying while the presidential mansion was renovated.

More curious, and less cautious than I later became, I ran east toward the scene of the action. The firing had ended. Bodies lay in the street. Secret Service men swarmed. In the moments before they ran me off, I looked up at the second story of Blair House. President Truman was standing there in his underwear looking out. Although none of us knew it at the moment, the assassination attempt had been by radical Puerto Rican nationalists.

My next association with a president was equally distant. Early in my time with CIA, I participated in preparing Director of Central Intelligence Allen Dulles for a briefing of President Eisenhower in connection with an official visit by Prime Minister Jawaharlal Nehru of India. After the session was over, it occurred to me that "Ike" might be expected to have trouble with Nehru's complicated first name. I said so to Allen Dulles. Maybe we should render it phonetically? He replied that he had already put his script into the typewriter. "Give me a separate memo on it," he ordered. A week later I got the memo back. Scrawled across it was: "Allen: The P.M. was surprised I could pronounce it. Good work. My thanks to whoever thought of it! D.D.E." It was heady stuff for a twenty-eight-year-old.

I later got to know Ike better. After he had retired to his farm in Gettysburg, distinguished official visitors to the United States wanted to see him. The State Department's Protocol Office always seemed to have difficulty arranging it, so I took to calling Gettysburg directly. It turned out to be no trouble at all to convince son John (who served as secretary) that it was worthwhile to receive a string of South Asian cabinet ministers—whom I accompanied. Ike gave them tea and talked to them benignly. After he found out that I had been in the army, he always found an opportunity to refer to me as "my fellow soldier here."

I never voted for Ike, but I liked him. He seemed to like me, too. One day, waiting for a tire to be fixed on the car that was to take a visiting dignitary back to Washington, I asked an aide (not son John) why. He grinned. "I think I can tell you that. You said that you were a soldier in the Pacific, but you never mentioned Douglas MacArthur's name. The Boss doesn't like to hear it."

It took me years to realize that Eisenhower ran the government well—or so it seemed from my level. Papers by officials informing each other on this and that were not encouraged. It was assumed that whoever was responsible knew what he was doing. When a decision was needed, it was made and carried out promptly. And the twinkle in the presidential eye was real.

Edith noted that I must be very fond of Chief Justice Earl Warren. Whenever I had a "bumper-thumper" accident on the streets of Washington, I was particularly nasty to a driver who carried one of the in-those-days-common "Impeach Earl Warren" stickers. She was right. I had had on my hands a visiting Pakistan Advocate General. Protocol wouldn't touch him. I tried out on the Supreme Court the technique that had worked with Eisenhower. Yes, said the chief justice's friendly secretary, she would ask. Back came an invitation to tea. The two legal lights had a pleasant discussion. I got into an argument with the chief justice on the desirability of having a nonlawyer on the court. Thereafter, whenever I brought another visitor over, Warren picked it up again. "Ah, the young man who doesn't like lawyers!"

To finish my account of great souls of the Eisenhower days, let me revert to CIA Director Allen Dulles. The story is from an eyewitness. One evening Dulles took an aide with him on the 5:00 P.M. Constellation shuttle flight from Washington to New York. He was supposed to make a speech there at 7:00 P.M. After half an hour in the air, the pilot came on the loudspeaker to announce that bad weather had closed down both Laguardia and Idlewild (the name in those days of Kennedy International). The flight was going on to Boston.

"He can't do that. I'll miss my speech!" Dulles said to the aide. "Go up and tell him to land in New York!"

In those preterrorist days, it was easy enough to drop into the cockpit, but even then pilots were absolute masters of their craft. The aide did not have high hopes of accomplishing his mission. On the way to the cockpit, he stopped to think over his problem in the toilet. While sitting there, the loudspeaker came on again. The flight would land at LaGuardia after all. Breathing a sigh of relief, he went back to his seat next to the director. Dulles turned to him and casually said, "Thank you."

Despite Ike's twinkle, I shared the enthusiasm of my fellow bureaucrats when the benign old gentleman gave way to the vibrant young Kennedy. We did not realize before the fact that it was "Camelot," but we were ready for a change. Thanks to television and Kennedy's 1956 abortive effort at the vice presidential nomination, many felt that they knew him as they had never known Ike, despite all of Ike's wartime publicity.

Not yet anywhere close to meriting official government seats for the Inauguration, Edith and I bought four on Pennsylvania Avenue from the Democratic National Committee, intending to take Patrick and Sikandra (ages nine and seven) to see a piece of history. We awoke to a blizzard on the appointed morning, with cars buried and streets blocked all over the capital. We left the children at home and walked an hour through the snow to our places. The extra clothes that the weather required left the two of us barely fitting into the space for four.

A few weeks later the beginning of another snowstorm caused government offices to close early in the afternoon. Edith and the children drove down to pick me up. At the last minute I was told that the new president was coming to visit Director Dulles in his office. I should stand by in case I was wanted. The family was waiting in the little courtyard of the main CIA buildings off E Street Northwest when a limousine and a single follow-car pulled in. As I watched from my window near the entrance, the president emerged with two companions, hatless and coatless amid the steadily falling snow. At the same moment the phone rang and I got word from Allen Dulles's office upstairs that I would not be needed after all. I could go home.

Disappointed, I stepped out into the corridor. Kennedy was going by. He stuck out his hand, said "Glad to see you working on a day like this. Hope to see more of you!" and swept on. I went outside to go home, comforted a little by the family's excitement over having seen the new president from a dozen feet away. It was the only time I was ever to talk to President Kennedy.

But twenty years later, when I was ambassador to Turkey, Kennedy's voice came back to me from the grave. The memo I had done for CIA Director McCone on my weekend in Rome with Pope John XXIII's associates had, it developed, been passed on to the president. It lay unnoticed for decades in the Kennedy Memorial Library. Then, Roland Flamini, a journalist, found it and drew on it for a 1980 book, *Pope, Premier, President: The Cold War Summit That Never Was.* I was described as a "CIA agent" who misled innocent Vatican circles to serve the base interests of the Agency.

Not long afterward an English journalist, Peter Hebblethwaite, featured me again, in his book *John XXIII, Pope of the Council.* To him I was a hero, dispelling unfounded suspicions among conservative American Catholics and inspiring a friendly message to the Pope from Kennedy: "Lots of journalists were drawn to Rome by the lure of the Council, but few of them managed to give such a revealing glimpse as Spain's subtle and accurate report." I preferred Hebblethwaite's interpretation.

Like most Foreign Service officers, I would rather have someone else defend me than do it myself. I had thought that was the end of the matter. However, after another symmetrical seventeen years (1963, 1980, 1997), the canard popped up again, just as I was finishing this book. *Man of the Century: The Life and times of Pope John Paul II,* by another journalist, one Jonathan Kwitny, has me sent to Rome as an undercover CIA agent on Kennedy's and McCone's orders to "infiltrate the Vatican." Kwitny seems to imply that my report on John XXIII was critical and that President Kennedy overruled it.

Basically, I approve of popular history. It is easier to read and remember than the scholarly kind. But when, as with Flamini and Kwitny, it is a mishmash of unsubstantiated quarter-truths put forth without firsthand knowledge of the people and events involved, it is better offered in a novel. I find myself longing for old-fashioned academic accuracy. Anyone who is interested can find my memorandum, dated May 13, 1963, in the Kennedy Library.

Returning to the living President Kennedy, he did call desk officers. I knew two of them. One hung up on him the first time, responding to a voice that announced "This is President Kennedy. I want to ask about . . ." by saying "This is Nikita Khrushchev, and I don't have anything to tell you." Kennedy called back and convinced him it wasn't a joke.

The next two and a half years were turbulent ones (in the White House bedrooms as well as in the world, although we didn't know that then). We stored emergency supplies in the basement during the Cuban missile crisis. We watched domestic turmoil as federal troops enforced desegregation in the South. We felt Kennedy's presence in government in innumerable ways, even though I never got to see him again.

Pretty soon there will be no one left old enough to indulge in what was once a universal pastime: recalling where one was when Kennedy was killed. Back in the State Department by that time, I was lunching in the eighth-floor dining room with James Grant, later director-general of UNICEF, and Howard Wriggins, now a Columbia University professor emeritus. The news came to us when a secretary rushed in and handed Under Secretary

Averell Harriman a message. He jumped to his feet and said, "The president has been shot!" Being the State Department, several voices called out "Whose president?" Then the real horror sank in, and we went home to the television sets.

For two days Edith and I didn't leave the house. The television screen would not let us. Then, the night before the funeral, after Lee Harvey Oswald had been killed before the whole nation by Jack Ruby, we went down to the Capitol to pay personal tribute. At 2:30 in the morning, the line of mourners stretched twenty blocks. We were told that we didn't have a chance of getting in before the funeral began. So we went home to drink coffee and look at television with our uncannily silent and sober children. Eventually, the funeral Mass at St. Matthew's Cathedral, a mile or so from our house on Cathedral Avenue, came on the screen.

We walked out on the porch beside the TV room to hear the bells tolling as the cortege left the cathedral and did so again a half-hour later to hear the sound of the final guns in Arlington Cemetery across the Potomac in Virginia. It was cold. There were frozen tears on all our faces when we came back in.

Ten years later, during my "academic year" at Florida State University at Tallahassee, I teamed with a professor of Diplomatic History to teach a course on "U.S. Foreign Policy since World War II." We organized our lectures by administrations: Truman, Eisenhower, Kennedy, Nixon. We both rhapsodized on Kennedy. During the discussion period, a young woman (in the starched white dress still common at what had been Florida College for Women until a few years earlier) remarked that both of us seemed very high on Kennedy. But what did he really do?

We mentioned the Cuban missile crisis but then found ourselves at a loss. We agreed that we would consult and offer a full answer next class. We spent much of the evening together in the local bar but were unable to come up with much—to which we confessed when the group met again. Nonetheless, we emphasized, his "spirit" was great.

"Yes," she responded. "That's what my father said: 'All spirit and not much else.'"

We chewed that over again in the bar. We were sure our view of John F. Kennedy was sound; we just couldn't prove it. Camelot was really over.

* * *

Lyndon Baines Johnson was the quintessential joker in the American pack. He used superb political skills and very real humanity to contribute to equal rights for the poor and the dark-skinned. Those same qualities disappeared as far as Vietnam was concerned, and he gave us the only war we ever lost. He brought his "lion-tamer" personality with him from the Senate to the vice presidency. Before he had been in the executive branch for a year, stories about his antics abounded in Washington. He told off-color stories about the Kennedys long before anyone else did. When he traveled abroad, he browbeat embassies, insisting on discount prices on souvenirs and freshly ground pepper in the middle of the night.

He visited Turkey in 1962. When I arrived there eight years later, one story about him was still repeated. He had sent advance warning that he wanted to meet the people and "press the flesh." Ambassador Raymond Hare in his cables cautioned against the vice president's expecting much enthusiasm from the dour Turks, who were in the middle of a terrible winter. He sent his DCM, Robert Barnes, to Tehran to ride in on the Johnson plane and brief the vice president. Barnes repeated Hare's caution and got a tongue-lashing for his pains.

Johnson arrived on an unexpectedly glorious spring day with everybody strolling the streets. On his way into Ankara from the airport, he stopped frequently along the road to light cigarettes and distribute pens. He collected large happy mobs (most of whom probably didn't know who he was). It took three hours for him to reach the city.

A few days later, just before leaving Turkey, he had a final session with embassy officials. He thanked them for their work but also warned them. President Kennedy had asked him to report on the caliber of our people overseas. Hare and Barnes claimed to know about Turkey, but he couldn't help wondering. They had warned him that there would be no popular enthusiasm. They had seen what had happened. Hare, an experienced old hand, kept quiet.

Barnes couldn't hold back. "With all respect, Mr. Vice President," he said, "Ambassador Hare and I do know a lot about Turkey. What we didn't know about was our vice president!" Six months later, Barnes was ambassador in Jordan.

By the time Johnson became president, I had risen enough in the State Department hierarchy to be invited occasionally to a Washington embassy party. Edith and I were at the Turks' one night for a reception for visiting

Prime Minister Ismet Inonu. The president came in and promptly focused on Edith.

"Where are you from, young lady?"

"Montana."

"A great place, just like Texas. I love your Charlie Russell's pictures. Did you know he wrote great things too?"

He fumbled inside his dinner jacket and produced a scrap of paper.

"I copied this out of a book this morning. Listen!" he ordered, reading a few sentences about freedom, equality, prosperity, and the West.

"That's what I'm trying to do with the Great Society, young lady. Do you understand?"

She said she did. After he moved on, she remarked that Lyndon Johnson was brilliant and fascinating. But she did wonder if he had fifty pockets in that jacket!

At the height of the Vietnam War, Afghan Prime Minister Hashim Maiwandwal, an old friend who had begun as a diplomat, came to Washington on an official visit. As a State Department country director, I was not important enough to be invited to the White House lunch, but I was ordered to appear for the substantive discussions at 2:30 P.M. Sulking over being excluded from lunch, I listened to Johnson deliver a two-hour monologue on Vietnam to a disconcerted and bored prime minister, who wanted to talk about economic and technical aid. I tried to divert the conversation. The president waved me down. Victory in Vietnam, he insisted, was more important to Asia than to America.

After that Johnson closed the meeting. He knew Secretary of State Dean Rusk, Assistant Secretary Phillips Talbot, and National Security Council staffer Howard Wriggins seated on the American side of the table. He could have had no idea of who I was. His eyes flicked down at the briefing memorandum in front of him, then focused on Maiwandwal.

"Now, Mr. Prime Minister, just because I talked to you so much about Vietnam, I don't want you to think that Afghanistan is not important to us. I gotta be honest with ya. Days go by when I don't think of Afghanistan at all. That's probably true of Dean, too. Phil and Howard are always interested, but they don't have all that much time either. Jim here, he watches everything. When he spots a problem, he gets in touch with me, and the two of us work it out right away."

Maiwandwal was charmed. So was I. My stock rose enormously with the Afghans. On departing, I offered my thanks to the president. He silently cocked a thumb at the door, "Shut up and get out!" it said. But I think that, like MacArthur, he winked.

No reminiscence of those Kennedy-Johnson days would be complete without mention of Averell Harriman. Already in his seventies, he served where he was needed, first as an assistant secretary of state, then as under secretary, and then again as ambassador-at-large. The word in the department was that he would cheerfully run the United Givers' Fund campaign if called upon. I never worked directly for him, but I kept being swept under his wing.

On an hour's notice he dragged me up to New York for a meeting at the UN. On the plane he told me he was speaking at a black-tie dinner of "Old New Yorkers" at the Century Club that night. I would attend. Somehow, between 6:00 and 7:00 P.M., I managed to rent a dinner suit. Seated next to a very old New Yorker, I listened to talk of a time before I was born.

In an interlude I remarked to my dinner partner that Harriman was certainly vigorous and active for his age. He looked at me coldly and said, "Young man, if I had never done anything but ride horses and chase women until I was forty, I would be vigorous and active too."

Harriman was wont to end any discussion about international transportation with a favorite remark: "I know a little about the subject. My father was in the railroad business." Enormously rich, money meant something different to Harriman than to most people. He never carried any. Those around him paid for his tips and small purchases, and he was slow to reimburse.

When I asked him to host a dinner for one of my high-level foreign visitors without protocol status, he said he'd be delighted and invited thirty distinguished guests to his Georgetown home. A couple of days later I got a bill, twenty-five dollars per person. The total would have broken the Spain budget for a year. I twisted in the wind for awhile and then managed to get Near East Assistant Secretary Luke Battle to pay for the foreigners out of his modest allowance. I collected from the Americans—except Chief Justice Warren, whom I refused to approach. I paid for him and myself.

On our trip to the Pakistani Mangla Dam dedication, Harriman said he wanted Edith to come with us. His administrative assistant protested that only wives of full delegates were authorized on the presidential airplane. Harriman told him not to worry. If there was any problem, he was sure Jim would take care of the costs himself. The matter was left unresolved. The thought of first class fare plus one dollar for the government airplane terrified us, but we decided to take a chance, and Edith came. I got the bill shortly after our return, five thousand and some dollars for a "nonofficial dependent" on Air Force Two. I mentioned it to Harriman. He shrugged and said not to pay it until he filed his report on the trip. In another week, he did. It listed the travelers: head, delegates, wives, officials (no wives). Edith was down as a personal assistant to the head. That took care of that.

Harriman was entitled to at least three titles, governor, secretary, and ambassador. The one he insisted on was governor, earned during a single term as governor of New York. The delegation for the Mangla trip included three sitting governors, those of Maine, Ohio, and Utah. When someone on the airplane called for "the governor," they all jumped up.

Harriman grew annoyed. He told me to explain to them that on his airplane, there was only one governor. I did so—in somewhat different words. Yet, as we flew through several long nights, he prowled the aisles, adjusting seats and putting blankets over sleepers, governors and clerks alike.

Traveling with the governor was always amusing, if intense. I happened to be in New Delhi on a trip from Washington when he came through on his way back from Saigon in Air Force Two. I hitched a ride home. Harriman had breakfast with Mrs. Gandhi in Delhi. He stopped in Pakistan for lunch with President Ayub and in Tehran for dinner with the shah. Thanks to the fact that we were flying against the changing clock, he had time to end the day with a late-night TV appearance in Rome.

As I sat near him on the plane, I learned one of the reasons he could do so much. When his pencil wore down, he simply held it up and an aide put a newly sharpened one in his hand. When his head was cold, he tapped it, and his homburg hat was brought. When descending the ramp in Tehran, a cold breeze wafted by. He put both hands on his shoulders, and someone brought him his coat. On the ground he kept the Iranian foreign minister waiting while he dragged me off to the terminal to stand by as he completed a telegram on his meeting with Ayub. When the wife of our ambassador to Iran was sent to persuade him to come away to the waiting shah, he looked her up and down silently, pulled the hearing aid from his ear, and went on writing.

In the 1960s I had plenty of worm's-eye experiences with Dean Rusk, note-taking when he met with visiting foreign ministers and playing "resource person" when he backgrounded selected journalists. Except when he spilled a drink on his trousers at one of the latter sessions, I don't think I ever saw him show emotion. That is not to suggest that he wasn't human.

During one critical stage of India-Pakistan relations, we in the Near East and South Asia Bureau tried for weeks to schedule a session with him to formulate a military supply policy for the subcontinent. Memo after memo from Assistant Secretary Luke Battle was ignored. Then one morning when I came into the office early, I was informed by a frantic secretary that Secretary Rusk was calling for someone from the bureau to come to see him. He wanted to talk about India. Neither Assistant Secretary Battle, nor Deputy Assistant Secretary William Handley, nor India Director Douglas Heck were in yet. As the Pakistan-Afghanistan director, I was to get myself upstairs at once.

There followed an impressive forty-five minutes with Rusk. He was thoughtful and well informed about India's problems and tested a few theories on me. I was thanked and dismissed with no instructions for action and no idea as to what it was all about. I reported to Battle and the others, but they had no clue either. The opportunity we had been seeking so avidly had come and gone.

A week later I asked one of Rusk's aides if he had any idea what had inspired the meeting. He chuckled. "His daughter's college roommate stayed with them the night before. She was a Peace Corps volunteer in India. She got him interested."

About the same time, the Pakistan foreign minister visited Washington. I took notes in the unspectacular session he had with Rusk at the State Department. That night he and the secretary had an hour alone together on a couch at a Pakistan embassy dinner. The next morning I dropped by the secretary's office and asked his secretary to make sure I got a copy of his memorandum of conversation on the meeting. Nothing happened. I tried again with the friendly aide. He reported back that the secretary said there was not going to be a memcon (memorandum of conversation).

Then the Pakistan ambassador asked me to arrange an urgent meeting with Rusk. He was under instructions from President Ayub to raise a vital matter. Rusk readily consented. Armed with notes, I took the ambassador to see him.

The ambassador said that President Ayub wanted confirmation and elaboration of the statement Rusk had made to his foreign minister that there was no longer a special U.S.-Pakistan relationship. Rusk looked at me and said, "I'm not sure I recall that. What do the notes of our meeting say?"

At less than my diplomatic best, I replied, "There's nothing in the notes like that, sir. You must have said it that night at the embassy dinner. I asked twice for a memcon, but you never did one!"

"Oh," said the secretary, "I don't recall that either," and he went on finessing the delicate subject.

What I had done, gratuitously revealing that our side did not have a record of an important conversation, dawned on me as I took the ambassador down in the elevator. Even he was perturbed: "You know we appreciate your understanding of us, but do you think you should have said that to the secretary?"

I got him away and shot back upstairs. The secretary was alone, reading papers before his next appointment. I apologized, acknowledging the egregiousness of my professional error.

He looked up calmly. "If you never do anything worse than that, you'll probably make out all right in the Foreign Service. Forget it."

Rusk's response, if less than complimentary, was kindly. I thought of it again just before Christmas 1994 when he died at the age of eighty-five.

14

More American Jokers

MY FIRST EXPERIENCE WITH new president Richard Milhous Nixon was more direct than had been the case with his predecessors. Lyndon Johnson's ambassadorial appointee in Islamabad, a wealthy corporate executive, had simply quit and paid his own way home early in 1969, when his pleas for prompt relief were ignored by the new administration. (Political appointees could do that sort of thing. Career ones could not.) Nixon had already appointed former Senator Kenneth Keating to India and was seeking urgently for a corresponding figure for Pakistan. He was fond of the country because it had been one of the few to receive him with warmth and respect during his eight years as a private citizen in the political wilderness. So, the State Department's "Mr. Pakistan" was temporarily assigned there as acting chief of mission.

One of my first duties when I arrived in Islamabad as the purest kind of chargé d'affaires *ad interim* was to receive our new president. The visit, August 1–2, 1969, was to take place in Lahore, because Islamabad airport could not take the Boeing 707 that was Air Force One in those days. Pakistan President Yahya Khan would leave his capital to greet and talk with Nixon in the "Queen City of the Punjab." National Security Adviser Henry Kissinger was coming. New secretary of state William Rogers was not.

I had never met Nixon but did not like him. My feeling was reinforced upon the arrival of two twenty-six-year-old "advance men" for his visit. During the recently concluded election campaign, they had handled publicity in some obscure California county. Now they were "presidential assistants" of awesome power and skill. They took over the embassy, insulted Pakistani officials, and made themselves obnoxious to everyone. I recall their names as Mutt and Jeff, but after all these years am not sure that is accurate.

The Pakistan chief of protocol, a tough Baluch, retaliated. He forbade them to come to the dress rehearsal for the presidential arrival. They showed up at the airport anyway. He ordered the police not to let them out of the terminal. They sneaked out onto the tarmac and began changing the cards designating the places the principals were to stand for the ceremony. The protocol chief waved up a platoon of police and walked over to Mutt and Jeff. "You are tiring yourselves, gentlemen," he said. He dug in a pocket and produced two rupees. "Here, take these. There is a nice machine in the terminal. Go get one of your Coca-Colas." The police nudged them away.

By 11:00 A.M., August 1, 1969, the temperature in Lahore was 115 degrees Fahrenheit. The welcoming party kept shuffling feet to prevent their becoming embedded in the melting tarmac. No less than six Boeing 707s preceded and followed Air Force One onto the airport, blocking all traffic in and out of Lahore for twenty-four hours. The motorcade into town was a shambles, with National Security Adviser Henry Kissinger's driver getting lost.

At a previous stop on the trip, the accompanying American press had gotten sick from bad water. So U.S. officials and their wives had been up all night boiling and bottling water for the press's hotel rooms. They took their revenge by labeling the bottles "U.S. Drinking Water. Passed by American Officials!"

Arrangements to protect Government House, where both Pakistani and American presidents were staying the night, had been painfully negotiated for days in advance. Pakistani security men would be responsible for the inside, U.S. Secret Service personnel for the outside. We forgot about the

U.S. chargé d'Affaires Spain and Mrs. Edith Spain greet visiting President Richard M. Nixon and Mrs. Patricia Nixon, Lahore, Pakistan, August 1, 1969. *Courtesy USIS/Lahore*

veranda. In the middle of the night a Secret Service man stepped up onto it. The Pakistani stalwarts came out boiling. I was dragged out of bed to prevent a "shoot-out" and found the two groups lined up on the disputed veranda, hands on guns. Somehow, we reached another compromise.

A meeting *à deux* between the two presidents was scheduled for after lunch. Just before the meeting Pakistan President Yahya took me aside. "I'll be alone," he said, "and President Nixon should be too. Is that understood?"

I checked with Nixon and said that it was. The meeting was at our request. It was the one, I subsequently found out, in which Nixon asked Yahya to see what he could do to promote a dialogue between the United States and China. As I edged Nixon into the room, a Secret Service man clung to him. I cut the bodyguard off and closed the door, standing with my back to it.

"The presidents are meeting alone," I explained.

"Where our president goes, I go!" he countered, trying to jostle me away from the door.

"Not this time!" I said. "I'm the chargé d'affaires."

"I don't care about your sex life, Buster," he responded. "Get out of my way!" He grabbed my arm and twisted it behind my back. Others of his kind swarmed to his assistance.

The crowd of Pakistanis and Americans coming out of the dining room began to take notice. I caught a glimpse of Henry Kissinger. "Dr. Kissinger! Dr. Kissinger!" I shouted.

Henry came over. "It is all right. The presidents are meeting alone. Let that man go!"

The bodyguard did so, snarling as Kissinger walked out of earshot, "Big shot! Interfering with my duties! I'll report this!"

In sharp contrast to their entourage, the Nixons themselves were as gracious as they could be. Mrs. Nixon asked advice on her program from Edith and other American women. The president thanked me and the staff for every little arrangement he noted. At least in that early stage of his presidential career, there was nothing even remotely arrogant about him. Later I discovered that that's the way great men—politicians anyway—are. Sometimes I suspect, too, that they are perfectly aware of and even encourage their staffs' nastiness. It makes it unnecessary for them to be that way themselves.

As Air Force One lifted into the sky, the Pakistan Chief of Protocol remarked: "You know that in the old days we said that when a man killed his tiger, he never feared again. We, my friend, have killed our tiger!"

Henry Kissinger added a coda to the visit. When the party was leaving I asked him if he would see to it that I got a memcon for the two presidents' private meeting. He responded coldly that if the president did a memcon, and if he and the president wanted me to have it, he would. A few days later Yahya asked me to pass a personal message to Nixon. He had promised to have an answer to the president's request within a week, but it would take longer. Yahya had assumed his ambassador was in Beijing. In fact, he was in the hospital in Shanghai. He had instructed the ambassador to send the reply direct to Washington after he got back to the Chinese capital.

I thought it over, made my own guesses as to what was going on, and sent the message to Washington. Feeling that I was doing less than justice to my own State Department, for the only time in my life I used a "back channel" (CIA communications), addressing it to "Eyes Only. Dr. Kissinger. The White House." Back came a message from Henry upbraiding me in the strongest language for violating security, unwarranted interference in his and the president's business, and ordering me never to do so again in my career in the Foreign Service "insofar as I had one." I drafted a "Screw you, Herr Doktor" response, but Edith talked me out of it. To this day, I can't imagine how else I should have handled the situation.

There was a further gothic footnote to the Nixon visit. A few days before the president arrived, Agha Hilaly, President Yahya's ambassador in Washington, who had returned for the Nixon visit, came to see me privately, at Yahya's behest. Would I object, Hilaly asked, if Yahya were to ask Nixon to keep me on in Pakistan as ambassador? I responded that I was a career diplomat and did as my president told me. At the airport after the Nixons had left, Yahya called me over to report, "He said yes!"

A week later a cable from Washington directed me to request *agrément* for one Joseph Farland, a Republican political appointee, as the new U.S. ambassador to Pakistan. I delivered the request to the foreign secretary and heard no more about the matter, except that Edith and I exchanged a few private remarks about the trustworthiness of our new president.

Almost a decade later, during an R&R visit to Pakistan from Dar es Salam, a long-retired Ambassador Hilaly gave us lunch. I said something less than adulatory about the by-then disgraced Nixon, and Hilaly reprimanded me: I certainly had no reason to criticize President Nixon; he had wanted to make me ambassador to Pakistan. I sneered.

"Oh," said Hilaly, "don't you know about that? I was still in Washington at the time. President Nixon sent word to the State department proposing your appointment, but some of your senior Foreign Service people objected. They said you were too young and inexperienced." Hilaly also thought that some of them might have wanted the job themselves, leading President Nixon to settle the problem by sending a political appointee.

In 1973, when I was deputy chief of mission in Ankara, the Watergate scandal was unraveling around the Nixon White House. Bereft of American newspapers and television, we did not get the full flavor of it until a large delegation of senators and representatives arrived in the Turkish capital for that year's meeting of NATO parliamentarians. Twenty-four hours later came "the Saturday Night Massacre," when Nixon fired Attorney General Elliot Richardson. The representatives, led by the fiery Wayne Hayes, insisted on returning immediately. Ambassador William Macomber tried to persuade them to remain a little longer, asking why the great rush. To the ambassador's consternation, Hayes answered in a loud voice within earshot of Turkish reporters: "Because I can't wait to impeach the son of a bitch. That's why!"

That night I reviewed my high school civics knowledge. The House of Representatives impeached. The Senate tried. It seemed right. The trial wouldn't happen for a time. The senators stayed in Ankara. Sitting on the sofa in our house with Senate Majority Leader and Mrs. Mike Mansfield, old friends from Edith's Montana days, I searched my mind for something to say. With Vice President Spiro Agnew already driven from office and Nixon facing impeachment, this quiet, pipe-smoking man might soon be determining what happened in our country. I asked: "How do you think things are going to come out in Washington?"

The majority leader puffed on his pipe for silent moments. Finally, he said: "I'm afraid we're going to have to get rid of this fellow."

I knew things were serious.

In 1976 my first ambassadorial appointment—to Tanzania—came from President Ford. Apart from his machine-drawn signature on my commission and a nice ashtray when he left the White House, I never saw anything of him.

Henry Kissinger, however, was still very much around. I described earlier how at a late date he "discovered" southern Africa, and the considerable good that came of it. During his three visits to Dar in 1976, he claimed to enjoy riding about in my little Australian Ford, after I blocked use of the bulletproof limousine he'd had flown in. He insisted that he was intimidated by an African president who spoke "so much better English than I do." He warned me that I must keep trying but must also remember that "this fellow Nyerere is not on our side!"

My sharpest memory of Henry Kissinger now, almost twenty years after I last saw him, has nothing to do with reality. It is of a story that drifted to Dar from Washington. President Nixon, Henry, an army chaplain, and a Peace Corps volunteer were riding in a single-engine plane with a solitary pilot. The pilot got up and announced that the plane was going down in five minutes and there was nothing he could do about it. He was sorry that for the five of them there were only four parachutes. He put one on and jumped.

President Nixon arose and stressed that there should be absolutely no mistake. He was as brave and unselfish as the next man. But, after all, he was the president of the United States. He put on the second parachute and left. Henry pointed out that he was as noble as any man, but he too must go. "After all, I am the world's greatest intellect and it must be preserved!"

The chaplain told the Peace Corps kid to go with the last parachute. He had his life, family, and career before him. The chaplain was given to God anyway, and he may as well go to Him now.

The Peace Corps volunteer had a way out. "Let's both go, Father. The 'world's greatest intellect' just went out of here wearing my backpack."

When Jimmy Carter replaced Ford and Cyrus Vance succeeded Henry Kissinger in 1977, a new flavor came into our dealings with southern Africa. Andrew Young, our ambassador to the United Nations, became a frequent visitor, together with Richard Moose, the new assistant secretary for African affairs. These men were a refreshing change. They traveled with few aides, played whimsical tricks on each other, and scooped up souvenirs.

From left: U.S. Representative to the UN Andrew Young, Ambassador James Spain, Tanzanian ambassador to the United States Paul Bomani, and President of Tanzania Julius K. Nyerere, Dar es Salaam, 1978. *Courtesy USIS/Dar es Salaam*

At one point, I had to hastily extract them from the wood-carving stands along the Bagamoyo Road when a carload of photographers showed up. They were trading American blue jeans and beer for handicrafts. They agreed that it was not the image we wanted on the front page of African or any other newspapers. Andy Young turned a farewell party we had arranged for him into a birthday party for Sam Nujoma, and the first American-Namibian social contact was established. Often the Americans were a bit much for the sober David Owen, British Labour Party foreign secretary, who came to join in negotiations on Rhodesia with Nyerere.

Secretary Vance came to Dar only once. The courteous, soft-spoken lawyer was superb at personal relations. He treated President Nyerere as the protocol superior he was (something Kissinger had never been able to bring himself to do). He laughed at himself and brought the dour Welshman Owen to do the same. He got the deadly serious Zimbabwean, Robert Mugabe, to tell a funny story. He spent two hours at three in the morning with Sam Nujoma, who had come to Dar to plead his case on Namibia.

He helped me out of a tight corner with the small local American community. Led by a fiery Maryknoll nun, it was rabidly opposed to what it considered U.S. policy in favor of the South African–supported, white-settler government of Rhodesia. Many of the American black "political refugees" in Tanzania echoed this position loudly. Months earlier, I had taken a petition from the protesters and had routinely sent it into the Washington maw. In the car on the way to a gathering at the Embassy Residence for all Americans to meet the secretary of state, I warned Vance that he might face hostility and recalled the petition I had sent along. He merely grunted.

At the reception he climbed on a chair, resting his hand on my shoulder to do so, and announced: "See how I depend on our ambassador!" He said that he knew of their concern about U.S. policy, because I had sent word of it to Washington in their own words. As American residents in East Africa, they had something worthwhile to say. He had talked to the president. Our policy was even now being reviewed.

The nun kissed him and promised a prayer as he left. My black friend who would ordinarily meet me only on street corners had come to the party. He confided that he knew that our Marine security guards were present in civilian clothes; he recognized them by their haircuts. He thanked me for not letting them beat him up and asked me if it was all right to take home one can of cold American beer. He hadn't had that for a long time.

In the middle of all of this, Carter invited Nyerere for an official visit to the United States. Now with enough rank to participate fully in such affairs, I went along. Nyerere was established in Blair House. We spent the afternoon at the White House in a working session with Carter, Vance, Moose, National Security Adviser Zbigniew Brzezinski, and some note-takers.

Carter invited Nyerere to speak first. He did, almost exclusively about Rhodesia and Namibia. His approach was moderate. Something had to be done to ensure their independence and the establishment of a democratic system of government without massive bloodshed.

Carter shuffled through a pile of papers in front of him while Nyerere was speaking and then replied. His knowledge of detail was amazing. He knew and pronounced correctly the names of the Africans involved, Mugabe, Nkomo, Muzorewa, Nujoma. He isolated the key issues—the makeup of the armed forces of the new states, the future of their white populations, and the kind of economic support that would be needed from the outside world. He and Nyerere, American Baptist and African Catholic, hit it off famously.

After two hours Carter drew the session to a close. "Mr. President, I think we've covered everything. . . ."

Brzezinski coughed loudly.

Carter drew a memorandum from his pile. He studied it glumly. "Well, there is the question of the Cubans in Angola. . . ."

"Ah, Mr. President, I'm so glad you brought that up," Nyerere responded. "I thought we were going to agree on everything."

"Well, the fact is that we'd like to see them out of there."

"They'll go as soon as the South Africans stop interfering in Angola. I have the Angolans' word on it. You needn't worry."

Brzezinski broke in. "Are you aware, Mr. President, that the number of Cubans in Angola, in proportion to the total number of Cubans, is greater than the number of Americans in Vietnam at the height of that conflict, in proportion to the total population of the United States?"

"No, I was not, Mr. Brzezinski. What an interesting statistic!"

"And, Mr. President, are you further aware that the number of Cubans in Angola is larger compared to the total population of that country than was the number of Americans in Vietnam compared to the population of Vietnam?"

This time Nyerere's eyebrows rose, and he simply waved an open hand.

"Down, boy!" the gesture said.

"Well, I guess now we have finished everything," Carter proclaimed, and the meeting broke up. I later checked the transcript with Brzezinski's note-taker. Both his boss's questions were there. So was the first of Nyerere's responses. The gesture was not recorded.

That evening, before the official stag dinner, I stopped in to chat with Nyerere at Blair House. I found that Dominic, years ago mainstay of our little cocktail parties on Cathedral Avenue, was major domo there. He promptly presented a Scotch and soda.

Then we crossed Pennsylvania Avenue to the White House. Among the thirty or so dignitaries present were Vice President Walter Mondale and Senator Daniel P. Moynihan of New York. President Carter was in less than his best mood. Not expecting him to remember me from the afternoon session, I began "I'm Jim Spain, ambassador in Dar es Salaam . . ."

"I know perfectly well who you are," he responded. "I met you this afternoon."

When he had moved on, I joined a group with Moynihan. He was staring in affected horror at a tray of drinks being offered by a butler. "What! Wine, beer, and Coca-Cola!" he thundered. "Is there no whiskey in the Carter White House?"

"No, sir," said the butler.

Trying to make small talk, I remarked that I'd just had a couple of good Scotches at Blair House. Then I saw the president a few feet away glaring at me. Shortly afterward the chief of protocol hissed in my ear. "You've really fixed things up, smart guy. Now we can't have any hard liquor in Blair House either!"

During dinner, Mondale got up, whispered in the president's ear, and left. "The vice president extends his apologies," said Carter to the table. "There's an important vote coming up in the Senate, and he may have to break a tie." He looked at Moynihan. "In that case, what are you doing here, Senator?"

The next time I met President Carter was at a White House reception for Donald McHenry, Young's successor at USUN. This time I knew better than to introduce myself. Anyway Carter was in a good mood. "Secretary Vance and I have been talking about the fine work you've done," he said. "We want you to . . ."

Mondale, next in the line, reached over and grabbed my hand. "Great occasion, isn't it?" he enthused. "So nice to see you." He passed me on promptly. "Here, say hello to Secretary Vance."

Vance was grinning. "The vice president likes to keep the line moving, but there is something I want to ask you about . . ."

Mondale broke in again. "Can't you State Department fellows do your business in the office? The president has to shake a lot of hands here, and you're holding him up!"

Vance shrugged. I fled—to spend the next few days wondering what was up. Then a telephone call came from the department. The president and the secretary wanted me to be ambassador to Turkey. Would I? That and India were the only two jobs in the Foreign Service I had always really wanted. After doubts about Edith's health were resolved, I said, "Of course!"

It was great while it lasted. I knew and liked the Turks and spoke the language passably. Keeping them in NATO after a cutoff of U.S. military aid over their invasion of Cyprus was one challenge. Encouraging them back to representative government after a military takeover in September 1980 was another.

After Vance had resigned over the fiasco of the hostage rescue attempt in Iran, his replacement, Senator Edmund Muskie, came to Ankara for a NATO ministerial meeting, accompanied by his wife and aides. They had not been in the Residence for more than an hour before, in that wonderful way politicians have, we were all old friends.

One night, after a press conference in which Muskie had said something about China slightly off the main U.S. policy line, we were sitting around at the Residence. The phone rang. It was Acting Secretary Warren Christopher. After a brief exchange of cordialities, I put the secretary on the line. What I overheard went something like this.

"Hello, Chris. Everything's going well here."

[Christopher inaudible.]

"Yeah, I said something like that. So what?"

[Christopher inaudible.]

"Who's complaining? Oh, that little fellow!"

[Christopher inaudible.]

"Well, you just call him back and tell him to stuff it. If he gives you any trouble, ask him what he's ever been elected to and, if it comes to a spitting match, who he thinks the president will support, me or him."

Poor Zbigniew Brzezinski had been batted down again.

* * *

America shuffled its cards in the November 1980 election, and a new set of powerful jokers appeared in the pack. Muskie left office. I was replaced by President Reagan's political appointee.

When I returned to Washington, I was told by Alexander Haig, the new secretary of state, that I had been given another academic year away from the department. "Maybe we'll find something better for you later," he told me. "Meanwhile, go read a couple of books—or write one!" A young FSO on the National Security Council staff whom I had once treated kindly gave me a more down-to-earth commentary on my status. He had overheard me referred to in the Reagan White House as "Andy Young's friend, who helped give away Rhodesia."

I was still reading and writing more than two years later when word came that Secretary George Shultz, who had replaced Haig, wanted me to try to do a Foreign Service inspection of the U.S. Mission to the United Nations in New York, headed by Reagan favorite Jeane Kirkpatrick. The law required one at least every five years, but Mrs. Kirkpatrick was resisting. Maybe I, a bland career man, not a professional inspector, could work something out with her.

As described earlier, we did manage something, and the episode seemed to put me back in the State Department's good graces. I was directed to return to the building and stand by for an assignment. The deputy secretary's Ambassadorial Assignments Committee recommended me to Shultz for India, and he approved. But the day the secretary signed off on my appointment, he got a call from presidential aide Michael Deaver: never mind sending any name over for India; he and the president had decided on a man for the post.

That was that. I was offered Sri Lanka instead, unimportant but pleasant and interesting. In due course, President Reagan put through one of his famous telephone calls to tell me of his desire for me to go there. I was tempted to tell him that I would rather have gone to India, but years of habit held. I said merely, "Thank you, sir."

Except for a prolonged and painful confrontation with Senator Jesse Helms and a pleasant social meeting with President Bill Clinton, about which I will tell later, my days of consorting with the big jokers in the American political pack were over.

In ending this series of anecdotes about the men who come from all over the country to run our affairs in Washington, there remains the question of what is to be said of them as human beings.

First, in my experience they are mostly competent and decent human beings. To anyone interested in public affairs, they are to be admired for the skill and energy with which they wield power and influence over what are truly important affairs.

But they are also subject to the temptations of power and position, so graphically described in George Reedy's book, *The Twilight of the Presidency.* Many become austere and withdrawn or vain and arrogant, according to their personalities. Some simply turn corrupt. Few manage to retain a sense of humor. The processes of their own government, never mind the machinations of foreign ones, make them calculating and cynical. Aware that their days of glory are transitory, they aim at mention in the history books rather than the right or the good.

Only rarely are they to be envied.

15

Advice and Consent

ARTICLE II, SECTION 2, OF the Constitution gives the president the power to appoint ambassadors "with the advice and consent" of the Senate. In my early days around the State Department, the Senate Foreign Relations Committee (SFRC) was the key element in the process. Its chairman, the stern but gentlemanly J. William Fulbright, believed in letting the president have the political appointees he wanted as long as they were halfway competent. Career people were presumed to be competent because they had worked their way up through the Foreign Service system. With a rare exception for "senatorial courtesy"—when a senator took exception to a nominee from his state—approval by Fulbright was enough. If I ever made it to an ambassadorial nomination, the last place I thought to encounter trouble was with the Senate.

In those days, I had never met a senator I didn't like. The first one I ever knew was Edith's uncle, Edward Burke of Nebraska. I admired both his populist sentiments and the brief fame he had won by being "purged" by Franklin Roosevelt for his vigorous opposition to FDR's "court-packing" scheme. In those early days, I was charmed with the casual ways of George Malone of Nevada, my father-in-law's buddy from their times together as state engineers. I admired Majority Leader Ernest McFarland of Arizona, my mother-in-law's friend, who snubbed my first awful ambassador, who so often snubbed me.

Foreign Service officers who meet members of Congress abroad have an advantage. The contact takes place on their "turf." They are in control of arrangements and appointments, and they can show off their local knowledge and skills. They can also, if they want to badly enough, avoid a visit entirely. In Istanbul in 1971 Bob Dillon, then deputy consul general, and I devised a scheme for so doing. We had one congressional delegation (CODEL) with genuine work to do coming in. Then another, with no definable interests other than a weekend's shopping, announced its imminent arrival. The morning papers had headlined the annual cholera epidemic in Istanbul (not significant for healthy, well-fed adults). Terrorism was on the rise. We sent a telegram warmly welcoming the second CODEL, quoting the most sensational of the newspaper accounts on cholera and violence. We explained the need for the sternest medical and security precautions. The CODEL decided to overfly.

I found most senators I met an admirable breed, direct, outspoken, concerned about others, the opposite of many Foreign Service colleagues. Over the years, I dealt with, among others, Hubert Humphrey and Rudy Boschwitz of Minnesota, Mike Mansfield of Montana, Charles Percy of Illinois, Joseph Biden of Delaware, John Glenn of Ohio, Howard Baker of Tennessee, Richard Clark of Iowa, Ernest "Fritz" Hollings of South Carolina, Robert Byrd of West Virginia, John Warner of Virginia, John Tower of Texas, Patrick Leahy of Vermont, Edward Zorinsky of Nebraska, Charles "Mac" Mathias and Paul Sarbanes of Maryland, and Alan Cranston and S. I. Hayakawa of California. Senators seemed to like me too. I was less staid, noncommittal, and respectful than most FSOs. (At least I thought so.)

Two illustrations from my last assignment in Turkey reflect what I mean. The notoriously gruff chairman of the Senate Armed Services Committee, John Tower, sent word of a three-day visit—commencing on the exact day Edith and I were planning to leave for a long-planned thirtieth anniversary trip up the Nile. I cabled back, explaining this and that I could see him at the airport as he arrived and we departed. I would change plans if he wished. Back came a reply: "Happy Anniversary! Do not change plans!"

Tower showed up alone on a commercial flight. We had a few minutes' talk in the terminal. He said he just wanted to see what the new Turkish military regime was like. He didn't want a press conference. Journalists never understood him anyway. At USIS's urging, I persuaded him to agree to a meeting with the press. A few days later in Cairo, I saw a copy of the *Jerusalem Post.* "Tower Approves Turkish Torture!" read the headline. There had been a hostile Israeli reporter at the press conference. I cabled apologies. He responded: "No harm. Don't let it spoil your second honeymoon."

Senator Patrick Leahy of Vermont, then a member of the Select Committee on Intelligence, appeared with two staff aides to look at the many U.S. electronic intelligence collection facilities in Turkey. Look they did, allowing themselves only one hour for shopping and sightseeing. They waived pouch and APO privileges (always accorded to CODELs), asking only for string to carry their modest purchases with them. Borrowed books were returned and generous tips left with the household staff.

In a long and friendly meeting with the prime minister, which I, not Leahy, insisted on, the senator got across a brief and graceful statement on the importance the United States attached to a return to democracy. The prime minister got an impression of a courteous and well-informed American lawmaker. It was good for both sides.

Back on the senators' turf in Washington, I found things somewhat different. The first time I went up for confirmation (for Tanzania), Senator John Sparkman of Alabama had just replaced Senator Fulbright as chairman of the Foreign Relations Committee. A gracious southern lady from the State Department's Congressional Relations Bureau took me over for a meeting in advance of the committee hearing. The courtly Sparkman asked a few questions about me and Tanzania. Then he said, "It's been a pleasure to meet you, Mr. Ambassador. I'll see you again at the hearing."

As we left, the lady whispered "You're in!" When the chairman calls someone who isn't an ambassador yet, 'Mr. Ambassador,' that's it."

At the public hearing, I listened as a half-dozen senators gently questioned an ambassadorial nominee for an important post in Europe. Sparkman then called a ten-minute recess while all the other senators except Clifford Case of New Jersey disappeared. I sat down at the big oval table and eavesdropped while two or three newspapermen debated whether or not to stay for Tanzania. I was less than flattered that they decided neither it nor I were important and left.

Newly elected senator and former high school teacher Richard Clark of Iowa, chairman of the Africa subcommittee, strode in. He was accompanied by an equally fresh young woman staffer, about whom I knew nothing other than that she was soon to marry an aide of Senator Humphrey's. It looked as if that was all there was going to be. Most senators on the Foreign Relations Committee apparently agreed with the newspapermen.

Sparkman posed the same few questions he had asked in our private meeting and indicated he was content. Case waived questions and offered congratulations. Clark wasn't having any of that.

Fueled by the staffer, who kept pushing pieces of paper under his nose, he hurled a series of questions. Would I characterize President Nyerere of Tanzania as an important Third World leader inherently suspicious of the United States? What did I think he thought about the CIA? How would Nyerere feel about having a former spy as an ambassador? Was it not true that Henry Kissinger, who had removed that great and good black American, Beverly Carter, was replacing him with one of his hatchet men? At the very least, should not Nyerere be informed in advance of my sinister connections and his acceptance of them assured?

I answered as best I could but made no impression. I did not realize it at the time, but I now think that day was the beginning of the end of the old wise and rational senatorial way of implementing "advice and consent." Fortunately, the newspapermen were gone, and no word of the diatribe ever appeared in print—which might well have induced Nyerere to withdraw *agrément*.

Then Hubert Humphrey, whom I'd never met, appeared. He was accompanied by an aide. My God! The one the other one was going to marry! He too was pushing papers at his boss. I figured the hope for which I had given up ONE fifteen years before was going down the drain. The kids were still in school, and I needed tuition money. I wondered if the Agency would take me back. The former vice president and presidential nominee listened to Clark for awhile. Then he asked his "distinguished colleague from the great neighboring state of Iowa" if he could ask him a few questions. The aide pushed forward another piece of paper, but Humphrey ignored it.

"How many people has the Office of National Estimates bribed or poisoned?" he asked. Without waiting for an answer he explained what Sherman Kent and his people at ONE did. "Does Nyerere—I know him well; do you, Senator?—think the Chinese ambassador in his country has spent his life as a Confucian missionary and the Soviet one as a rug salesman? What do you want to do? Embarrass him?" He didn't wait for an answer to that either, but added that the last time the Senate had heard talk impugning the personal integrity of career government servants, it had been from Senator Joseph McCarthy.

Sparkman said he thought the nomination had been explored fully and adjourned the session. I was promptly confirmed.

A year later, I was in Washington with Nyerere on his state visit. The Senate gave a lunch, and I found myself sitting next to Humphrey. I tried to thank him and told him of encouraging developments in Rhodesia. He waved the thanks off. "Now you see," he said, "public service can be a burden, but it's worth it, isn't it?"

He was already dying of cancer. A few months later, he succumbed. Edith and I happened to be in Washington again. All we could do was to stand in line for an hour to file past his bier in the Rotunda of the Capitol where he had served so faithfully and well.

My next encounter with "advice and consent" was the only one of the four to go smoothly. In the fall of 1979, I appeared before the Senate Foreign Relations Committee for confirmation as deputy U.S. permanent representative to the United Nations in New York.

Only Senator Hayakawa asked questions. "How many ambassadors do we have at USUN?"

"Five."

"Which one are you?"

"The second one, deputy permanent representative."

"Do we need them all?"

"I'll be able to respond better to that, Senator, after I've been there awhile."

Then: "Do you know the language they speak there?"

Not sure what the senator was getting at—perhaps he was asking about my French?—I said that I could get along in it.

"If you were with some of the people there in a bar outside the office, could you order a drink?"

I was sure about that. "Yes, sir!"

Confirmation came the next day.

* * *

My appointment to Turkey a few months later did not go so easily. The State Department was trying to rush me out so I could sign the long-pending Defense and Economic Cooperation Agreement. The Turks took their usual three weeks to grant *agrément*—which must precede announcement of the appointment by the White House. The embassy in Ankara added three days by sending the *agrément* back to Washington by routine rather than immediate cable. State sent the papers to the White House requesting that it be announced and sent to the Senate immediately to allow time for action before the Congress adjourned for Christmas in mid-December.

A punctilious White House Press Office person held things up another three days. My biography showed that I had an M.A. from the University of Chicago and a Ph.D. from Columbia University. But it said nothing about a B.A. Where was that from? I responded that I didn't have a B.A. How could that be? In my day at the University of Chicago, one could go straight for an M.A. without a B.A. She called the university to confirm. Only then was the announcement made. The nomination finally reached the SFRC on December 14, 1979. Its last meeting before recess was scheduled for December 18.

The SFRC chairman, Senator Frank Church, agreed to waive the committee's rule that nominations must lie before it for six days before action. The prospects for prompt confirmation, which would enable us to send off our household effects so they would be waiting for us on arrival, seemed good. So did those for a family Christmas in Washington coupled with a holiday swearing-in, at which Patrick, Stephen, and William could be present.

Then the head of the committee's minority staff, a former Foreign Service officer who considered himself an expert on all things to do with the State Department, raised an objection. There was a problem about which he would have to confer with Senator Jacob Javits of New York, the SFRC's ranking minority member. Action was postponed until the committee met again in January.

The problem, it turned out, was once again my ancient link with the CIA—except this time it was me rather than the host government that the staffer was thoughtfully worrying about. A CIA station chief had recently been assassinated in Athens. Violence was even greater in Turkey than in Greece. Was not the State Department being reckless in sending me off to be killed? And, oh yes, my CIA connection had not been mentioned in the biography sent over by the State Department. What other information was being withheld from the Senate?

In the single SFRC hearing on the nomination (an "executive" session in early February), Javits took up his aide's cudgel. Both of them refused to talk to me either privately or publicly. I sat silently without a single question being asked while Senator Church sought unsuccessfully to persuade Javits to drop his objections on the grounds that a decision on the CIA connection was one for the Government of the United States, not the Government of Turkey.

This time there was no Hubert Humphrey to cut through the chaff. S. I. Hayakawa tried. He cited my qualifications (including speaking Turkish) and moved to approve. Javits refused, putting a "hold" on the nomination until he was assured that Turkey knew I was a former CIA employee and was still prepared to accept me.

Both Secretary of State Cyrus Vance and Deputy Secretary Warren Christopher tried to reason with Javits. The Turks, they pointed out, were our close allies. They knew me well and were almost certainly already aware that I had once worked for CIA. They had already given *agrément*. Javits was adamant. He would not remove the hold until Vance assured him that he had consulted with Ankara.

I and the few other senior Foreign Service officers aware of the issue objected to giving in. To do so would establish a frightening precedent. I offered to withdraw. A tired Vance said no. He and the president wanted me to go to Turkey. I wanted to go. Javits's condition would be met. We'd worry about precedent later.

So, one night about 8:00, the Turkish ambassador in Washington received what must surely have been a surprising call from Christopher. After a few minutes of small talk, Chris described the situation. Would the ambassador make certain that the Government of Turkey had no objections to my one-time association?

The ambassador called Chris back the next morning to say that Prime Minister Suleyman Demirel considered the matter to be none of the Turkish government's business. He also called me to ask what the hell was going on. I tried to explain traditional Senate quirks. He didn't believe me. He considered Javits to be pro-Greek. "He's setting something up to embarrass us!" he warned.

Vance informed Javits that the Turkish prime minister saw the matter as none of his business. The senator said he would remove his hold. When we tried to move ahead, we found that the nomination was still blocked on the Senate's books. A call to the senator's aide revealed that this was his doing. He wasn't going to remove "his" hold, he announced, until Secretary Vance called him personally to give assurances. The Vance aide who was doing the telephoning was stung enough to say that if the secretary got back on the phone, it wouldn't be the staffer he would be calling, but he could assure him that he would not like the results.

The SFRC reported the nomination to the floor, recommending approval by a vote of 9 to 1. Curious as to the lone dissenter, I did some probing with staff friends. It had been not Javits but Hayakawa. The gentleman from California, I was told, approved of the nominee, but after the Javits intervention had concluded that the whole thing had become so fraught with silliness that he voted against it in the SFRC. Apparently, he switched in the floor vote a few days later when I was confirmed with unanimous consent.

All of this was but prelude to my next struggle with the Senate, in 1985. I did not expect it. I couldn't imagine anyone objecting to a senior, proven career diplomat going to little Sri Lanka and the tiny Maldives. That, unfortunately, is the way Foreign Service officers tend to think.

But Jesse Helms of North Carolina had emerged as a new force in the Senate. Not satisfied with electoral victory over the Democrats, he was doing everything he could to force Reagan further right. His holds on ambassadorial nominations became commonplace. He collected a group of reactionary staffers and let them target the State Department on anything that took their fancy. To Helms and his crew it was not the qualifications of the nominee or the importance of the country to which he was going that counted. It was the opportunity to embarrass the administration and the State Department. He was still doing so a dozen years later, as I wrote these lines.

The first hint that trouble was brewing came when a friendly staffer from the House Foreign Affairs Committee called me to say that he had been at a congressional staff dinner the night before and heard a couple of aides—he didn't know their names but thought they belonged to Helms—talking about me and Winston Lord, president of the Council on Foreign Relations, who had just been nominated as ambassador to China. They were gleefully telling each other how they were going to have Lord and me "twisting in the wind."

I asked the Congressional Relations Bureau person who had been assigned to my nomination to try to find out what was going on. The opposite of the gracious lady who had shepherded me through my first nomination, intellectually she belonged more with Helms's crew than in the department. She returned to report that Lord and I had written "awful things." She wondered if, perhaps, the nominations might better be withdrawn.

Her bosses did not agree with her, and in due course I found out what the issue was—or was supposed to be. The Senate system on hearings for ambassadorial nominees had changed over the years. Now, instead of the SFRC chairman's presiding, the subcommittee chairmen did. For the Middle East and South Asia this was newly elected conservative Republican Rudy Boschwitz, the "Plywood King" of Minnesota. My initial meeting with him was amicable. We talked a little about Sri Lanka. He mentioned my writings in the scholarly quarterlies during my recent foreign affairs fellowships at Carnegie and Rand and said I should be prepared for a few questions on them, but he thought that everything would be all right.

At the hearing, Boschwitz read quotes from my writings. He remarked that I seemed to imply that the Senate did not take its responsibilities on confirming ambassadors seriously. Was that not being proven incorrect at the very moment? One paragraph might seem to suggest that ambassadorships were sold to political appointees, but he was sure I didn't really mean that.

Then liberal Democratic Senator Alan Cranston, presumably trying to help, took up the subject. "It seems to me that someone who professionally has tried to improve the system should not be pilloried for criticism of a system that has much in it to criticize. I admire the frankness with which you have dealt with these issues. I think you are a highly qualified person for this ambassadorial post and I will do what I can to support you!"

Jesse Helms never showed up for the hearing, but the Cranston remark clearly did not sit well with one of his minions sitting behind the podium. He passed up a set of questions he said Senator Helms wanted answered in writing. Boschwitz handed the questions on to me, saying that if they could be answered promptly, he would try to get confirmation before the upcoming recess. He added that he would send my name to the full committee "suggesting that we speedily approve [it] and get you out to your new post."

Helms's questions were cutthroat, mostly of the "When did you stop beating your wife?" variety. Having been evicted from my apartment near Dupont Circle when the lease expired, I stayed up all night at the house of Steve and Sue Low, who had given me refuge, using their new computer to prepare as thorough a response as I could. I "respectfully declined" one question that demanded I list the names of all ambassadorial nominees of all administrations whose financial and political connections were responsible for their appointments. To avoid embarrassment to anyone, I had listed no names in the article and I wasn't about to do so now.

The next morning the full SFRC met to consider ten nominees. Boschwitz presented a mildly favorable report on me. Eight of the ten were approved. Helms again was not present but sent a message asking for "a week's delay" on Winston Lord and me. Such a request is any senator's privilege, the idea being to give him time to collect information or resolve doubts.

The delay was approved when Senator Claiborne Pell of Rhode Island associated himself with it. His problem, he explained, was that he had long objected to our having an ambassador accredited to the Maldives when that country did not have one in Washington. He wanted time to arrange separate votes on me for Sri Lanka and for the Maldives. He would enthusiastically vote in favor of me for Sri Lanka and against me for the Maldives. Nothing personal.

Senator Zorinsky pointed out that with a recess impending, the "week's delay" would be seven weeks. That didn't matter to the others.

I settled in at the Cosmos Club to wait things out. I had originally planned a leisurely father-and-son trip to Colombo with youngest child Bill. He had been shattered by the deaths of his mother and sister, and we planned stops in familiar places in Europe and Asia for distraction and happy memories. Now I sent him off on the trip alone. After he had been in Turkey for more than a month, he telephoned asking what he should do next—and implying that he was wearing out his welcome with the friends who had put him up there. I told him to go on and use his ticket to Colombo. I might never see the place, but he should.

I cabled the Colombo chargé d'affaires, Victor Tomseth, saying that Bill would be showing up. Victor cabled back. No problem! The ambassadorial residence was staffed. He would put him in there. Helms's crew, it struck me, would love that. Not even confirmed, I already had a son in the official house. No, I replied. Keep him out of the Residence. Find a cheap hotel. Victor "compromised." He took Bill into his own house.

When the Senate reconvened on September 9 for its second session, everyone was prepared to play hardball. Helms's crew pointed out that Lord and Spain were defunct. If a nomination laid over for more than thirty days, it had to be resubmitted. To its credit, the Reagan administration promptly did so.

Next, a letter came to me from Boschwitz. He was disappointed at my answers to Helms's questions. He understood that they were a group effort in the department. If the Senate were to accept them in their present form, it would be guilty of the very criticism I had leveled against it. An hour later the explanation for Boschwitz's hostility came via the grapevine. Helms's staff was circulating a story that I and some other FSOs sitting in the department, giggling and poking fun, had casually pounded out the answers amidst a flood of disparaging remarks about the Senate.

The full Foreign Relations Committee met on September 24. Helms did not attend. The rest of the committee reported out the Lord and Spain nominations 9 to 0. Then Helms put a floor hold on both nominations.

His crew now honed their attack. Lord was a monied, East Coast, liberal Republican, the "wrong" kind of political appointee. China used abortion in its population control program; Winston Lord wanted to be ambassador to China; thus Winston Lord favored the murder of unborn children.

As for me, I was the "wrong" kind of career appointee, shifty, indecisive, and self-serving. I was "disloyal to the president and disrespectful of the Senate." By refusing to name specific examples of the kinds of ambassador I had criticized, I was preventing the Senate from carrying out its constitutional responsibilities. If necessary to save the Republic from such people, Helms would keep his holds on forever.

At this point, I discovered that there was an opposing view in the Senate and that the minority could play rough too. I stopped in to see Ed

Zorinsky one day. There had been a sentimental tie between our families since we realized that he was the first Democrat to fill his Senate seat from Nebraska since Edith's uncle almost fifty years before. (And like Edward Burke, he was as much Republican as Democrat.) He was on the SFRC but normally devoted little time to it. All I expected was the opportunity to cry a little on his shoulder.

Grinning, he said, "You know I agree with everything you wrote. Senators don't give enough time and attention to ambassadorial nominations. I've reformed. Let me tell you what I did yesterday. I sent a pretty little girl on my staff over to see Helms's people. She told them she needed to advise me how to vote on nominations. Who were the good ones and who were the bad ones? You'll not be surprised to know you were one of the bad ones. But, when she brought me back the good ones, I slapped holds on all of them for as long as Helms's holds stand on you and Lord."

Meanwhile, the White House sent down a large slate of judicial nominations, for which minority consent is traditionally necessary. In a Democratic caucus, Senator Patrick Moynihan of New York proposed withholding that consent until action was completed on the nomination to China of his constituent, Winston Lord. Pat Leahy amended the proposal to include me. Agreement was unanimous. Minority Leader Robert Byrd joyfully conveyed it to Majority Leader Robert Dole.

The newspapers were also getting into the act. On October 31, the *New York Times*'s lead editorial proclaimed "Free the Helms Hostages!" Terming the senator from North Carolina "a windy bully," it called for removal of the Lord and Spain holds, "a mean abuse of senatorial courtesy to turn prejudice into a blackball." On November 3, the *Washington Post* sounded off: "Mr. Helms, . . . no small embarrassment to the United States, to the Reagan Administration, and especially to the Senate . . . has held up appointments before and has been routed . . . once the Senate roused itself to stare him down. The Senate must do so once more!"

The morning of November 5, some thirteen weeks after my nomination had first gone to the Senate, I was sitting in the State Department. A secretary came in to say, "There's a man on the phone who wants to speak to you. He says his name is Bob Dole or something like that." I jumped for the phone. It was the majority leader. "Why did you say that ambassadorships could be bought for five thousand dollars?" he began.

"Come on, Senator. I didn't say that."

"I know you didn't, but you and Winston Lord are tying up this entire session. Come over here this afternoon. I'll get Jesse in and we'll straighten this thing out."

At 2:00 P.M., I was in the majority leader's cozy, open fire-warmed office in the Capitol. The assistant secretary of state for congressional relations and a White House personnel man were already there. Dole, Boschwitz, and Helms soon arrived. For the first time, I met my adversary face-to-face. Helms and I were the principal speakers in the ninety minutes that followed.

He began by saying "This nomination never should have come down here in the first place!" and continued with a steady flow of abuse about me, the State Department, the Foreign Service, the *New York Times,* and the *Washington Post.* He pulled out a piece of paper and demanded, "Look me straight in the eye! Remember you are under oath!" (That was the first I'd heard about that.) "Did you not say this: 'I have never agreed with President Reagan on anything. He and I have practically nothing in common!'" A *sotto voce* exchange between Helms and Boschwitz made clear that the alleged source was a Sri Lankan.

I replied that I had never said anything remotely like that. Even if I believed it, after all my years in diplomacy, I would hardly have said it to a foreigner, especially one from the country to which I was assigned. (I remain convinced to this day that the quote was a fabrication by one of the meaner of Helms's staff.)

Helms sneered and got up to leave. I made a consciously patriotic little speech to the effect that forty years ago I had left my country for the first time to serve in uniform in the Pacific. I had worked for my government ever since as a civilian, dragging my family into dangerous places. He had a perfect right to think I was a bad diplomat. What I was not prepared to accept was anyone's impugning my devotion to my country, my respect for our government, and my loyalty to every president I had ever served.

It didn't seem to me that much had been accomplished, but that evening, while I self-indulgently read Richard Marius's *Thomas More* in my room at the Cosmos Club, the phone rang. It was a caller from the floor of the Senate. To this day I have no idea who. Over the background noise of a vote in progress, I was told, "You've just been confirmed, 94 to 1, with Senator Helms announcing that you admitted you 'misspoke yourself,' finally answered all his questions, and apologized for critical references to the

Senate. He still voted against you. . . . Just a second! Win Lord's through too, 87 to 8." (All three points of Helms's announcement were wrong.)

I had, of course, been something of a tail on the prominent Lord dog all the way through. The TV coverage that night and the press the next morning featured his victory, barely mentioning me. That was just fine. All I wanted to do was to get off to Sri Lanka. One newspaperman did call. He offered congratulations and asked me if I had anything to say about Senator Helms's charges that I was "disloyal to the president and disrespectful of the Senate." I indulged myself once again. The first charge, I said, was 100 percent untrue; the second 99 percent so. We both had a laugh, but the quote never saw print. The story was over.

What do I make of the process of advice and consent with which I had so intimate and painful an experience? Two points are clear.

The "hold" courtesy is intended to provide limited time for a busy senator to check out a fact or two. Helms's use of it for personal and political vendettas is a vicious perversion. A Senate tradition that allows the "holder" to remain anonymous is an abuse of basic American principles. The Senate should change or end it. Despite Helms's flirtation in recent years with Democratic Secretary of State Madeleine Albright and his replacing the worst of his staff, in my view he remains, as the *New York Times* said, "a windy bully," who will do and say anything to forward his private agenda and who, I suspect, likes to hurt people. To stop or change him is up to the voters of North Carolina, who are probably only vaguely aware of the havoc he wreaks on the national and international scene while serving their state interests as well as or better than the next senator.

The rest of the process, even given the idiosyncratic blocks I encountered from Clark and Javits, is good and necessary. It is part of our representative system. It digs out real dirt, as well as imaginary blemishes. It gives the ambassador who gets through it extra prestige and influence—and something to write about in his memoirs.

16

This and That

RUDYARD KIPLING, IN ONE OF his lesser known poems, "Chant-Pagan," gives voice to an "English Irregular Discharged":

Me that 'ave been what I've been,
Me that 'ave gone where I've gone,
Me that 'ave seen what I've seen—
    'ow can I ever take on
With awful old England again,
An' 'ouses on both sides of the street,
And 'edges two sides of the lane,
And the parson an' "gentry" between,
An' touchin' my 'at when we meet—
    Me that 'ave been what I've been?

The old soldier recounts his adventures watching "'arf a world 'eave up all shiny with dew, kopje on kop to the sun . . . an' the silence, the shine, an' the size of the 'igh unexpressible skies. . . . Me that 'ave followed my trade in the place where the Lightnin's are made, 'twixt the Rains and the Sun and the Moon. . . ."

If the master of words were writing today, he might put the lament in the mouth of "American Foreign Service Officer Retired."

Some retired FSOs find it easy to accommodate. They may always have preferred the regular and predictable life of Washington to the uncertainties of overseas assignments. They may still have tuition, mortgage, or alimony bills to pay off, and the capital city remains the most likely place to find remuneration for their experience and talents. They may be so devoted to government and foreign affairs that they would rather contribute from the fringes than experience absolute deprivation. One sees them everywhere in Washington, lobbying for this or that cause, managing foundations, lunching and attending seminars at the International, Cosmos, or Metropolitan Club. In a way they are the fortunate ones. They have found a familiar place and are happy with it.

Me, I've avoided the "'ouses both sides of the street" and "'edges two sides of the lane" by retiring in Sri Lanka. Edith and I used to talk about what we would do when the time came. When the children were small and trying, we pledged that when they were grown I would become a monk or a mercenary and she would join a convent or a bridge club. Later, we discussed other choices. Mine was a ruined Norman keep in Ireland. Hers was a villa on the Costa Brava in Spain. She would visit me in summer, and I would travel to her in winter. Finally we settled on togetherness on a ranch in Montana or a bungalow in Peshawar. When retirement suddenly took on reality (isn't that the way it comes to most of us?), she was gone, and I was sadly free to do anything I wanted.

My ties are deeper with Pakistan and Turkey, but the gentle, smiling people of Sri Lanka were kind to me when I most needed it. There is still much of the comfortable, servant-supported life that I knew when I first came to Karachi in 1951. I live in a lazy, tropic mode: up by nine in the morning, tennis or swimming in the afternoon, a cocktail party most evenings, boar hunts on the tea estates in the hills a couple of times a year, a lot of reading, and some writing. Spice is provided by the local stock exchange, small enough that even an amateur can comprehend it. Purpose comes from an effort that will take years to organize, a multi-million-dollar public-private power and irrigation project in the southern corner of the island. Diversion can always be had by choosing which of the dozen cotton slacks and shirts that constitute my wardrobe to wear on a given day and by trying to tell if it's winter or summer by the fifteen-minute variation in sunrise and sunset that indicates the difference. (The temperature is always the same.)

There is an occasional adventure. One week the pope visited Sri Lanka. As I tried to drive to a Colombo hotel, I cursed the security precautions that blocked off the streets. I was not very happy with His Holiness either. Fragments of a Clancy Brothers song, "The Old Orange Flute," came into my head. The only line I could remember was "Oh! We'll dip the Pope in Boyne wah-ter." (The reference is to the Battle of the Boyne River in Ireland in 1689, when the Stuart Catholic cause was crushed by Protestant King William.) I pulled into a parking place at the hotel singing it at the top of my voice.

A man sitting in a neighboring car scowled at me. I got out. He did too—with a fist cocked. "Sure, that's not a nice thing to be singing on a day like this!" he challenged. "What sort of a man are ye anyway? A foine English bigot, maybe?" He drew back for a good round swing.

I mumbled: "No, no, an American. Just a whim. No offense intended. Apologies to you and to the Holy Father . . ."

My antagonist relaxed, and I found out that he was a correspondent for a Dublin newspaper in town for the day to cover the papal visit. I realized that my talent for trouble, which had been so faithful during my encounters with the U.S. Senate, was still alive. I had chosen to park next to the one man in all Sri Lanka capable of recognizing and being offended by the ancient jibe!

Sri Lanka is an easy place from which to travel to the Central Asian haunts of my youth. A few years ago, youngest son Bill and I went up through the Karakoram and Kun Lung Mountains from Pakistan to China. It took two weeks in a variety of vehicles, but it was worth it to travel the sixteen-thousand-foot Kunjerab Pass and to see Kashgar. (When Edith and I talked about a similar adventure forty years before, it would have taken two months walking and riding.) The previous year I visited second son Steve in Quetta, where he was stationed with the United Nations High Commissioner for Refugees trying to help the millions of Afghan refugees in Pakistan. The fighting had died down in southern Afghanistan. He was moving the UNHCR office up to Kandahar.

I persuaded him to take me along for my first visit to Afghanistan in a quarter-century. Our two-vehicle convoy was attacked and shot up west of Spin Baldak by *mujahidin* or bandits (or both). Fortunately no one was hit, but we were kidnapped into the hills. The UN vehicles and all our personal possessions except the clothes on our backs were taken.

We left while our captors squabbled over the loot. Making our way by walking and hitching rides on passing lorries and buses and finally hiring a taxi, we got back to Pakistan within twenty-four hours. Steve got a letter of reprimand for taking an unauthorized person in a UN vehicle, but I had my visit, however brief.

The taxi, naturally, evaded the Pakistan Customs and Immigration post when it crossed the border, and I found myself trying to fly out of Karachi a few days later with a passport already stamped in and out of Pakistan and without any right to be in the country at all. There could have been trouble, but the friend who had taken me to the airport was a schoolmate of the former inspector general of police—whose son was now a deputy inspector general—so there was no problem. Those who have lived in South Asia will appreciate the phenomenon.

Sri Lanka is also a good place from which to go farther afield. Halfway around the world from the United States, one can take advantage of the cheaper Pacific air fares and the cheaper still "around-the-world tariffs." After a lifetime of being bound to the worst of American carriers by government regulations, it is a pleasure to be able to pick and choose, even at my own expense, between Emirates and Singapore and a host of other airlines for comfort and service.

With these advantages—and "frequent flyer" coupons (which I can now keep for myself)—I might finally get to make the last check on a list Edith and I compiled just after our wedding of places we wanted to see. Most of them we checked off together—Westminster Abbey, l'Arc de Triomphe, the Colosseum, the Taj Mahal, Sancta Sophia, Lake Van, Zanzibar, the Great African Rift, and more. There were three left when she died—Kashgar, the church at Limassol on Cyprus where Richard the Lion-Hearted married Beregaria in 1191 on his way to the Third Crusade, and the Gorges of the Yangtze. In retirement I have made it to the first two. Only the Yangtze

Gorges remain. Who knows? It is always good to have something left to do—and they are just a few thousand miles away.

Travel to the United States is easy. I normally do it twice a year. I can leave Colombo for Singapore or Bangkok late at night on Friday, go on to Tokyo Saturday morning, and thanks to the magic of the International Date Line, be in San Francisco or New York Saturday evening. Passage via the Persian Gulf and Europe is even faster, albeit more expensive. With sons in Austin, Chicago, and Boston, I get to combine family visits with the "re-Americanization" that was so important a purpose of Foreign Service home leave.

I may have developed a greater interest in Turkish food, Pakistani antiquities, and Sri Lankan folklore than our own varieties. It is true that, despite frequent visits to Washington, I have never been back inside the main State Department building since I was there immediately after resigning, to find out how much my pension would be. On the other hand, there is nothing to beat American politics. On visits in the mid-1990s, I watched Ann Richards campaign in Texas and Teddy Kennedy in Massachusetts. I talked with Oliver North as he trolled the James River Valley for votes in Virginia. And, when Pat Leahy unexpectedly took me along to the White House, I chatted about nothing in particular with President Clinton. It was easy to tell that the years had passed and my hair had grayed since I had last been at 1600 Pennsylvania Avenue. Clinton is the first President ever to call me "sir"!

And there are always little bits of history reappearing to remind an aging retiree of his active years. In 1997, for example, on my way to the United States, I stopped off in Turkey for a few days to be with son Bill, who was there doing a magazine article. The visit began badly when I got off the Emirates Air Line plane from Dubai to find myself on the verge of deportation. It seemed I had an honorary diplomatic passport (one of the few gracious things the Department of State does for its retired career-FSO ambassadors). For reasons never clear to me, the Turkish immigration authorities will not issue a tourist visa for such passports. The Emirates captain who had flown me from Dubai was brought in and told he had to take me back when his plane left in two hours.

Reverting to what I could remember of my Turkish and flourishing a U.S. Embassy Ankara cable that said I had an appointment the next day to

A postretirement visit at the White House, 1995. *From left:* U.S. Senator Patrick J. Leahy of Vermont, James W. Spain, Mrs. Marcelle Leahy, and President William J. Clinton. *Courtesy White House*

see longtime friend President Demirel, I finally talked my way into a special six-day temporary visa, for which the Turks would not take the twenty U.S. dollars normally extracted for a visitor's visa. It took two hours, but I was let through with smiles and arms around my shoulders. Turkish procedures with which I first lived a quarter-century earlier had not changed. What at first seems harsh arbitrariness almost always turns into helpful friendliness.

My six days in Turkey were a delight—as my many retirement visits to closer-by Pakistan have been. As a one-time consul general in Istanbul, I was allowed, together with old friends, a cruise up the Bosphorus on the *Hiawatha,* still in good shape after surviving a bombing during the years I was away. Bill and I had a sentimental forty-five minutes with President Demirel in which he was as warm to my son as he had been to me years before.

We took the bus to Ankara—air-conditioned, stewards and stewardesses serving tea and cold drinks, five hours on a six-lane highway. What I had known as a barren plateau with scattered villages was now an almost continuous ribbon of habitation dotted with factories and workshops. In Ankara we met with opposition leader Bulent Ecevit in the Parliament building and reminisced some more. Frank Ricciardone, who must have been at least the tenth lineal successor to me as DCM and was vice consul in Adana during my time, put us up in his house.

After my return to Colombo, another bit of history unfolded. One Laurent Kabila began to appear in the newspapers and on the television screen as the new ruler in Congo (Zaire), replacing Mobutu Sese Seko. The sleek, heavy figure struck no chord of memory, but the name teased me. Then I remembered. He was the somewhat pathetic character with a few dozen followers who had kidnapped the foreign students from Tanzania in 1975, causing Ambassador Beverly Carter's removal by Henry Kissinger and bringing me my first ambassadorship. He too had come a long way.

Sri Lanka itself has an abundance of charms. White sand beaches and warm blue waters run for hundreds of miles around three sides of the island. Sigiriya, the lofty royal rock fortress with its stunning murals, provides a setting for some of the best fiction produced by my neighbor and

Recalling old times with President Suleyman Demirel of Turkey during a 1997 vacation visit in Istanbul. Youngest son Bill is at left. *Courtesy Government of Turkey*

friend, Arthur C. Clarke. Anuradhapura, the great ruin in the northwest, was a larger city than Augustus's Rome in the first century A.D. Much of it is still there. The same may be said about Pollonaruwa, which dates merely to the seventh century. Only Jaffna in the north is inaccessible, due to civil war.

Sri Lanka abounds in artistic talent—painting, sculpture, batik, woodcarving, cabinet-making. After departing the Embassy Residence, I found a spacious apartment in one of the oldest buildings in Colombo and had a fine time decorating it with local paintings and furniture. The outside of the building and its public areas are shabby, leading another retired diplomat, an executive with an international oil company who flew to town in his own airplane, to comment: "When I came in downstairs, my first thought was, 'It looks like poor old Jim has fallen on hard times.' I was wrong. This is a great apartment, twice the size of what I have in London."

Later, youngest son William (a frequent visitor) and Geethanjana, his Sri Lankan artist friend, cooked up a scheme to have a skilled sculptor, Gustinna Wadu Somarathne, do a portrait bust of the old man, which another noted sculptor, Sarath Chandrajeewa, would cast in bronze. I was neither so modest nor so ungracious as to refuse. I like the representation and counter my vanity by thinking of the splendid work as my "Ozymandias caper."

There are other things to do on the island. After two years of lazing about, I brought in a modest amount of money and became a "guest resident investor." The small and almost comprehensible Colombo Stock Exchange provides enough excitement to keep anyone's adrenaline running. Each year I have been involved with it, it has gone up a hundred percent and fallen back fifty. I have stopped telling my sons of these ups and downs. As one of them said: "Sometimes it seems we are all going to be rich heirs. Six months later it looks as if it is time to start setting money aside to take care of you in your old age." In terms of private investments, I've lost money in a snack food company and made it on stock in a grocery company. And there's always that $325 million power-irrigation project to dream over.

Such is one FSO's retirement. It's not bad. Before leaving the subject, though, I want to muse a little about the advantages many retired American FSOs have today. Pensions 50 to 80 percent of a decent salary with cost-of-living

Sculptor Gustinna Wadu Somarathne working on the "Ozymandias caper" at Spain's retirement apartment in Colombo, 1997, with artist Geethanjana and Spain.

additions are not everyone's lot—at home or abroad. Most of my British peers in the service went away with something like half that, perhaps added to by £2,500 a year for company directorships, if they had been lucky enough to be knighted. Few other Americans have had the advantages of school, housing, and hardship allowances, or of owning houses in the Washington area that could readily be rented while overseas and increase tenfold in value over their working careers. All of this makes possible, in most cases, some savings and investment to supplement retirement income. (There are other things, of course, that most Americans have not had either—cobras in three of the four bedrooms in Dar es Salaam; assassination attempts, one each in Istanbul and Ankara; and hepatitis, three of the family six, with three-week to four-month hospitalizations).

Let me make clear that I am not advocating the elimination of all this. A good pension is fair for a hard life—especially one in which many fall by the way. The point I want to make is that the retirement system in force for much of America today is a unique creation of those seventy years of the twentieth century that I have lived through. Before our time people seldom "retired." Those who had wealth by inheritance or booty simply lived on it and passed it on or lost it. The rest worked to live. When they weren't able to, they died. As late as the 1930s, the chief objective of my union-minded father was no more than a pension. What he got—and grateful he was for it!—was Roosevelt's Social Security.

In this closing decade of the twentieth century, we have not only the 80 percent of "high three" that I walked away with from the Foreign Service and the 50 percent retirement pay for twenty years' service that keeps our armed forces filled without a draft. Corporate "golden handshakes" run into hundreds of millions. In the case of government servants, there is now the Thrift Savings Plan into which the employee puts his own funds. It came too late to make much difference to my generation, but it may help reduce the taxpayers' costs for retirees of the future. Who can doubt that a better system is good?

My own "golden years" have one great shadow across them. I am alone. For a while after Edith died, I could think of nothing but things that might have been. How often had we hoped for a holiday in Florida when coming back in winter from a foreign posting. But always a tuition or new car bill showed up and we ended by taking the shortest and most economical route to Washington.

As those who have been through the loss of a long-beloved spouse know, things get better eventually. I can now buy a ticket and enjoy a trip to Florida—or Kashgar—without measuring the cost against next month's household budget. What I am not able to do is to savor and remember the experience with the zest I once had. Her eye for the interesting and exotic was much better than mine. Often I got more from listening to her talk about a place or a person we had seen than from the experience itself. To couples who are still together in retirement, I say: How lucky you are!

My first purpose after retirement was to see if I could write fiction. I was pretty sure I could. My early books on the Pathans in the 1960s readily found publishers in both Europe and the United States. Oxford University Press kept *The Way of the Pathans* in print for more than thirty years and solicited me to do another during my retirement. In 1984 my book *American Diplomacy in Turkey* won acceptance on the first try. The Office of National Estimates taught me how to write clear and concise prose. In my later years, I came to be able to use four-letter words without flinching. I had a lot of experience in exotic places to provide ambiance. Colombo's comfortable, slow-paced lifestyle offered an excellent environment for writing. A school chum, Andrew Greeley, the Chicago priest-sociologist, had become a best-selling novelist. My Colombo friend, the scientist Arthur C. Clarke, was a world-renowned science-fiction writer. Surely, my conversion from bureaucrat to novelist would be easy.

I subscribed to writers' magazines and literary quarterlies. I laid in a supply of paper and bought a computer and a printer (in each case, the first of three). I studied the mysteries of 220-volt electrical connections, modems, surge protectors, and the like. I hadn't grown up with such contrivances and couldn't comprehend their manuals. I soon discovered that a computer was not just another form of typewriter. It could do marvelous things, changing typefaces and moving sentences about at will. But it could also gobble up irretrievable hours of work and drive me to howling at the ceiling in frustration. It took me almost two years before the first manuscript was ready to submit for publication.

Arthur Clarke's top-flight New York agent agreed to take a look at it as a favor. He returned it, saying that it was not badly written. He'd learned a lot about the Foreign Service from it. But where were the strong characters, the conflict, the human emotion that made a story? The *Foreign Service Journal* confirmed his judgment by turning down almost all of the short stories that made up the manuscript. Eventually, in 1997, a fellow retired FSO, Robert Keeley, getting his satisfaction by running a mini publishing operation, the Five and Ten Press, published eleven of the stories in *Innocents of the Latter Day: Modern Americans Abroad.* Foreign Service people seemed to like them, but others perhaps might not.

Another friend told me that Jane Alexander, a great lady of the American theater whom she knew, was looking for a new vehicle. Turn a fantasy novel I had written about a female God and a bumbling IRA hit man trying to reform the world into a script. Jane would love it. I did. The distinguished actress read it and replied: "The idea is a cute one but I don't feel it could get a commercial production. There doesn't seem to be a market for this kind of material anymore. Some theological seminary that does an annual play would love it."

Andrew Greeley arranged a luncheon with Tom Doherty of Tor Books, his favorite publisher. I tried another manuscript (I had five by this time) on him. Doherty was not impressed but offered some advice:

> You know, the deck is stacked against a first-time fiction writer. As best we can figure out, about 35 percent of the customers buy a book because they've read and liked something by the same author. Another 5 or 6 percent buy for subject matter. There are enough people interested in medieval England that any book on Richard the Lion-Hearted will sell. Another 3 or 4 percent buy on the basis of reviews. About the same percentage buy because of promotion or placement in the book shops. I have no idea what motivates the other 50-plus percent, but you don't even have the first 35 percent going for you.

I complained to Arthur Clarke. All I wanted was for someone who knew to give me one of three answers on my writing: (a) "It's great. We'll have an auction next week. How much advance do you want?" (b) "Not bad. If you did this, and this, and that to it, we'd like to look at it again." or (c) "Stop bothering us. You may have been a good diplomat but you can't write worth shit!" The old pro grinned. "You're asking the impossible," he said. "You can get all three responses to the same piece of work. You'll just have to design and polish and keep trying until you hit."

I set out to learn about the "trade," meaning the popular national publishing business. It was appalling. Publishing remains entrenched in the thirteenth century. Decisions on hardcover editions are made on the projected amount of cleavage for the cover of the paperbacks.

Alone among manufacturers of consumer goods, the people who make books put them out for sale on consignment. If a distributor orders a hundred copies of a volume and six months later has fifty unsold, he can return them to the publisher for full credit. A novel that costs $29.95 in a bookshop today can be had in less than a year for $3.95 from "disposal specialist" Daedalus Books, of Hyattsville, Maryland, my favorite bookseller. Neither Detroit nor Tokyo sells cars that way, and even the least popular of their products do not depreciate by 75 percent the first year.

The "literary" quarterlies and presses live a life of their own. It is apparent from first glance that they prefer fiction without a beginning, middle, and end and, if possible, without plot. A second look reveals their penchant for incest. Editors and authors write for their own or each others' magazines and award grand-sounding prizes to their own or kindred authors and staff. The writers' magazines are great on "how to" articles, lists of foundations that support indigent authors, and advertisements from vanity presses eager to publish at the author's expense.

But I've never seen a single ad from an established agent soliciting manuscripts. The ad I took myself in the *New York Review of Books* ($500 for three inches) describing my material and asking interested agents to contact me elicited one reply—and my second exchange with him was returned marked "Moved. No forwarding address."

Then I recalled an episode in the 1970s when I got mad—not for the first time—at the Foreign Service. I told Edith I was going to quit. "Fine," she responded. "What are you going to do then?"

"I'm a good writer, aren't I? I'll turn out best-selling novels and make a lot of money."

"Well, your Pathan books are good, but now you're talking about fiction. No offense, but I've noticed that what seems important and intriguing to you leaves most other people cold, and what they consider tragic or joyful passes right over your head. Are you sure you could write stories that a lot of people would pay to read? We still have four children to put through college."

Maybe that bit of wisdom, rather than the idiosyncracies of the publishing trade, is the answer to my problem. My publisher son thinks books are going out of style anyway. On-line coverage and compact disks are the things of the future. I like the feel of paper and will be sorry if that happens. However, ten dollars for something that costs thirty dollars today is not a bad deal—even if I have to spend another ten to print it out. As for me, only the university presses remain faithful to their calling. Oxford University Press solicited and published another Pathan volume, *Pathans of the Latter Day,* in 1995, and Kent State University Press graciously accepted and published this volume.

* * *

My world is now a small one. My thoughts are more on the past than the future. My seventy years of the twentieth century have given me more important things than pensions, publishing, and stocks to ponder. Not all of these stem from my official activities. The high-riding CIA people with whom I had most trouble are convicted (and pardoned) criminals. Jesse Helms cost me money and agony for six months. But what difference do these things make less than a decade later—never mind a hundred years from now?

There are a few things that might have made a difference, and of these I am proud. My 1963 memorandum on Pope John XXIII and his collaborators bolstered acceptance of new forces sweeping the ancient institutions of the Church. In 1978 my persuading David Owen to accept the independence fighters as the armed forces of Zimbabwe helped ward off a blood bath. In 1980–81 my tightrope-walking with both Washington and the Turkish generals contributed to keeping the country in NATO and returning it to democracy.

Personal decisions were also important. I am glad that I went to Quigley, learned Latin and Greek—and did not become a priest. I am glad that I went to the University of Chicago, learned how wide and glorious is our world—and did not become an atheist. I am glad that I served in the armed forces and learned how varied are the American people and how easily even the most regimented organization can be circumvented. I am glad that I discovered the Pathans when few other Americans knew them. I am glad that I joined the Foreign Service, left it for the Office of National Estimates, and returned again. I am glad that I caught a personal glimpse of the Chicago gangster phase of our history, and of the Old West from my in-laws.

I am grateful that my father lived long enough for me to know him a little and to realize how different his youth was from my own. I am grateful for a mother who still worried and fussed over me when I was in my middle years. I am grateful for four children who, pretty much on their own, weathered the perils of "Foreign Service brats" in the 1960s and '70s and who became adults in time to talk with their parents as equals. I am grateful for American, Indo-American, and Chinese grandchildren bubbling over with the freshness and charm of childhood (and who I hope, in my old-fashioned way, will carry on my name). Above all I am grateful for a young woman from Montana who married me somewhat against her better judgment and then spent thirty-three years loving and cherishing me without stint or reservation.

Whether evident in this narrative or not, the Spains have a high regard for history. It doesn't tell what is coming next, but it explains better than anything else why men do the things they do. We measured our life by it in our own peculiar way, as in "the day after President Kennedy was killed," or "the summer we couldn't take leave because Daddy had to stay in Dar es Salaam when Henry Kissinger was there."

Only belatedly did I realize that the name of Justinian's great church in Istanbul, Sancta Sophia, means not Saint Sophie but Holy Wisdom. Wisdom became another source of inspiration. It would take another book to tell how and why, but Greeley puts it simply in his autobiography. Wisdom is "God's attractive charm as revealed in the order, beauty, and graciousness of the creative world." His image of God is that "She is a Comedienne—and an Irish one at that." He may be right.

One Sunday while visiting Washington, I listened to the Lesson from the Book of Wisdom read at St. Matthew's Cathedral. A few words bore into my mind. "Beyond health and comeliness I loved her. I chose to have her rather than the light because the splendor of her never yields to sleep. Yet all good things come to me in her company and countless riches at her hands."

To me the words described Edith. I found a King James Bible to get the rest of them. None were there. The Book of Wisdom does not appear in the revised authorized canon. A note in the back dismisses it as mystic rambling put in the mouth of Solomon by a latter-day Greek. Only the prosaic Douai version carries it and associates it with divine revelation.

How Edith would have enjoyed that! And, with her, the Irish Comedienne!

Index

In Those Days

was designed and composed

in 10½/14 Adobe Minion with Castellar display

by Will Underwood

at The Kent State University Press

on a Power Macintosh 7100/80

using Adobe PageMaker 6.5;

printed by sheet-fed offset lithography

on 50-pound Turin Book natural stock

(an acid-free, totally chlorine-free paper),

Smyth sewn and bound over binder's boards in

Arrestox B cloth, with dust jackets printed in three

colors on 100-pound enamel stock finished with

polypropylene matt film lamination

by Thomson-Shore, Inc.,

and published by

The Kent State University Press

KENT, OHIO 44242 USA